PORTFOLIO / PENGUIN

I KNOW HOW SHE DOES IT

Laura Vanderkam is the bestselling author of *What the Most Successful People Do Before Breakfast*, *All the Money in the World*, *168 Hours*, and *Grindhopping*. She is a frequent contributor to *Fast Company*'s Web site and a member of *USA Today*'s board of contributors. Her work has also appeared in *The Wall Street Journal*, *The New York Times*, *Fortune*, and other publications. She lives with her husband and their four children outside Philadelphia.

I KNOW HOW
SHE DOES IT

How Successful Women
Make the Most of Their Time

LAURA VANDERKAM

Portfolio / Penguin

PORTFOLIO / PENGUIN
An imprint of Penguin Random House LLC
375 Hudson Street
New York, New York 10014
penguin.com

First published in the United States of America by Portfolio / Penguin 2015
This paperback edition with a new afterword published 2017

LIBRARY OF CONGRESS CATALOGING-IN-PUBLICATION DATA

Names: Vanderkam, Laura, author.
Title: I know how she does it : how successful women make
the most of their time / Laura Vanderkam.
Description: New York : Portfolio/Penguin, 2016. |
"This paperback edition published with a new afterword 2016." |
Includes bibliographical references and index.
Identifiers: LCCN 2016009845 (print) | LCCN 2016015960 (ebook) |
ISBN 9780143109723 (pbk) | ISBN 9780698162846 (ebook)
Subjects: LCSH: Work-life balance. | Working mothers—United States. |
Women executives—United States. | Women in the professions—United States. |
Success in business. | Businesswomen. | Time management.
Classification: LCC HD4904.25 .V364 2016 (print) | LCC HD4904.25 (ebook) |
DDC 650.1/1082—dc23

Printed in the United States of America
3   5   7   9   10   8   6   4

Set in Minion Pro
Designed by Alissa Rose Theodor

TO RUTH

Contents

I KNOW HOW SHE DOES IT

Introduction

"Remember the berry season is short."

I came across this poignant thought the other day in the most pedestrian of places: on the basket our local pick-your-own strawberry farm gives visitors before they hit the fields. I was there on a sunny June day with my seven-year-old, Jasper, and four-year-old, Sam. My husband, Michael, had taken our two-year-old daughter, Ruth, fishing at a nearby pond. I was woozy on the hay ride to the fields, from the heat and the bumps on the rutted road, and also from what was then still a new secret: another baby on the way, joining the crew when all this hilly green in southeastern Pennsylvania would be covered with snow. As I fought back my dizziness, I stared at the found poetry on this empty box: "Remember the berry season is short. This box holds approximately 10 lbs level full, 15 lbs heaping full."

It is a metaphor for life, perhaps, in that everything is a metaphor for life. The berry season is short. So how full, exactly, do I intend to fill the box? Or, if we slice away the metaphor, we could just ask this: what does the good life look like for me?

I think about this question frequently, writing in the genre I do. While self-help gets a reputation for flimsiness, at its best it takes a practical look at this eternal question, with a bonus not all philosophers offer: ideas and strategies for figuring it out.

I write about the good life through the lens of time, because a life is lived in hours. What you do with your life will be a function of how you spend the 8,760 hours that make a year, the 700,000 or so that make a life: at strawberry farms, rocking toddlers to sleep, and pursuing work that alters at least some corner of the universe.

The good news for those often told to limit their aspirations is that the box will hold all these things. It can hold all these things and more.

This book is about how real people have created full lives. It is about how you can borrow from their discoveries to do so too. It is about how you can move around and rethink the hours of your weeks to nurture your career, your relationships, and yourself, and still enjoy more open space than most people think is possible. It is, in short, about how to enjoy and make the most of your time, by which I mean investing as much as you wish in everything that matters: work, family, community, leisure. It is about celebrating abundance rather than lamenting choices or claiming that no one can have it all.

I find the subject of how we spend our time fascinating. I approach time management as a journalist, studying data sets and interviewing successful people about how they use their hours. In my previous books (*168 Hours* and *What the Most Successful People Do Before Breakfast*), I've tried to share these discoveries and tips for making readers' lives work. But as I wrote these books, I realized two things. First, I was most drawn to the stories and strategies of women like me, who were building careers and families at the same time. Second, for all I probed my subjects to describe their lives, I was mostly relying on their anecdotes and storytelling. I wanted to see people's schedules in all their messy glory. I wanted to look at their time logs and see the curious places the data led. That's why I wrote this book, adding a researcher hat to my journalist one, trying to understand what 1,001 days in the lives of professional women and their families really look like.

There is much to learn from seeing how people use their hours to achieve their goals. Learning their strategies can be empowering; it reminds us that we have the power to shape our lives too. Years ago, when I filled out my first 168-hour (one week) time log, I thought that it seemed strange to view life as cells on a spreadsheet. But over time I came to see that I could view myself as the artist deciding on those cells. I became a mosaic maker, carefully placing tiles. By thinking about the arrangement, and watching others, and trying different strategies, over time I could create an intricate and satisfying pattern. I could create a mosaic that embraced new things: new opportunities in my working life, the new children whose lives I've loved watching unfold. Sometimes the larger world delights in telling people that a full life will be harried, leading one to being maxed out, or torn. But while it is the rare artist who can create a perfectly blissful mosaic, focusing only on the stressful moments ignores the other sweet moments, like making strawberry shortcakes with those bright red berries, and getting a note from someone who tells you your book has changed her life.

Life is simultaneously complex and compelling. It is stressful and it is wonderful. But if you believe, like I do, that the good life can be a full life—a level full life or even a heaping full life—then I invite you to study how you place the tiles of your time, energy, and attention. I invite you to think about the pattern with the goal, over time, of making an even more satisfying picture.

After all, the berry season is short. I believe in filling it with all the joy that is possible.

. . . .

CHAPTER 1

The Mosaic

L ife is not lived solely in stories. Yet this is the way we talk about our lives: in moments that must impart a lesson. Consequently, in much of the literature on work and life, our tale would begin with a Recitation of Dark Moments: a snowstorm threatening to maroon me in Los Angeles while my husband is in Europe and my three young children are with a sitter in Pennsylvania who wasn't planning on keeping them for several snowy days straight. Or, perhaps, I am in New York City overnight in order to be on a morning show at dawn. I am trying to turn in early when my husband calls to report that, after taking the kids to the circus, he's realized they're locked out of our new house. He's in problem-solving mode, calling me to get the numbers of people with a spare key, and when they don't pick up the phone, letting me know that the locksmith will be there in two hours. I shouldn't worry. They have adequate bottles! But of course the net result is that I am pacing around my hotel room, picturing my five-month-old baby out in the car in the middle of the cold night. How am I supposed to sleep after that?

I could begin with such tales, and then lament the craziness of modern life, and the impossibility of having it all. Ever since *The Atlantic* put Anne-Marie Slaughter's manifesto on this topic on the cover, and scored millions of reads, it's a truth in media circles that the phrase "can't have it all" lures women in. Tales that let us be voyeurs to such foibles draw clicks. People hunt for more extreme examples. An editor seeking submissions for a book of such stories suggested, as an example of what she wanted, "getting a text message from a sick child while flying an F-16 over Afghanistan." In 2012, the legal world posted reams of comments in response to a widely circulated departure memo from a Clifford Chance associate with two young children. In it, she chronicled an awful day, describing middle-of-the-night wake-ups from the kids, a colleague who sat on a note until day care was closing, a bad commute, a not-exactly-helpful husband, and a long to-do list waiting for her after she wrestled the kids into bed. "Needless to say, I have not been able to simultaneously meet the demands of career and family," she wrote her colleagues, and so the only choice available, the choice we all seem to understand, was to quit.

But in this book, I want to tell a different story. The key to this is realizing that life *isn't* lived in epiphanies, and that looking for lessons and the necessity of big life changes in dark moments profoundly limits our lives.

I came to see this not in an aha moment but in an accumulation of conversations that convinced me that my research into time use might be giving me insights that the larger world was missing. As one example, in summer 2013, I talked with a young woman who'd formerly worked at a consulting firm. She was thinking of starting a coaching company that would counsel women like our Clifford Chance heroine to negotiate for part-time or flexible work arrangements. It was a perfectly good business idea, but her explanation for why she liked the concept stuck in my mind: *I looked at the senior women in my firm,* she told me, *and there was no one whose life I wanted.*

Normally, I might have let that go as background noise, the sort of thing young women say to one another, but I had been reading a lot of Sheryl Sandberg. So I began formulating a response that I eventually realized needed to become its own treatise.

It starts like this: Several years ago, I wrote a book called *168 Hours: You Have More Time Than You Think.* One happy result of releasing the book was that numerous companies asked me to come speak about how people should manage their time. To make my workshop more useful, I started asking a few audience members to keep track of their time before our session. These time logs, which are half-hour-by-half-hour records of an entire week, revealed what issues people in the audience cared about, and how much time they spent at work, at home, and on personal activities.* I'd analyze these logs with my audience guinea pigs so I could talk about the challenges people faced. These audience members could then tell their colleagues how they dealt with them. Our sessions were interactive and, I hoped, enlightening.

I speak to all sorts of audiences, but often the women's networking group at whichever company I was visiting decided to sponsor my talk. Many of the time logs I collected for my talks, therefore, would come from the female executives who ran these networking groups. Many of these women had children. And, over time, I noticed something.

Their lives didn't look that bad.

Perhaps it speaks to the pervasiveness of those Recitations of Dark Moments that I thought I'd see perpetual chaos, or at least novelist Allison Pearson's *I Don't Know How She Does It* scene of an executive distressing pies to make them look homemade, but nope. There were tough moments, to be sure, but I also saw kid time, husband time, leisure time, sleep. I'd even seen time logs from senior women in consulting firms, that industry in which the entrepreneur who wanted to start the coaching company hadn't seen anyone whose life she wanted. To be sure, not everyone would want such a life. In the log she kept for me in March 2014, Vanessa Chan, a partner in a major consulting firm and mother to two young girls, woke up Wednesday morning in one city, which was a different city from the one she woke up in Tuesday morning, which was not the city she lived in either. She arrived home late Wednesday after her girls were asleep. She gave the sleeping children a kiss before going back to work. If we wanted a tale inspiring work/life lamentation, we could focus on that scene.

But when you see the whole of a week, you see different moments too. Chan missed Tuesday and Wednesday, but she put her girls to bed more nights that week than she didn't. She read them multiple chapters in *Little House on the Prairie*. I tallied it up, and she logged more time reading to her kids than, according to the Bureau of Labor Statistics' American Time Use

---

* Why thirty-minute blocks? I have found that few people spend an entire waking hour on one activity aside from work, but fifteen-minute (or ten- or five-minute) blocks seem too numerous and discourage many people from completing the log. Some people voluntarily opt to use different-size cells or time-tracking apps.

Survey, the average stay-at-home mom of young kids reads to hers. She visited one daughter's school and set up playdates with other parents while she was there. She did very little work on the weekend (not that it never happened, she told me, but she tried to keep a lid on it). Instead, she organized a game night for her family and went skiing, and took her daughters to the Lego movie. She had a coffee date with her husband. She watched TV and did a session on the spin bike. Far from distressing pies to make them look homemade, Chan spent a reasonable amount of time designing a Pokémon cake for her daughter's upcoming birthday. In all her busyness, she had time to indulge her hobby of making and decorating Pinterest-worthy cakes.

Not everyone would want Chan's life. Chan herself didn't want it forever. She had entrepreneurial aspirations for a second career, and when I checked back a year later, she was starting a company called Head First Ventures, which focused on bringing to life product concepts that Chan developed to solve a wide range of consumer gripes and pet peeves. But even if not everyone would want Chan's life, I couldn't claim that no reasonable person would want this life either. Cake designing, skiing, and snuggly bedtime stories do not imply a work/life horror show.

I saw this same phenomenon in many allegedly horrid industries: finance, law, medicine. Women were leaning in to their careers, and they were leaning in to the rest of their lives too.

How did they do it? The math is straightforward. There are 168 hours in a week. If you work 50, and sleep 8 per night (56 hours per week in total), that leaves 62 hours for other things. If you work 60 hours and sleep 8 hours per night, that leaves 52 hours for other things. Time diary studies (mine and others) find that very few people consistently work more than 60 hours per week, even if they claim they do.

The time is there to have what matters. Like Chan, though, we have to choose to see this, and many people choose not to. In the discussion of women's life choices, we often focus on the crazy moments, or the difficult moments, which makes sense. They're darkly entertaining. These get the press. Other moments—like eating breakfast with your kids or playing board games together on the weekend—aren't talked about. High-powered people may not mention them, partly because they absorb the not-unfounded message that talking about family at work could hurt you professionally. Leisure also isn't something people stress in conversation. They may mention, casually, something that happened on *The Bachelor*, but they won't introduce themselves by announcing they spend their evenings watching it. When people ask how things are going, the modern professional answers this: "Busy." I do it myself.

But what if this logical leap—these stressful things happened, and therefore life is crazy and unsustainable—limits our stories? The human brain is structured for loss aversion, and so negative moments stand out more starkly than positive moments, particularly if they fit a popular thesis. We lament the softball game missed due to a late flight, and start down the road of soul searching and the need to limit hours at work or perhaps resign, but we don't rend our garments over the softball game missed because another kid had a swim meet at the exact same time. No one ever draws the conclusion from that hard-choice moment that you need to get rid of the other kid. We could draw numerous conclusions from our Clifford Chance associate's horrible day—she needs a different child care arrangement, she needs a different division of labor at home, she needs to be more clear about her boundaries at work, or some days are just miserable and such is the human condition—but these are not the conclusions that fit the chant of our modern Greek chorus: no one can have it all, *so don't you even try.*

I've been pondering this aspect of narrative, and why certain moments turn into stories that then develop their own power as they get repeated. Influential economist Robert Shiller explained the phenomenon best in a different context when he told *The Wall Street Journal* why people cling to the idea that they can pick hot stocks, basically because they like these companies' stories: "Psychologists have argued there is a narrative basis for much of the human thought process, that the human mind can store facts around narratives, stories with a beginning and an end that have an emotional resonance. You can still memorize numbers, of course, but you need stories. . . . We need either a story or a theory, but stories come first." Language existed long before literacy. We absorb information as tales you might hear around a campfire, with points of evidence leading to an epiphany that teaches a lesson, a lesson that matches what the larger culture wants you to believe, even if (another narrative device) it sometimes masquerades as a "hidden truth."

I love stories as much as anyone, but these campfire stories built around dark moments miss the complexity of life. You cannot look at Chan's long Wednesday without seeing *Little House on the Prairie* too. The traditional format leads to the conclusion that life is madness. It is either/or. A commenter on the *Modern Mrs. Darcy* blog summarized this worldview, explaining why she'd opted out of the workforce: "If you get your joy from a paycheck and a pat on the head, go for it. I prefer hugs and dandelions."

Look at the whole of life, though, all the minutes that make up our weeks, and you see a different picture. Those questions lobbed at successful women as if any given cocktail party were a presidential news conference—*How do you do it? How do you manage? How do you balance?*—have a straightforward answer. Life has space for paychecks *and* dandelions, business trips *and* Pokémon cakes. We can carry many responsibilities and still revel in our own sweet time.

I am more interested in this entire mosaic. Many people have placed the tiles of their professional and personal worlds together in ways that give them space to strive toward their dreams at work and home. As I tried to convey this holistic view to people, though, I often hit this problem: I had no statistics I could call upon. Some organizations do phone surveys, but there are vast problems with just asking people how they spend their time (more on this later in this book). Time diary studies are more accurate. The American Time Use Survey and studies from the Pew Research Center and elsewhere look at how mothers and fathers spend their time, breaking it down by whether people work full-time or part-time, in or outside the home. Full-time jobs, however, are a diverse set, as are jobs held by people with bachelor's degrees (another common demographic cut).

I wanted to get at the idea of "big jobs," and understand what the lives of people with marquee careers and families looked like. But I had nothing beyond the stories of people I interviewed, and the slowly accumulating pile of time logs from speeches to document the reality. As I read more "can't have it all" stories, I realized that people were arguing or, worse, making huge life decisions based on anecdotes.

I wanted data. The best way to get that data, I decided, was to produce some.

The Mosaic Project

In 2013, I began seeking out time logs from women who, by at least one definition, had it all:

- They earned more than $100,000 per year
- They had at least one child (under age eighteen) living at home

I recruited women who might keep track of their time via my blog and various professional networks I'm involved in, and I branched out from there. I sent volunteers a spreadsheet and asked them to record their time for a week. Most received these instructions: "Write down what you're doing, as often as you remember, in as much detail as you wish to share. Keep going for a week, then send it back, and we can discuss it." Some people used Word documents so they could describe their lives more at length. Some used apps such as Toggl to produce more precise measures than my spreadsheet with its thirty-minute cells allowed. Some altered my 336-cell spreadsheet to turn it into a 672-piece mosaic of fifteen-minute blocks.

When people sent the logs back, I tallied hours spent on work, sleep, TV, exercise, reading, and housework/errands. I had conversations by phone or e-mail with most of the women. I wanted to learn more about their strategies, and many people asked for feedback about their logs: how they might solve time management challenges and find more time for fun. I approached these time logs partly as an anthropologist, studying these new ways of making work and life fit together.

This book is about the results of what I came to call the Mosaic Project: a time diary study of 1,001 days in the lives of professional women and their families. Everyone has opinions on having it all. I want to show, moment by moment, how it's really done.

At least that's the hope. Any project like this raises questions. Perhaps most obvious, why women? I hope this book will be useful for anyone who wishes to have a full life, which these days certainly includes many men in demanding careers as well. I overheard my husband's half of a conversation once with a new father who was trying to figure out how he could build a career at his firm and spend time with his son. It was the same work/life balance conversation women have been having for decades, even if neither guy would ever host a panel discussion on the topic.

I focused on women for a few reasons. First, highly successful women are still more likely to be in two-career families than men in similar positions, with all the juggling that implies. One study of medical researchers who won K08 or K23 grants, which are early career National Institutes of Health (NIH) awards that demonstrate high potential, found that only 44.9 percent of these up-and-coming male researchers who were married/partnered had spouses or domestic partners who worked full-time. For women, the figure was 85.6 percent. That's not to say that men with partners who work part-time or who stay home with their kids don't also want to have full lives. Likewise, a number of women in the Mosaic Project had stay-at-home partners, or partners who didn't work as many hours as they did. These categories are not cut-and-dried.

However, I have found that, on the margins, successful women still have a certain vision of what their involvement with their families should be. I suspect it is benchmarked against a false perception of how stay-at-home mothers spend their time, but to put a positive spin on it, women really want to spend time with their families. They want to be intimately involved in their home lives. So a breadwinning mother with a husband who stays home with the kids tells me that she gets up with her children in the morning so she can spend time with them before work and her husband can sleep. Another describes her husband "punching out" when she gets home from work in the evening; she takes over the evening shift. Few men with stay-at-home partners expect to come home and enjoy a martini while their wives keep the children hushed. Still, they aren't facing a social message that they are somehow neglecting their children by spending their days earning the cash that keeps their families solvent.

People often speak of the work/home roles that high-earning women navigate as a second shift. But they can be viewed less pejoratively too. Because women are navigating these dual roles, they produce new and creative ways to move around the tiles in the mosaics of their lives. I'd seen this anecdotally in time logs, and I knew this from my own life, but as a work-from-home, entrepreneurial sort, I assumed I had freedoms others did not. Indeed, in

Anne-Marie Slaughter's *Atlantic* article, the conclusion was that women who managed both to be mothers and to have big careers "are superhuman, rich, or self-employed." As the Mosaic logs poured in, though, I soon saw that even conventionally employed women developed creative strategies for building lives that allowed them to have it all, not just in theory, but reflected in how they spent their hours.

That's why I studied women. But here's another question: why *mothers*? Certainly, it's possible to have a fulfilling life without having children, and one recent poll done by Citi and LinkedIn found that women are more likely to believe this than men. Some 86 percent of men said having children was part of their definition of success, but only 73 percent of professional women included children in their definition of having it all. I hope that, in time, the investments people make in extended family, friends, and community will become a bigger part of the work/life conversation. Right now, however, people with children are the vanguard. As they create new ways of placing their tiles, the strategies they employ can be instructive, whether your definition of success includes having children or not.

As for the $100,000 salary requirement, I needed an objective number. I know this measure of success is incomplete as well. I am aware on an extremely *personal* level that some careers pay more than others. A few minutes spent perusing the Bureau of Labor Statistics' Occupational Employment and Wage Estimates files convinced me that if I wanted to assume a good living, I went into the wrong line of work. The median wage for "writers and authors" is $55,870; the 90th percentile is $115,740. Meanwhile, the median wage for lawyers is $113,310. This means that an utterly middling lawyer will earn as much as a writer at the top of her game. I know that by using $100,000, I'm going to wind up with some mid-level lawyers in my sphere of "successful women," and I'll wind up not counting enormously influential people who have achieved success in lower-paying fields.

Nonetheless, earning six figures indicates you have achieved financial success, even if you're not in the 99th percentile for your industry. You can support a family on your own, whatever any other adults in the household choose to do. Very few women (in the United States, less than 4 percent of employed women overall) earn six figures. I wish that figure were higher, but it isn't, which suggests that women who have achieved it are doing something worth studying. Even if it's true that some careers readily yield six-figure incomes, one reason many women *don't* choose these high-paying fields is a perception that you'll work crazy hours and have no control over your life. From these time logs, I found this was not true, though I also found that another objection I heard—it's easy to have it all if you earn six figures because you can just outsource everything!—wasn't automatically true either. Many women made their lives more difficult than necessary by not taking advantage of their affluence, a phenomenon I'll explore in later chapters.

I had collected 143 complete logs when I and the researcher who worked with me crunched the numbers to understand these 1,001 (143 × 7) days from a quantitative perspective. I received dozens more logs I couldn't use in the quantitative half of this project because they were missing a day or two or were not detailed enough to provide an accurate daily count of time spent working and sleeping (the two categories that generally occupied the largest chunks of hours in people's lives). They still provided qualitatively interesting fodder. I interviewed some of these women for the book, and others who met the criteria but didn't keep logs, to learn their strategies. Many more logs have continued to come in since I stopped "officially" collecting them for data, and this book reflects insights from those logs too.

I appreciate all these logs, because tracking time takes time and effort. This is why most people don't undertake a study like this when they want to understand how many hours people devote to things. Instead, researchers ask people to estimate: How many hours do you work? How many hours do you spend taking care of your children? The study on K08 and K23 grant recipients, which I mentioned above, used this method to estimate how many hours men and women spent on household tasks. They asked.

Asking people to estimate how they spend their time is simple and straightforward. Unfortunately, it produces unreliable answers. Most of us don't know how many hours we devote to different things. We don't know how many hours we work or sleep or watch TV. People will give answers to survey takers, but those are just guesses. And worse, they're guesses influenced by systematic bias. If everyone in your industry talks about their eighty-hour workweeks, even if logs show they're probably averaging fifty-five hours, you will talk about your eighty-hour workweeks too. In a world where we complain about how busy we are, we're not going to mention that five out of seven nights per week we sleep just fine. It's the night that a kid woke up at two a.m. and you had to catch a seven a.m. flight that you talk about at parties or mention in your departure memo. It's not that the horrible night didn't happen. It's just that it's no more emblematic of life than any other night. It must be taken in context.

A 168-hour time log removes most of these problems. People can lie on these logs, to be sure, but it's harder to do. You'd have to systematically input more work and less sleep on the log itself, and most people aren't that intent on lying. Phone survey lies are lies of ease, not nefariousness. A time log reminds the respondent that a day has 24 hours, and a week has 168. No matter how amazing we are, all of our activities must, and do, fit within these bounds.

To be sure, a time diary study has limits too. As one woman aptly pointed out, when you have a baby, morning, evening, and weekend time rarely involves doing anything for thirty minutes straight. Here's an entry from one woman's weekend: "Check on work/[son] play outside/read book while watching/wash/hang/fold laundry." Many people described the mishmash of what happens after dinner or on weekend mornings as "family time." There may be puttering around the house, some housework, some child care, some TV, some playing, but those time blocks probably aren't devoted to one single activity. I don't discount the "?" entries on time logs. Modern life features a lot of "?" time. Furthermore, a key requirement of a time diary study like the Mosaic Project is that you have to be able to describe time in words. This seems straightforward to me. I'm working. I'm driving. I'm sleeping. If I'm multitasking by checking e-mail while watching TV, I'll write that too.

Not everyone thinks this way. One of the most poignant scenes in Brigid Schulte's 2014 book, *Overwhelmed: Work, Love, and Play When No One Has the Time*, involves her attempting to fill out sociologist John Robinson's time spreadsheet, then abandoning the Excel format when she decided she could not shoehorn her life into a grid. Instead, she created a rather dramatic document: "2 am–4am Try to breathe. Discover that panic comes in the center of the chest—often in one searing spot. Fear in the belly. Dread just below that. The should haves and self-recrimination oddly come at the left shoulder . . ." I have had a few people, often extremely creative entrepreneurs, describe the same challenge. People have different personalities. To stick with a time log for 168 hours, you probably need a practical personality closer to mine ("it's good enough") than a free-form or perfectionist sort.

There is also the question of whether the weeks logged are "typical" or "atypical." I maintain that there are no typical weeks. Attempts to label weeks as atypical are what create faulty impressions of our lives. I don't instruct people to start filling out their time logs at a given day or hour. Starting a log on Monday morning is good, but you can also start the log on Wednesday at two a.m., as long as you keep going for the next 168 hours. Yet for the Mosaic Project, I saw that people generally aimed to log weeks they saw as more typical than atypical. A number of women started over with new logs when they lost workdays due to illnesses and snow and other unforeseen events, even though these atypical events add up. Most didn't log weeks with holidays or vacation days, though these things happen too. Overall, I suspect this tendency to hunt for typical weeks—often weeks spent at work in a significant way—means people's work hour totals for their diary weeks were higher than one would find averaged over a longer period of time.

I had to make judgment calls on what to count in different categories. Everyone in the Mosaic Project e-mailed me at some point, and I spoke with most on the phone too, so I tried to clarify anything ambiguous, for example if "coffee with Lou" was a work meeting or a personal one. If a log was too sparse, I chose not to include it.

A few other sources of bias: The act of observing something changes the thing being observed. I don't always read to my kids as much as I would like, but when I record my time, I'm more diligent about it. I spend less time perusing social media, if for no other reason than I don't want people to know I check Twitter fifteen times per day. I imagine others do the same thing.

The women in this data set aren't a representative sample of all high-earning women with children. No doubt the truly overwhelmed couldn't (or wouldn't) find time to fill out a time log. Also, many Mosaic Project participants read my blog or have read my books. The vast majority of humanity has not, so that's one difference. I think of my readers as extremely competent people, though another possibility is that people become heavy consumers of time management literature because they think they need help in this area. About a third of participants worked for companies where I bartered speeches in exchange for time logs. They came from a variety of different fields and regions, though they often lived in or near major cities, because that's where six-figure jobs tend to be concentrated. Their children ranged from babies to teenagers. Their family sizes ranged from one to four kids. I had married/partnered moms and single moms (I didn't make having a partner a criterion for having it all, though some might argue it is).

I won't claim I've done things perfectly, but despite the limitations of my study, I think the Mosaic Project captures a more holistic picture of the lives of professional women and their families than I've seen elsewhere. In these logs, we see how people truly spend their hours. We see life moment by moment, rather than hearing about these moments after they've been twisted by the human impulse to turn life into a story with a conclusion ("Life is crazy!").

To be sure, the logs did *not* show that life was a breeze. I am not a Pollyanna; all is not perfect. There were moments on these time logs when people *were* crazed, and some people were more crazed than others. Some women described their lives in great detail, stretching those Excel cells to convey moments that made me cringe. One woman locked her keys in the car on the first day she was dropping a child off at a new day care, thus making that already traumatic morning even more traumatic. Another woman, awakened in the night by a newly potty-trained child's accident, left the house at 5:45 a.m. to squeeze in a workout and "halfway to gym realize I don't have my sneakers, have to turn around, no Spin class today."

But these logs did not indicate a 168-hour show of desperation, as you might expect from the "maxed out" anecdotes dominating the literature about women, work, and life. There are sweet moments of joy and fun, too. A lawyer's 8:30 p.m. Friday night entry shows this: "See a sign at favorite wine store that says they have a 'life changing pinot noir.' I can't pass that up." A manager at a chemical manufacturing plant went to a balloon festival and an alligator festival with her family on the same weekend and also squeezed in "Shopping by myself!!!"—those three exclamation points summing up the happiness of this experience. There are snuggles in bed. There is space for blowing bubbles on the driveway. In a beautiful meta-moment, a woman wrote of attending a mosaic-making class to tap the artistic side of her personality. There are strange juxtapositions: a woman ironing on a Saturday, followed immediately by a facial, perhaps as a reward. Such is the mishmash of life.

This varied nature is what I want to convey every time someone asks

"How does she do it?" What we think of as either/or is often not so stark. The logs from the Mosaic Project show what life really looks like for women with big careers and families. It is about the strategies people with full lives use to make space for their priorities, and what we can all adopt from these strategies to make space for priorities in our lives too.

The Good Life

I wrote in the introduction that I am interested in what it means to live a good life, and how one can construct a good life. As I was compiling the data, a reporter asked me if the people in the Mosaic Project were happy about their strategies.

It makes sense that the good life should be one that makes you happy. Some women were voluntarily introspective after keeping their logs, and I have shared their insights throughout this book, but I didn't ask people whether they were happy, partly because the question is so fraught. Happy when? While on the phone with me? Life is not static. Some participants recognized elements of life that didn't work; when I circled back six to twelve months later, they'd made major changes from leaving jobs to moving. One woman who'd moved and switched day cares actually used the word "glorious" to describe her new morning routine.

We know from surveys of moment-by-moment contentment that people are happier while engaged in "intimate relations" than while driving to work. Any given week likely features both. Hour-by-hour happiness doesn't rise with household incomes past $75,000 a year, though overall life satisfaction keeps climbing well past $100,000. Random phone polls don't find many very high income households—because there aren't that many, one constraint I faced in enrolling people in this study—but one survey found that the vast majority of people in high-income ($100,000-plus) households called themselves "very happy." None called themselves "not too happy."

Be that as it may, here's an interesting statistic from one Pew Research Center analysis: women find every activity more tiring than men do. This is true for work, child care, and housework, which might make sense, but it's even true for leisure (though we're talking low absolute numbers in this category). I don't know why this is. It may be the stories we tell ourselves that there is always more we should be doing. It may be a comparison to our partners. In two-income households with kids, fathers have about 4.5 more hours of leisure per week than mothers, though they also log 10.7 more hours at the office. Perhaps women feel constantly "on call" in their lives, at work and at home. Stress can lead to complaints, even if objectively things look good. After I shared one woman's work and sleep hour totals with her—a perfect 40 for work, and about 8 hours per night for sleep—she wrote me that "On paper, it kind of seems like I have nothing to complain about! And yet I still do."

It is the *and yet I still do* part that inspires much angst and speculation in work/life literature, and it is no doubt at the core of why plenty of women in the Mosaic Project, and in the world at large, feel that they don't "have it all," even if they meet my definition. People seek answers: maybe it's that we're not mentally present, or that our leisure time comes in bits of "time confetti," to use Schulte's memorable image. But no one gets a perfect life. Not people who stay home with their children, not those who are married or not married, not those who have kids or don't have kids.

I want to push back against this expectation of a stress-free life, because it keeps us from seeing the sweet moments that already exist. Counting blessings is trite, but there's something to it. My friend Emma Johnson, known online as the Wealthy Single Mommy, and a participant in the Mosaic Project, started a blog series in 2014 she called "First World Fridays." In it, she wrote about whatever idiotic thing she complained about during the previous week, mocked it, and turned it around toward gratitude for the amazing life she has. Some entries: "My friends are buying second homes and I'm falling behind." Or my personal favorite: "My cleaning woman was slow with the laundry which made me late for my vacay."

None of this is to argue that problems don't exist. Johnson's life hasn't been bump free; see the "single mommy" part of her blog title (there's more on this in chapter 9). Some women in the Mosaic Project had children with special needs, with all the challenges inherent in that. A few women (though not many) averaged less than seven hours of sleep per day over the course of their diary weeks. Nothing in this book should be construed as an argument that society couldn't choose to adopt policies that are more supportive of working parents. That's an important topic and great thinkers have written about it, though issues of universal maternity leave and affordable child care are somewhat separate from the subject of what people do to make big jobs and families work. Women who earn six figures generally have access to paid leave (or can bankroll time off if they're self-employed). They can afford quality child care.

Instead, I want to argue for perspective. When I'm in LAX wondering if my flight will be canceled due to the impending snowstorm on the East Coast, I can be grateful that I have a phone to text my kids' sitter to strategize. She's totally ready to spend the night if need be, and my husband is on the case too, rebooking himself back to the United States on a flight that will take him around the storm path. I can be grateful that I'm not living in far more stressful circumstances, like the saga I read recently of parents in the Rwandan genocide seeing their children hacked to death in front of their eyes. My irritation when my beautiful, brilliant, and healthy children all want something from me simultaneously just as a source has finally called me back at 6:30 p.m. is pretty trivial compared with that.

Not only are such moments trivial, they are also just some of the tiles in my mosaic, in anyone's mosaic. There are many other moments, a full 10,080 minutes each week in total. The rest of this book, looking at all those minutes, is divided into three parts.

First, I look at how people spend their time at work. The good news is that successful people work more reasonable hours than we might assume. Indeed, some people, looking at their logs, decided they could work *more* if they wanted to achieve a breakthrough, without trading off anything of consequence. I found that Mosaic Project participants had much control of their time, not just as stated in corporate policy, but in how they operated day to day. They used this control to create space for personal and family time, even as they worked more hours than the average person. Of course, there are always ways to work more effectively in whatever hours people choose to work, and the last chapter of the work section covers strategies people used to spend more hours on career-building activities, and fewer hours on the useless parts of work that can expand to fill the available space if you let them.

Second, I look at how people spend time at home. I look at the ways women create meaningful interactions with children and partners, and identify strategies for making life, and life maintenance tasks, easier. Mosaic

Project participants spent vastly different numbers of hours on chores and errands. People choose different ways to structure their lives, but I think it's important to know what the ramifications of those choices are.

Finally, I look at how people spend their personal and leisure time. I look at sleep, something that occupies more time than people think, and perhaps the biggest source of distortion between impression and reality in people's lives. I look at exercise. I look at television, reading, and other leisure pursuits, and discuss strategies for making time for leisure, or at least enjoying it more when it happens. The final chapter, on mastering the tiles, contains advanced time management and productivity techniques, from learning how to estimate and budget time to using those little bits of time that exist in all our lives.

Since I am primarily interested in data, I allowed Mosaic Project participants to be anonymous if they wished. Others wanted to share the particulars of their days, so you'll see interviews about their challenges and strategies. You'll see time logs throughout this book, some in all their glorious detail, some more abstracted to show a strategy or common characteristic. What I love about these time logs is that they really look like mosaics, arranged in interesting patterns to allow for work, family time, personal time, sleep. No two women's mosaics look the same, but when they are taken all together, they answer that perennial question of *how does she do it?* A life is lived in hours. Having a full life is possible if you place the tiles right.

•

This book features dozens of time logs. Here's mine from a week in mid-March, to give you a sense of how to read them (p. 22).

There are no typical weeks, and I worked more that week than usual. I was uncommonly diligent about getting up at six a.m. to work because I was writing a post for *Fast Company* on what I learned from a week of waking up early (I learned that I worked more!). I worked Friday night, which isn't an entry I'm thrilled about. Indeed, I was downright sarcastic; see the "fun Fri night" comment. Part of the reason I was working on Friday and so much on Sunday is that I didn't work on Thursday afternoon. I'd also taken a day off the week before. My work total was 56.5 hours for the week. I've tracked my hours dozens of times over the years, and I know I usually work closer to 50 hours per week.

How to Look at a Time Log: My Week, March 17–March 23, 2014

	MONDAY	TUESDAY	WEDNESDAY	THURSDAY	FRIDAY	SATURDAY	SUNDAY
5AM							
5:30							
6	Up, work (Mosaic Project)	Up, work	Up, work (Mosaic)	Up, work (Mosaic)	Up, work		
6:30	Work (Mosaic Project)	Work	Work (Mosaic)	Work (Mosaic)	Work		
7	Work (Mosaic Project)	Work	Work (Mosaic)	Work (Mosaic)	R up, breakfast	Up, work	J in bed with us, up
7:30	Hang out with M, kids' bfast	Kids' breakfast	Hang out with M, kids' bfast	Kids' breakfast (banana bread!)	M, R, then boys up	Breakfast for R	Run
8	Kids (play; get ready)	Kids, work	Kids (15), work (15)	Work (Fast Company)	Nanny chat, then work	Read to R	Make coffee, shower
8:30	Work (Mosaic Project)	Work	Work (Mosaic)	Work (Fast Co)	Work	Clean kitchen	Work
9	Work (Mosaic Project)	Work	Work (Mosaic)	Work (Fast Co)	Work	Clean, get J out door	Primp, kids ready
9:30	Work (Mosaic)	Work	Work (Mosaic)	Work (Mosaic)	To KOP Starbucks	Play piano while kids watch TV	Ready, to church
10	Work (Mosaic)	Work (brainstorm ideas)	Work	Work (email)	Coffee with L	To Pinewood Derby	Church: bluegrass mass
10:30	Work (Mosaic)	Work (brainstorm ideas)	Work	Work (Mosaic)	Coffee with L, home	Pinewood Derby	Church: bluegrass mass
11	Work (Mosaic)	Work	Work	Run to post office (actual run)	Work	Pinewood Derby	Leave church, to Peace a Pizza
11:30	Work (Mosaic)	Work	Work	Primp, pick up Sam	Work	Pinewood Derby	Lunch at Peace a Pizza
12PM	Lunch with kids	Lunch with kids	Lunch with kids	Lunch with kids	Work (give webinar)	Pinewood Derby	To Y, kids to playroom
12:30	Work	Work (admin)	Work	Work	Work (give webinar)	To YMCA	Run (2 miles) and lift

How to Look at a Time Log: My Week, March 17–March 23, 2014

	MONDAY	TUESDAY	WEDNESDAY	THURSDAY	FRIDAY	SATURDAY	SUNDAY
1	Work	Emails	Work, primp for video call	Work	Work	Run while J at bball	Lift, play bball with boys
1:30	Brisk walk outside	Emails (+10 min call)	Video call doesn't happen, inefficient!	To Eaves with friend	Work (Oprah)	Watch rest of bball	Bball with boys
2	Work (Mosaic)	Work (interview)	2pm call also doesn't happen	To Eaves with friend	Work (Gifted Exchange)	Drive home	Swim with boys
2:30	Work (Mosaic)	Work (interview)	Work (call re book publicity)	To Eaves with friend	Work (USA Today)	Fill in taxes, get lunch	Drive to REI/pet store
3	Call re potential speech	Work (15), run (15)	Work (call re book publicity)	To Eaves with friend	Run	Play outside	Pet store and REI
3:30	Work	Run (15), work (15)	Work (Mosaic)	Learn J has Chinese performance	Work	Play outside	To IKEA, then trip aborted, home
4	Work	Work (draft Oprah piece)	Work (USA Today)	Chinese performance	Work	Play/yardwork	Finish taxes
4:30	Work	Work (Mosaic)	Work (Mosaic)	Chinese performance	Work	Read	Taxes, desk, dinner in oven
5	Work (15), kids, TV	Work (15), to library (15)	Work (15), kids, pick up J at school	Home, email, triage	Work	Read	Work (inefficiently)
5:30	Watch TV with kids	Work (novel)	Home with J, read, kids	Work (Fast Company)	Kids, read	Shower, dress	Make dinner, eat
6	Read NY Times online, cook	Work (novel, 2000 words!)	Start dinner, read	Work (Fast Co)	Make dinner, eat dinner	Kids dinner	Eat, clean up
6:30	Eat dinner	Read	Dinner with family	Work (15), dinner (15)	Boys to Derby, R & me to McDs	Hang out	Work
7	Play with kids, clean R up	Read (15), to dinner	2 kids to Ikea, J watch Frozen	Dinner	Sundaes! then home	Play piano	Work
7:30	Play downstairs with S&R	Sushi	Work (Mosaic)	Work (Mosaic)	Bath for R	Put R down, to date night	Work (15), Frozen dance party (15)

How to Look at a Time Log: My Week, March 17–March 23, 2014

	MONDAY	TUESDAY	WEDNESDAY	THURSDAY	FRIDAY	SATURDAY	SUNDAY
8	Dessert, stories	Drive home, fill gas tank	Work (Mosaic)	Work (Mosaic)	Play with R, boys do Wii	Date night	Kids' bath, read to kids
8:30	More stories, work (15)	Read to kids, bed	Mix banana bread	Work (ideas)	All kids to bed	Date night (find restaurant)	Read to kids, kids bed
9	Work (Mosaic)	Read	Kids to bed	Kids to bed	Work	Date night (Morton's)	Work
9:30	Work (Mosaic, answer email)	Read, M home	Kids to bed, email	Work, starting to drag	Work - fun Fri night	Date night (Morton's)	Work
10	Shower, into bed	Watch TV	Shower, read	Shower	Work	Date night (Morton's/home)	Work
10:30	Sleep	Shower, bed	Bed	Kids! (15), sleep	Talk to M, ready for bed	Shower, etc.	Shower, etc.
11		Sleep			Bed	Watch TV	Bed
11:30						Bed	
12AM							
12:30							
1							
1:30							
2							
2:30							
3							
3:30							
4							
4:30							

The good news is that this higher work total didn't leave me sleep deprived. I slept 51.75 hours, or about 7.4 hours/day. I can see evidence that I'm getting enough sleep: on Saturday morning, I didn't set an alarm, but I was still up at seven a.m. after going to bed at eleven p.m., even though my kids didn't wake me.

Working 56.5 hours and sleeping 51.75 hours leaves nearly 60 hours for other things. I scored some reasonable personal time. I took myself out for sushi on Tuesday night. I ran five times (an activity I consider leisure), though I didn't run as much during any given session as I might have hoped. This week was largely about squeezing exercise in: see the "run to Post Office (actual run)" entry right before lunch on Thursday. On the decadent side, I went shopping with a friend in the middle of Thursday to use a gift certificate to a boutique called Eaves in Wayne, Pennsylvania. I played the piano, albeit not much. I also went to church, an activity I logged in the personal category. The choir performed a Bluegrass Mass in lieu of a regular service and it was like going to a concert without having to pay for a babysitter. It was an unexpected reward for hauling my family there on Sunday morning.

My husband and I went out for dinner on Saturday night. I had some good kid interactions, too. I got to see Jasper perform with the Chinese language club at his elementary school. I practiced basketball with the boys and went swimming with them at the YMCA. I took Ruth out for sundaes while the boys and my husband worked on their pinewood derby car, and later watched Jasper place in his age group for the Cub Scouts pinewood derby. That was thrilling for all involved. I ate lunch with Sam and Ruth four out of five workdays.

In the "needs improvement" category, my evenings weren't as effective as I would have liked. On Monday, Wednesday, and Thursday, my log shows a lot of multitasking. I'd play with the kids for a bit, then try to read the paper, then cook dinner while checking e-mail. When the weather is nicer than it was in March, my goal is to spend evening hours more mindfully: out playing in the yard, blowing bubbles and picking dandelions. If I intend to work in the evening, it would be good to have a plan for what I hope to accomplish, so I don't drift in and out of my inbox. These are all things I'm trying to do.

If you'd like to keep your own time log, you can sign up to receive a template via my Web site: LauraVanderkam.com.

．
．
．
．
．
．
．
．
．

WORK

．
．
．
．
．
．
．
．
．

.
.
.
.
.
.
.

CHAPTER 2

Seek True Balance

How much do we work? How much should we work?

These are important questions to ask if you're trying to make work and life fit together, and they're ones that Jessie Neville, an intellectual property attorney, wanted to think about when she chose to participate in the Mosaic Project. Married to a software engineer, and mother to a five-, three-, and two-year-old, she wrote me that she thought she'd be a good addition to the study because having three kids "seems to be unusual in the legal profession." Indeed, after working on some stressful projects before having her third child, she was fully prepared to quit. She took eighteen months off from work. But her firm wanted to keep her, and lured her back with a contract that released her from a billable hours target, that bane of lawyers everywhere. Neville would get paid based on what she billed and could choose what she wanted her work life to look like.

So what should it look like? What would represent the right balance between work, her houseful of little ones, and what she calls her highest priority—"trying to be sane"?

The answer evolved. When she first kept a time log for me in January 2014, she was dealing with both external and internal assumptions of what it meant to build a big career while having a full life too. "I feel a little bit like a social experiment here," she joked, with few other female attorneys matching her level of fertility. Colleagues watched to see how it was done or if it *could* be done. As she studied her time log, she saw that she was dealing with these worries too. "Fear does factor in," she told me. "I didn't know if I could do this." Unsure when various "mom work" (like running errands related to the kids) would happen, she'd do it after her nanny arrived at the house at 7:30 a.m., and before she started her workday. That was one solution, though these morning errands cut into potential billable time. She hired a cleaning service, then came in to work at 10:20 a.m. on the January Tuesday she logged because she spent two hours picking up around the house before they showed up. Unsure of whether she could set limits on e-mail and client demands at night, she often did household administrative tasks such as scheduling during the day. Work wound up "in last place, behind pretty much everything else." That January week, she worked about thirty-two hours, and couldn't bill nearly as much of it as she wanted. There was a psychological component to this, with Neville telling herself the story that "If I'm not going to succeed at work, I might as well go to Office Max and buy all this stuff." No one can have it all—right?

Except here's the thing: "I do like the work," Neville reminded herself during this transition. "It's suited to my skills. I like to problem solve. I like to help people. I like to look at details." She liked her colleagues too. Having taken eighteen months off, she had the opportunity to rebuild her portfolio to focus on projects that intrigued her. There were also huge financial upsides to leaning back in to her career. She could help her family more by billing time at a lawyer's rate than by spending that same quantity of time running errands someone else could do.

So, when I circled back in October 2014, I learned that Neville had made a choice: she would return to a salaried position. She would bring a billable hours target back into her life. It was a better deal financially and, with the support of her family, she decided to make it work. She had been quite intentional about the logistics. While her January time log showed long mornings of getting distracted by household tasks, by fall Neville had elected to start taking the bus to the office. This decision forced her to leave the house promptly, whether things were picked up or not. "I get here by nine every day. I leave a little after five every day"—or at least most days, she told me. She was figuring out ways that her nanny could help her at home. "I used to go do errands on the way in to work that she could easily do and now does do." Neville was also exploring ways to bill more of the hours she was at work. But part of billing enough time is simply putting in enough time. When she needed to hit her target, her husband would take the kids and she would stay a little later or give herself one weekend a month to go in to the office and make this happen.

In other words, Neville's answer to what would make a better work/life balance was to work *more*. Not around the clock, but more than she originally thought she would. The numbers were pretty stark. On the Tuesday from her January 2014 time log, she worked just 5 hours and billed 3.3. When I had her track a Tuesday in October 2014, she worked 9 hours and billed 7.5 of those. Yet despite this near doubling of work volume, she still played with her kids in the morning, had family dinner, took some personal time for a hair appointment, and read before bed. Working more didn't require short-changing her family or herself. It simply required focusing on what she did best and not the myriad other things that could occupy her time. Life was a work in progress. She was figuring out her exact boundaries, but "all I can say is that right now, this is working."

I don't think this realization is unique to her. Many of us have space to lean deeper into our careers if we wish, but stories and assumptions—that leaning in will require harsh trade-offs—have great power over our lives. When it comes to work, especially for people who are also trying to build families, these stories can limit our lives and our careers in profound ways. But we can change our stories if we want. Taking a clear look at work hours, and how much we can or want to work, is the first step to building a life that's truly balanced, and moving forward on all fronts.

•

When it comes to work, and how many hours we work, we make many assumptions. We repeat common phrases without thinking. But is it true, as pundits lament, that Americans are increasingly overworked? According to historical charts from the St. Louis Fed, the average workweek for an employed worker fell from about 42.4 hours per week in 1950 to 39.1 hours per week in 1970. In August 2014, the Bureau of Labor Statistics reported that the average private, nonfarm workweek was 34.5 hours, or about a full 8-hour workday less than people clocked two generations before.

To be sure, an average masks many things. There's evidence of bifurcation in the workforce. In a tepid economy, some people can't get as many work hours as they want, creating a cash crunch that makes it hard to enjoy excess leisure. On the other side, men with college degrees (a proxy for those on the upper end of the workforce) have seen their weekly nonwork hours (that is, time devoted to activities other than work, housework, and child care) fall slightly from 1985 to 2005.

We do know that women are working more hours for pay than they did in past decades although, again, the average workweek isn't that long. According to the American Time Use Survey, in 2013, the average employed mother with a child under age six engaged in work and work-related activities for 33.11 hours a week, and the average employed mother with kids ages six to seventeen logged 33.46 hours. Some proportion of women work part-time. Yet when the ATUS produced a report looking at married parents' time between 2003 and 2006, it found that married mothers who worked full-time and had kids under age six did 33.88 hours of work and work-related activities per week, which technically doesn't even meet the definition of full-time work (more than 35 hours a week). Those with kids aged six to seventeen worked 37.73 hours a week.

Looking at the numbers, most people aren't overworked. When it comes to questions of having it all, though, and the big jobs most cultural commentary involves, we assume a different reality. Sure, the average person doesn't work that much, but doctors, lawyers, consultants, people at tech companies, those in finance, and those in the upper rungs of corporations, making six figures a year? *They* must work extremely long hours.

I used to believe this. Back in 2002, when I was twenty-three, I wrote a column for *USA Today* called "White-collar Sweatshops Batter Young Workers" that, in the days before social media, managed to go viral by being e-mailed around a lot. I wrote about a young woman who was an investment banker with JP Morgan. She had been working on two projects at once. "One night after weeks of 18-hour days and constant travel, she staggered home at 7 a.m. Not to sleep. To shower. As she stood in the water, she started crying.

At age 25, she was having a midlife crisis. 'I started thinking, there's got to be more to life than this,' she says."

I noted that JP Morgan was far from the only firm driving its young employees insane; various banks (some of which disappeared later) and consulting firms did as well. "All hire the brightest Ivy League grads and make them a deal," I wrote—basically, that you'd get paid well and get "glimpses of corporate luxury, from ritzy hotels to jaunts on the jet. In exchange, you must work 70, 80, 100 hours a week through the best years of your life." But it was a scam, I noted: "Give a kid a signing bonus and a $500 bottle of champagne, and he doesn't notice that he's working for $12 an hour."

It went on like this, talking of exclusive firms keeping labor costs low by squeezing blood out of their hires. "People complain. Oh, they complain. You worked 80 hours this week? Well, I worked 90. You slept four hours? I slept at the office and showered there, too! The dirty secret is, many sweatshoppers actually like it. This generation vied for status in college by comparing workloads. Many of them then dove like lemmings off the cliff into corporate America. A high-wattage job fills an almost religious need to be part of something bigger than yourself, and 16-hour days mean you don't have to deal with the messiness of life."

A few things stand out to me from this, other than my editors' saintliness in indulging my overwrought prose. I simply accepted what my friends were telling me about their work hours, even though they found time to complain to me about those hours, usually in situations that clearly weren't work (for example, in one of New York City's numerous dive bars). I simply accepted the adage to think hard about your career because "you spend the majority of your waking hours working."

Is this true? In a decade of writing about time and careers, I've come across studies that show a fascinating tendency of white-collar workers, particularly inhabitants of those "white-collar sweatshops," to inflate their work hours. Many studies simply ask people how many hours they work. People respond with a number. In theory, even if no one knows the exact number, some people should be high and some people should be low, and together they should come to the right answer. But this is true only in the absence of systematic bias. Workweeks are prone to such bias because we like to think of ourselves as hardworking and, in a world of ongoing layoffs, no one wants to be seen as working less than the guy in the next cube.

Sociologist John Robinson has done some interesting work on this over the decades. In his and Geoffrey Godbey's 1997 book, *Time for Life*, they analyzed time diary data from 1965 to 1985, and found that people claiming 50- to 54-hour weeks were overestimating by about 9 hours compared with their actual diaries. People claiming 55- to 59-hour workweeks were off by 10 hours. People who estimated 60- to 64-hour workweeks were off by 14 hours. Those who thought they worked 65 to 74 hours were north of the mark by 15 hours, and those claiming 75-plus-hour workweeks overshot by 25 hours and more. As they concluded, "only rare individuals put in more than a 55–60 hour workweek." In an article for the June 2011 *Monthly Labor Review*, Robinson and his colleagues updated those figures with more recent data. Comparing estimated workweeks with time diaries, they found that those claiming 75-hour workweeks were still off by about 25 hours.

That's a big discrepancy. Indeed, I've started to call this eye-opening finding the "X - 25" rule. When people put an exact number on their long hours and that exact number is higher than 75, you can often mentally subtract 25 hours, if not more, to arrive at the correct tally. Yes, a few people consistently work 80-hour weeks (though some number of them may complain about their "120-hour weeks"). The longest workweek I've seen on a time log was 100 hours—from a self-employed woman, incidentally, not someone in finance, consulting, or a tech start-up. But in general, people don't work extreme hours. Even CEOs don't. The Executive Time Use Project, run out of the London School of Economics and Political Science, has been looking at CEO schedules across various countries and industries. One analysis of more than 1,000 CEOs in 6 countries found that the average CEO spent 52 hours per week on work activities, while CEOs in the bottom quartile worked 44.2 hours per week, and those in the top quartile worked 58.5 hours per week. Those aren't short workweeks, by any means, but they're not even close to flirting with the three-figure level.

On one level, this tendency toward inflation is what it is: more evidence that people lie about many things in life. When I get in a more somber mood, though, it makes me angry, because I think there's something insidious going on. By exaggerating workweeks, people can make some jobs appear off-limits to those who care about having a life. The competition toward the top of many fields is intense. Making women—and men—think that they must inevitably choose between a particular career and their families will knock a huge chunk of the competition out. A Mosaic Project participant who worked at a hedge fund noted that her field gets a reputation like this. "I was very intimidated in business school by guys with a background in hedge funds," she says. "They just had this attitude that they knew it all, and they'd make these pronunciations about the world." She wouldn't have considered the field until a roommate did a summer internship at a hedge fund and swore it was interesting, manageable work. This woman applied, got a job, and "after having the job for less than a year, I realized a lot of what [the business school guys] said was complete BS." She worked 45.75 hours during her diary week, and did no work at night or on the weekend. She gets five weeks of vacation a year, has the flexibility to go to preschool events, and gets paid *a lot*. But the industry's reputation "scares people away from even interviewing."

The truth about big jobs is far more positive. In the Mosaic logs, I found that women who earn over $100,000 do work more hours than the average mother with a full-time job (who works roughly 35 hours a week). This should not be surprising, given that even those with the lowest six-figure salaries earn about three times as much as the average woman (who earns about $37,000 a year working full-time). But six-figure earners do not work three times as many hours. They don't work twice as many hours. Mosaic Project women put in about 44 hours a week, on average. Some worked more, though not that much more. No one in the Mosaic Project topped 70 hours during their diary week, even though I included women in the sweatshop-tilting fields of finance, law, medicine, accounting, consulting, tech, etc. Only eight logs (6 percent) topped 60 hours, and for more than half of those, the participant offered reasonable evidence of why those work hours would not be repeated fifty times during the year. Further, an average, by definition, means that a number of people were lower than 44 hours a week. Of the 143 logs, 51 (36 percent) featured fewer than 40 hours of work.

A 44-hour workweek, or even a 54-hour workweek, can make for a reasonable life. And, indeed, high-earning women have more balanced lives than the popular narrative conveys. Jenni Levy, a physician who worked 48.5 hours during her diary week, tells me, "I talk to young women in college all

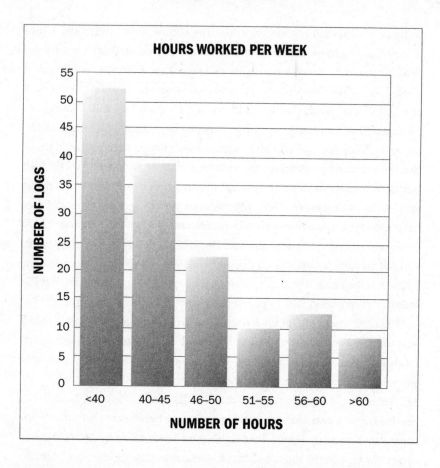

the time, and they say to me, 'I want to go to medical school but I also want to have kids,' and it makes me want to scream." No one says *I want to be a teacher but I also want to have kids* as if the two are incompatible, and yet "I see with my friends who are teachers that they have way less flexibility than I have," says Levy, "and they make much less."

Women massively limit their earning power when they choose not to consider "big" jobs that would require a few extra hours of work on the margins. While 9 hours certainly isn't nothing, in the context of a 168-hour week, and considering the potential salary variance, the difference between a job that usually requires a 35-hour workweek and one that requires a 44-hour workweek may not be as vast and life altering as we think it is. You can reap big rewards by being willing to work a few extra hours, the few that take you right up to the point of diminishing returns.

To be sure, I am not denying that long workweeks happen. If you are above the point of diminishing returns, there are ways to cut your work hours and still get a lot done, which this chapter will cover. But if you are *under* the point of diminishing returns, as lawyer Jessie Neville felt she was, it's okay to know that the usual work/life balance narrative—that you're probably over-worked, and achieving the good life means figuring out ways to work less—is not the only story out there. When we create enough time to invest in our careers, our careers grow. We can better support our families financially. Over time, that affluence can give us even more control of our time and our lives.

Much psychological research finds that the key to workplace happiness is a sense of progress. Day by day, you are getting somewhere. There is little more frustrating than working but not working enough to see that happen. When we work enough to see our careers flourish, we find work energizing. That gives us more energy for the rest of our lives. "I can't imagine anything better in the world than what I do for a living," Levy says.

·

Why is it so hard to work long hours? Why do we think we work more than we do? Partly it's that what we think of as work time doesn't always encompass work. I could describe my days like this: On a "serious" day, which I could decide to see as typical, I'm up around 6:15 a.m. and working by 6:20. I take a break for the evening at 5:20 p.m. That's eleven hours. I probably work for at least another hour most nights, and I work on weekends too. If I add this up, I should be hitting sixty-five hours regularly, let alone the weeks I travel. I travel fairly frequently, so let's say I work seventy hours a week.

But unless you get paid by the hour, you've probably never calculated exactly how many hours you work. In looking closely at my days (which ad-mittedly change year to year based on the kids and our child care schedules), I see that I sometimes work from 6:20 to 7:20 a.m., but then I spend time primping and hanging out with my kids. Our nanny comes most days at 8:00, but transitions aren't instant. I'm probably not back at my desk until 8:20. Even if I manage to work with no aimless wandering around the house (or naps) until noon, I almost always take a half-hour break then for lunch. I also tend to take at least a half-hour break in the afternoon to go for a walk or a run. So a 6:20 a.m. to 5:20 p.m. day isn't eleven hours spent working, it's nine hours. And that's before we get to the other activities that take place during the workday, which include doctor and dentist visits, school functions, snow days, nanny vacation days, occasional errands, or grabbing coffee with friends and the like. I'm more prone to this than others because I am self-employed, but I saw plenty of "life" during work time on time logs, and this time adds up. Here's the saga of a woman with a completely conventional job, who attempted to figure out which week would show a "normal" schedule:

> If anything, a "normal" week for me is one that includes one day in between Monday and Friday that is weird for one reason or another. For example, January 3rd is missing from my log because it was a snow day and my office and kids' schools were closed. January 6th is missing because my 8-month-old son was baptized the Sunday before and I took the day off to help get various grandparents and godparents to and from the airport. The next week, my husband had a planned minor surgery on the 14th, followed on the 15th by my 4½-year-old daughter coming down with croup, so I took a bunch of sick time. The 20th was the MLK holiday; the 21st my son was sent home sick from day care and I wound up taking more sick time, plus there was another snow episode that afternoon that shut down the office and schools early. This week, I worked from home on Monday morning so I could spend extra time with my best friend from college (also my daughter's godmother) who was visiting from Texas, and to help with getting the house ready for a second set of house guests during the week. I feel like 4 weeks in a row of planned/unplanned time away from the office means that it's a lot closer to normal than not.

I have never managed to work a "perfect" week either that's not missing at least a few hours during one workday. Even when my husband took the kids for a weeklong vacation with his extended family during the summer of 2014, and I had zero child care responsibilities for seven straight days, I still found that life intervened. I sprained my ankle on a run and had to deal with that. My neighborhood lost power for close to twenty-four hours after a thunderstorm, rendering my laptop useless. Given that the American Time Use Survey finds mothers with full-time jobs and young kids work fewer than thirty-five hours per week, I presume such interruptions happen for other people, too. Think of a typical full-time worker, who's in the office from nine to five daily, but takes thirty minutes for lunch, leaves an hour early on Friday, and comes in an hour late on Tuesday due to a dental appointment. That puts her at 35.5 hours for the week. One errand tacked on to the end of lunch one day or a longish midmorning break will pull her under that thirty-five-hour threshold that defines "full time."

This is why it is hard to work long hours, and it's why most people don't. To be sure, my method of counting work hours resulted in over- or under-counts for individuals. Some people just blocked out, say, nine a.m. to seven p.m. as work hours on their logs, though I doubt they were working the entire time. In the other direction, some women needed to run around frequently, and I didn't count time in the car unless it was multitasked work (for example, identified as time spent on the phone for a work call, or a real estate agent driving her client somewhere).

Of course, that raises these questions: What is work? Why didn't I count commuting time? The average commute time in the United States is about twenty-five minutes, and it seems like it would be easy to include commute time in work totals, but time diary studies have long struggled with how to count this. Direct travel is easy, but what if the person stops along the way? A ten-minute stop to buy milk on the way home might be a regular part of the journey, but that would go in the "purchasing goods and services" category, not work.

I decided not to count the commute as part of the workday, partly because I don't have an army of statisticians to help me figure this out, and also because commute time generally *isn't* contributing to your career trajectory. Your boss wouldn't accuse you of working less if you moved closer to work. You wouldn't bill less time or take on fewer projects. If anything, the opposite might be true. Two people may both have child care from eight a.m. to six p.m., but if one is driving thirty minutes each way, unless she consciously chooses to carpool with a colleague and hold meetings in the car, she most likely loses that hour. Whereas someone who's working from home or who lives close to work might use that time to do what she is paid to do. Over time, working nine hours per day (eight to six minus an hour for lunch and breaks) versus eight hours per day (eight to six minus an hour for driving plus an hour for lunch and breaks) adds up. Unless your work limit is below forty-five hours a week, you can get more done in nine hours versus eight.

Once I chose not to count commuting time, counting work was relatively straightforward. Most people called entries "work" or something that was pretty clearly work ("meeting with assistant"). I considered "Lunch with colleagues" as work, though not "lunch" (unless it was "worked through lunch"). Likewise, a work dinner with clients is work, even if you enjoy the people on their own. Travel counted as work only if it involved career-related activities. People will quibble with this, but to me, watching one of *The Hobbit* movies on the plane is not work. (In practice, this didn't affect totals much because women who traveled a lot used preboarding time for calls, takeoff time for work reading, etc.)

With this counting methodology, I found that 19 of the 143 logs featured fewer than 35 hours of work. Some of these women were entrepreneurs who had some ability to choose how much they worked. Interestingly, while a small number of women in the Mosaic Project mentioned that they had official part-time schedules, many of these women worked more than 35 hours (a phenomenon I'll discuss in the next chapter). In general, the sub-35-hour crew were people aiming to work full-time. Things just came up that precluded a 35-plus-hour workweek. The lowest number in my sample—a workweek just shy of 25 hours—came from a woman whose partner was traveling, and who had to cover two snow days with her child. In all, though, even if I don't include the 19 logs with fewer than 35 hours, the average workweek in the logs I collected only rises to 46 hours per week. If you work 46 hours per week and sleep 8 hours per night, that leaves 66 hours for other things.

•

Some women did work significantly longer than average during their diary weeks. I studied the eight women who logged more than 60 hours to figure out why their lives looked like they did. One woman chose to log a week during which she'd attended a weekend professional conference. Another woman had joint custody of her children. She sent me two recorded weeks.

In one, when her ex-husband had the kids, she worked 63 hours. When she had the kids, she worked 32.5. Both are equally typical, but they average out to a more reasonable 48 hours.

The biggest driver of extreme work hours, though, was a quirk in my sample. I gave speeches at a few companies in exchange for time logs from some of the participants. One major accounting firm offered logs from their female employees who met my criteria. I collected the bulk of my time logs, including ones from this company, in February and March 2014. Accounting can be a career with reasonable hours overall, but not during what these women referred to as "busy season," mid-January to mid-March for auditors, and up to Tax Day, April 15, for people who work in the tax divisions. Almost all of the remaining people logging more than 60 hours a week were accountants at that firm.

To be sure, even intense hours allow for space. The accountant who logged the longest week, 69 hours, managed to take Saturday completely off. If you work 69 hours and sleep 48 (as she did that week) that leaves 51 hours for other things. That's something, if not a lot.

I was curious about this accountant's life, so, after various accounting deadlines passed, I got back in touch. She told me that the week she logged "would have been one of my busier weeks, although my hours are fairly heavy." She shared a file of her billable hours from the previous fifteen months so I could calculate a more holistic average. While the first few months of the year stayed in the 50s and the 60s, things tapered off after that. Some summer weeks featured fewer than 40 hours. Her average over this long stretch of time encompassing two busy seasons was in the 50s. You can't bill all your time, and she worked long hours, but 69 hours was an outlier, even for her.

Everyone else worked less.

•

None of this should imply that anyone who feels overworked is fooling herself. You can work far fewer than 69 hours a week and feel legitimately like you are working too much. Indeed, you can work 44 hours per week and still feel unbalanced. Perhaps the hours of eight to five keep getting interrupted, forcing you to work early, or late, or on weekends to make up the time, and you don't get the concentrated downtime you want. Perhaps you find yourself making mistakes, and losing hours to digressions you know are unproductive. Perhaps you've decided you'd like to do something different with your life, but your long hours are preventing you from pursuing those dreams. Or your presence at the office is occasionally required for reasons that are questionable at best. I had an internship once in college where we got paid time and a half for overtime, and were allowed to order dinner if we stayed past eight p.m. Not surprisingly, if we interns had nothing better to do any given night, or the employees we were working with wanted to stick around, we'd find work that "needed" to be done, at least until the spicy tuna rolls arrived. Those were stupid hours. We all do have mental work limits. The exact number likely varies based on the work you do, but if yours is 45, and your boss expects to see you for 50, it is quite possible that you are working some stupid hours too, or to use a more nuanced, economics-sounding phase, "past the point of diminishing returns."

I started to recognize this point of diminishing returns on time logs, both over the week as a whole and within each workday. For the overall sample, Wednesday was the peak workday, with an average of 9.0 hours worked. People worked less as the week went on and they hit their weekly point of diminishing returns. Thursday totaled 8.5 hours, and Friday 7.1, or about 2 hours less than Wednesdays. As for daily points of hitting work limits, I noticed that when people didn't take intentional breaks, they took unintentional ones. One lawyer (not Neville) wrote on her log, "Begin drafting email. Realize I need a shirt for work. Buy 2 sweaters and clutch at J. Crew online. Decide to walk outside and get lunch." It might have been a more efficient use of that half hour, and cheaper, just to go to lunch first.

If you're stuck in an office that really values face time, you can play the game if you want. Start taking longer breaks. Maybe no one leaves before eight p.m., but no one really knows if you're in a meeting for an hour over lunch, or if you've just disappeared. Maybe people care more about one end of the long workday than the other. In general, managers who prize face time tend to value staying late more than coming early. It's more visible, even if total hours are the same. One woman who worked in an office where people sometimes worked until ten p.m. consciously came in around eleven in the morning, having used earlier hours for family and personal time. You can also recognize that these things are not either/or. You can choose to stay ridiculously late one night per week so everyone sees you doing it, and then cut out every other night at the time you choose.

There are also more productive things you can do to take control of your work life. You can take all your vacation days and personal days, which lowers your total work hours over time. If you're in an industry such as accounting that goes through peaks and troughs of busyness, relish the troughs. You don't have to seek out activities to fill space. You can if you want. Troughs might be a good time for big-picture projects such as starting a networking group, but if you're feeling overinvested in work and underinvested in your personal life, slow periods are a good time to rectify the problem.

You can attack root causes, too. One reason many women and men leave client-facing roles in consulting, law, and finance is the assumption that client service is incompatible with having a life outside of work. But this isn't inevitable, and a key part of making this work is negotiating expectations and workloads with an eye on sustainability for both you and your team. A client who wants a crash project will be given it, but she has to pay for a certain number of additional team members. The team can be there all the time, but you bring in the team in shifts. That way people can cheerfully work late two nights a week, knowing they'll get the others off. Flexibility is a team sport. Of course, this means that no one can be the 100 percent point of contact for a client. This is a mind-set shift, because in many professional service firms, owning the relationship with a client is a real currency. But it's a currency with downsides from an organizational perspective. It inspires internal bickering and jockeying, which isn't productive for anyone. Better to spread the love. Take turns delivering good news and bad news. Make sure everyone shines in the soft skills department.

Finally, you can promote quality over quantity. Some proportion of clients may not care if they are overworking your team members, but they do care about their business interests. A repeat offender can be told that a team member she desperately wants is not available, because she has other options with clients who don't suffer from late-night neediness. You can offer your difficult clients a star, if the clients agree to your star's demands. You can also be the star. In many fields, expertise and connections can be traded for a reasonable lifestyle. You can be, as productivity guru Cal Newport titled his book, *So Good They Can't Ignore You*. Some competitive sorts may jockey for advantage by being available when others are not, but from a long-term perspective, being able to crank out a report overnight is less valuable than spotting a huge opportunity right at the beginning of a project. When you are just starting out, you have to build your career capital. Over time, as you prove you're very good at what you do, you can cultivate managers and clients who value that in and of itself.

Even if you're not in client service, there are plenty of strategies for knocking time off your workweeks. The easiest way to find an hour a day? Study your schedule and choose one hour-long meeting or conference call that does not require your presence. When do you not add value? What recurring meetings could happen less frequently? What meetings are about information, rather than reaching a decision that requires everyone in the room? Figure out if you could send someone else in your place or possibly even cancel the meeting altogether.

You can also schedule meetings for shorter slots. Just because Outlook tells you meetings should take 30 or 60 minutes doesn't mean these blocks have been determined by divine decree. Shorten meetings you can't kill. Two 60-minute meetings turned into 45-minute meetings buys you 30 minutes a day. Personally, I like the idea of 22.5-minute or 37.5-minute meetings. Everyone will assume you have an incredibly detailed, thought-through agenda.

Another tactic for maximizing your working hours is to plan your toughest tasks for early in the morning. One study done by researchers associated with Johnson & Johnson found that people's energy levels peak around eight a.m. When you show up at work with your coffee, it is game time. You're pumped and ready to go. So that's the best time to schedule intense work that will require deep thought. By three p.m. or so, most people's energy levels are flagging. If you aim to tackle a vexing item then, you'll get distracted, and take twice as long as you would have at eight a.m. This buys you a late night.

You can also tweak social dynamics in the office to support a reasonable quitting time. Humans are social creatures, and our natural inclination is to end the day by circling around saying good-bye to people. It's a nice ritual but there's nothing stopping you from subtly training your coworkers to have these chats earlier in the day. Circle around after lunch, checking in with your team, so you don't face a choice between cutting a conversation short or staying late.

My personal favorite strategy is to perform a four p.m. triage. An hour before you aim to leave, revisit your to-do list. Pretend an evil villain, laughing maniacally, has informed you he will steal your phone and laptop at five p.m. and keep them until the next morning. Knowing that, what would you still do? What wouldn't you do? With a hard stop at quitting time, it turns out a lot of things can wait. Even if you generally work for an hour after the kids go to bed, which is a strategy I found many women employed, consciously choosing to log off until then can buy you a more reasonable workday over all.

Ultimately, though, the best strategy is simply to be bold. Building the life you want is about having the courage to do it. Unless you have officially scheduled work hours, you can leave the office earlier, even if your boss is still there. Not everyone is obsessed with face time. Try scheduling something in the evening that will get you out of the office early or on time at least one night per week. Some of the people who are best about getting out of work on time are, no surprise, those who must catch a train, or pick up their kids at day care by six p.m. Even if you don't have that, treating your personal life with the same importance and urgency as your work appointments increases the chances that you will leave on time. You'll also have a life worth leaving for.

•

Those are some strategies to trim your work hours if you think you're working more than you'd like. But what if you're not there? What if you'd like to work *more*?

Most productivity books don't address this question, because the assumption is that no one would want to work more hours, especially not someone with kids. Maybe we'll "lean in" before kids, to use Sheryl Sandberg's phrase for taking your career development seriously, but we won't lean in after they arrive. That's fine if you had a lot of time to build a career before becoming a parent, but some of us started our families on the earlier side. There's only so much pre-kid leaning in you can do if you have kids in your twenties. Eventually, if you have reasonable ambitions, you have to learn to lean in with them. Given how hard it is to work long hours, sometimes I struggle to achieve my optimum. Someone interviewed me recently during a string of snow days and asked what I'd like to spend more time doing. I said "work." She thanked me for my honesty though it was clear that was not an answer many other people had given her.

The truth is that while I work hard, and I sometimes work long hours, I know I underinvest in the soft side of my job. I do not put nearly as much effort into expanding my connections as I should. If my regular work consumes all my child care hours, then it is always easier not to get in the car and drive thirty minutes to go meet someone. If I'm navigating child care arrangements and I'm working with my husband's travel schedule too, it is easier not to go to that conference. I make these decisions even though I know my chances of hitting some sort of jackpot at any event are good. In recent memory, I've gone to a friend's cocktail party and walked out with an assignment for a feature at a major magazine because I kept yakking with an editor. I bumped into another editor at a conference and he hinted I should ask for a raise. I did—I'm good at taking hints!—and the raise paid for my conference. This book came about similarly: I attended Book Expo America and chatted with my former editor at Portfolio about this idea. I got positive feedback, and here we are.

I also know that when I go places, I find fascinating things to write about. I find stories that make me want to keep my foot on the gas with my career just so that I'll have the opportunity to tell these stories to as big an audience as possible. This process of discovery, this exploration, is what gets short shrift.

There's more about this soft side of careers in chapter 4, but as I study how people spend their time, I've started to see a few things. One is that if you want to work a few more hours, you won't necessarily need to make the harsh trade-offs people think you will. Try tracking your time for a week. See what time is spent on things you care about, and see how much time is spent on other things. That time can be redeployed if you want. Looking at how Neville changed her days, she found additional hours to work without giving up time with her children or her personal time. She just had to think about what she did best, and nix the mindless time that passes for all of us whether we think about how we use it or not. Even if you don't have the same options, you can probably increase your working time by moving the tiles of your life around creatively, a topic covered in the next chapter.

Semantics matter in this conversation, especially if we're talking about increasing the hours at a full-time job. "Full-time" implies that work consumes all your time—the full amount of your time—but it clearly doesn't. If you work 40 hours a week and sleep 8 hours a night, that leaves 72 hours for other things, which is almost twice as much time as you're working. The adage that "you spend the majority of your waking hours working" is only true if you're working more than 56 hours a week (if you sleep 8 hours a night). Most people don't do that, even those earning six figures, in big jobs with lots of responsibility. In only 11 percent of Mosaic logs did the person spend more than half her waking hours at work. You can work more than full-time and still have more time for nonwork things than you spend on the job.

Indeed, working less than full-time means you're not balanced in any linguistically correct sense of the word. In this instance, your life is weighted more toward the personal side. Working 25 hours per week and sleeping 8 hours a night means you have 87 hours available for other activities. That's a personal-to-work ratio of 3.5 to 1. If everyone is happy with the situation, that's great. There are plenty of amazing things beyond work one can do in life. But it's also okay to enjoy what you do for a living and *want to do more of it*. It's okay to be excited about moving into a season of life when more work is possible.

Calee Lee owns Xist Publishing, which creates children's books formatted for touch screens. When she and I first chatted years ago, she was mostly caring for her young children while freelancing a few hours on the side. That's a great choice, but she had additional dreams for a much bigger career. A few years later, she wrote a guest post for my blog about her decision to embrace these new ambitions. "Even though I promised myself I would never be one of those mothers who lets the laundry pile up, I am," she noted. "And it may be the best thing that ever happened to me."

On March 30, 2011, Lee wrote about finding herself "with an extra couple of hours before my mother was scheduled to bring my children home. I'd finished up my freelance projects for the week and looked at the pile of laundry located all of two feet from my desk. I posted a tweet, 'I have 2 (unplanned for) hours until the kids come home. I know @lvanderkam would not approve, but I'm considering doing laundry.'

"I didn't need to wait for Laura's reply," Lee said. "I knew the best way to spend those hours would not be folding clothes while watching Tivo'ed *So You Think You Can Dance*. As much as I love a good dance-off, TV and chores are for hours when my brain is done. Instead of completing one task, I started a new one—I began writing the children's story I'd been telling for years . . . I'd never bothered writing the story because frankly, I didn't think I had the time."

Fast-forward a few months. Lee used Amazon's publishing platform to launch *The Queen and the Cats* with help from an artist friend. She realized that "if I was going to go through the hassle of developing a contract, learning how to make an ebook and figuring out how to market from my home office, I figured I might as well build a little company and do this for others. Xist Publishing was born." Within a few more months, she'd signed several authors to produce touch-screen-friendly picture books. They released twenty books in 2012, and more books in 2013. By 2014, even with investing much of Xist's income back in the business, Lee was able to pay herself a Mosaic-level salary.

When she filled out this log (p. 48),* Lee was navigating how she thought of herself as an entrepreneur, and how work fit in her life. She had some preschool and babysitting hours to focus on work, but only enough to log just shy of thirty-two hours during her diary week. She'd schedule calls and intense work while her son was in preschool in the mornings, and then try to answer e-mails and work on small things in the afternoon while he was around and, unfortunately, no longer napping—a bittersweet milestone for people who work from home without much child care.

It was a difficult balancing act, but this phase would be ending soon. Her son would be going to full-day school, giving her space to lean in and achieve the work/life balance that comes from being able to build a business without as many limitations. Describing her current life with a four-year-old as her constant companion, she told me, "In some ways I really, really like it. I'm really happy with the way my life is structured right now. In some ways I'm also really happy that he starts full-day next year."

---

* Important note: Lee logged her time during Holy Week; hence the high volume of hours at church.

	FRIDAY	SATURDAY	SUNDAY	MONDAY	TUESDAY	WEDNESDAY	THURSDAY
4:30 AM				4:45 wake up - work			
5				Work		Wake up - read	
5:30				Work		Read	
6	Wake up and get self ready		Wake up	Get kids and self ready	Wake up and get ready	Send email	Get up with O
6:30	Breakfast and lunches			Breakfast and lunches	Breakfast and lunches	Email	TV with kids
7	Kids get ready	Wake up	Lounge	Kids	Kids	Email	Fall back asleep
7:30	Driving - school	Breakfast	Lounge	Driving - school	Driving - school	Email	Sleep
8	Work	Clean up	Lounge	Work - marketing	Work	Email	Wake up
8:30	Work	Laundry	Lounge	Work	Work	Driving - school	Get ready
9	Work	Get self ready	Get self ready	Work	Work	Driving - client	Get kids ready and dishes
9:30	Work	Get kids ready	Get kids ready	Work	Work	Driving - drop off stuff at J's	
10	Phone calls	Church	Church	Work	Work	Driving	Work
10:30	Load gear	Church	Church	Work	Work	Set up gear	Work
11	Pick up kids	Church	Church	O (son)	O (son)	Film interview	Work
11:30	Driving to in-laws	Church	Church	O/clean	Grocery	Film interview	Work
12PM	Driving/eating	Church	Church	Lunch	Lunch	Driving	Work
12:30	Drop off kids at in-laws	Make palm crosses	Lunch	Work	Work	Driving	Kids/work
1	Driving to Palm Desert	Make palm crosses	Clean/kids	Clean	Work	Driving	Lunch
1:30	Driving	Look for paper w/ my article in it (work?)	Clean/kids	Grocery	Work	Driving	Work/ kids interrupting

	FRIDAY	SATURDAY	SUNDAY	MONDAY	TUESDAY	WEDNESDAY	THURSDAY
2	Set up gear	Kids/clean	Clean/kids	O (son)	Work & errands	O (son)	Work
2:30	Film interview	Kids/clean	Read	Pick up A	Pick up A	Pick up A	Work
3	Film interview	Kids/clean	Read	Library (work?)	Work	Church	Work
3:30	Film interview	Kids/clean	Read	Library (kids play)	Work	Church	Kids - Easter eggs
4	Film interview	Kids/clean	Read	Work	Work	Church	?
4:30	Film interview	Birthday party (kids; guest)	Movie night w/ kids	Kids	Kids to choir	Church	Make dinner
5	Film interview	Birthday party	Movie night w/ kids	Make/eat dinner	Dropoff	Make dinner	Eat dinner
5:30	Film interview	Birthday party	Make dinner	Clean up	Car wash w/ O	Eat & clean up	Clean up
6	Driving/eating	Birthday party	Dinner	Baths	Dinner out	Wine w/ husband	Email
6:30	Driving	Birthday party	Bath time	Get ready	Driving	Putter	Get ready
7	Visit at in-laws	Kids	Church	Church	Church	Putter/play	Church
7:30	Visit at in-laws	Laundry	Church	Church	Church	Play	Church
8	Visit at in-laws	Laundry	Church	Church	Church	Bath	Church
8:30	Visit at in-laws	Put kids to bed	Church	Church	Church	Put kids to bed	Church
9	Driving home	Get ready for bed/ read	Put kids to bed	Put kids to bed	Church	Read	Church
9:30	Driving home	Read	Read/get ready	Read	Put kids to bed	Sleep	Church
10	Read	Sleep	Sleep	Sleep	Work		Church
10:30	Sleep				Work		Church
11					TV		Settle
11:30					Sleep		Sleep
12AM	O - awake				O - awake		

	FRIDAY	SATURDAY	SUNDAY	MONDAY	TUESDAY	WEDNESDAY	THURSDAY
12:30					Sleep		
1							
1:30							
2							
2:30							
3						Awake	
3:30						Awake	
4							
4:30	X	X	X	X	X	X	X

As she said, "It was a personal choice to be a primary caregiver as long as I have, but we are transitioning out of that. It will be a good thing for my business and my children and everyone involved. We had a good run, but now they can go away a little more." The children grow into becoming their own independent people, and Lee's business will grow into its own too. That's a balanced life. It's one that embraces ambition, rather than some old story of what balance should be.

•
•
•
•
•
•
•

CHAPTER 3

Take Charge of Your Time

When we talk of combining work and a life outside of work, we often come to the idea that work must change. We believe that jobs requiring longer-than-full-time hours must be off-limits to people who want to be deeply involved with their families. We've internalized this so much that, for all people talk of being overworked, most women, even professionals, don't work all that many hours. Joan Williams, a professor at the University of California's Hastings College of the Law, accurately pointed out in a post for *Harvard Business Review* that only 9 percent of American mothers work more than fifty hours per week. She wrote that she'd asked numerous people to estimate what proportion of mothers work those kinds of hours, and "Most guess around 50 percent." Look at employed mothers with college degrees and the proportion of those who work fifty-plus-hour weeks increases slightly, though it's still less than 14 percent.

If 14 percent sounds familiar, Williams observed, that's because it's about the proportion of top jobs—law firm partners, top paid employees at public firms—that are held by women. This is probably not a coincidence. Working hours that are slightly longer than average opens up career possibilities. Given the way the workplace is widely perceived to work, though, Williams was resigned to female representation remaining at about 14 percent of these jobs: "We can't get mothers to work more hours," she wrote. "We've tried, and failed, for forty years. Mothers won't bite for a simple reason: if they work 55 hours a week, they will leave home at, say, 8:30 and return at 8:30 every day of the workweek, assuming an average commute time. Most moms have this one little hang-up: they want to see their children awake. Increasingly, many fathers do, too."

I believe that parents do want to see their children. I also know there are some organizational cultures out there that view work as an in-the-office, 8:30-to-8:30 deal, and pockets of bad management lurk in even excellent companies. But as someone who's worked fifty-five-hour weeks in my life (please see the time log in chapter 1), and who sees my children regularly, and who's studied time logs from women working fifty- or fifty-five-plus-hour weeks who also see their children, and exercise, and see their husbands, and blow bubbles in the backyard, I think this argument presents a false choice.

When it comes to making the pieces of work and life fit together, flexibility matters more than keeping a strict limit on total hours. Taking charge of your time is more important than working full-time or part-time, which is good, because there are often huge financial and career consequences to switching to part-time work, while there aren't necessarily consequences to moving your work hours around on dimensions of time and place. Indeed, about a third of full-time workers already work "remotely"—that is, away from the corporate mother ship. Little-known fact: the majority of these people are men. In this new world, no one necessarily knows whether you're traveling between two clients at eleven a.m. on Friday or you're at your son's preschool brunch, which is what my husband did the other day. If you can choose which hours to work, and, to some extent, where to work them, you can still have the sort of personal life you want while working more hours than someone whose hours and location are more strictly controlled.

The good news is that the vast majority of women in the Mosaic Project had flexibility in their work schedules, and they used that flexibility in creative ways. This meant that some worked at hours that sound, to someone picturing the old model of working, insane. In the context of these women's lives, however, these strange hours worked. Yes, workplaces can do a lot more than they currently do to accommodate working parents. There are also ways working parents can structure their lives to go full on in building their careers while building their families too. These desires need not be either/or. If you take charge of your time, it is completely possible to work fifty or fifty-five hours a week—the point that makes people eligible for the biggest and highest-earning jobs—and still enjoy a full personal life as well.

•

Finding out exactly how much flexibility people have at work is a tricky question. A 2014 survey from Cali Yost's Flex + Strategy Group/Work + Life Fit, Inc., found that 97 percent of full-time employees had some sort of work-life flexibility, which is an encouraging statistic, though 45 percent said they weren't so sure their companies were all that committed to the idea. Some companies market themselves as flexible, but aren't. Other companies start with flexibility, then build a gleaming new headquarters and end work-from-home practices because, darn it, they built this edifice and want to see people there. Within companies, flexibility varies among managers. One may require anyone leaving before five p.m. to take a personal day, whereas another figures that if the work gets done, the particulars are irrelevant. There are also some companies and industries that no one perceives as flexible, but in which people create flexibility anyway, following that old adage that it's easier to ask for forgiveness than permission.

Flexibility is less about policy than about the reality on the ground. Instead of asking people how much flexibility they had, I looked at their time logs. Did people do anything personal—more substantive than eat lunch, or make a quick call, or check Facebook—during what appeared to be their core work hours?

Most—75 percent—did. The activities varied. Some women went to their doctor or dentist appointments or their children's. They volunteered at schools. They exercised. They went shopping. Plenty worked from home at least one day a week, and did some personal activities during breaks on those days.

Of course, there is a flip side to this flexibility. I also tracked how many women did something work related, beyond briefly checking e-mail, during what one might think of as core personal hours (early mornings, nights, and weekends). This number was similar: 77 percent.

When people write articles about the craziness of modern life, they focus on and lament this latter figure. Our inboxes and cell phones can indeed follow us everywhere, and we work with people in different time zones who expect replies at times that imply we live on the same continent. There are few of the 168 hours in a week that at least one person from the Mosaic Project did not work. If I wanted to write about the horrors of being on a conference call with a team in Asia at ten p.m. I could. People worked on weekends. A lawyer got up around 4:30 a.m. to start billing work.

Many of the same pundits who lament the 24/7 work culture, however, speak positively about flexible work, and working from home. In 2013, the American Time Use Survey found that 36 percent of Americans with college degrees did some or all of their work at home on the days they worked. Some of this resembles my setup—working in my home office full-time except when I'm traveling—but in some cases, this means a professional takes a longer lunch to take a yoga class, then works at home at night to complete the tasks that didn't happen during that time. She visits her son's school during the day and is back on e-mail after the kids go to bed. The two are completely connected. It is the ability to do the latter that enables the former, which means it misses the mark to label one "good" and the other "bad."

To be sure, not all work can be shifted around this way. If your job involves patient procedures, for example, you will generally need to do those procedures at appointed times in whatever facility is set up to do them, though people with these more regimented schedules still figure out ways to create lives that work. The rise of group practices is partly about the need to accommodate family responsibilities. People cover for one another if one person needs to attend to something in her personal life. It's harder to pull off than in a corporate environment, but it is flexibility in a different format.

My definition of flexibility has its limits. I may be undercounting flexibility in an absolute sense, as some women in the study had flexibility, judging by their colleagues' more porous schedules, but chose not to use it. A few women chose to work just as Williams described: a traditional Monday to Friday schedule, worked straight through. Here's what one such log from an accountant, featuring fifty-one hours of work, looked like (p. 57).

There is a certain simplicity to this log. Work is work and home is home,

	MONDAY	TUESDAY	WEDNESDAY	THURSDAY	FRIDAY	SATURDAY	SUNDAY
5AM	Sleep	Sleep	Sleep	Sleep	Sleep	Sleep	Sleep
5:30	Sleep	Sleep	Sleep	Sleep	Sleep	Sleep	Sleep
6	Sleep	Sleep	Sleep	Sleep	Sleep	Sleep	Sleep
6:30	Family time	Family time	Family time	Family time	Family time	Family time	Family time
7	Meal	Meal	Meal	Meal	Meal	Meal	Meal
7:30	Family time	Family time	Family time	Family time	Family time	Family time	Family time
8	Travel time	Travel time	Travel time	Travel time	Travel time	Family time	Family time
8:30	Travel time	Travel time	Travel time	Travel time	Travel time	Family time	Family time
9	Work	Work	Work	Work	Work	Travel time	Family time
9:30	Work	Work	Work	Work	Work	Volunteer time	Family time
10	Work	Work	Work	Work	Work	Volunteer time	Family time
10:30	Work	Work	Work	Work	Work	Volunteer time	Family time
11	Work	Work	Work	Work	Work	Volunteer time	Family time
11:30	Work	Work	Work	Work	Work	Volunteer time	Family time
12PM	Work	Work	Work	Work	Work	Volunteer time	Family time
12:30	Meal	Meal	Meal	Meal	Meal	Meal	Family time
1	Work	Work	Work	Work	Work	Volunteer time	Meal
1:30	Work	Work	Work	Work	Work	Travel time	Meal
2	Work	Work	Work	Work	Work	Family time	Family time
2:30	Work	Work	Work	Work	Work	Family time	Family time
3	Work	Work	Work	Work	Work	Family time	Family time
3:30	Work	Work	Work	Work	Work	Family time	Family time
4	Work	Work	Work	Work	Work	Family time	Family time
4:30	Work	Work	Work	Work	Work	Family time	Family time

	MONDAY	TUESDAY	WEDNESDAY	THURSDAY	FRIDAY	SATURDAY	SUNDAY
5	Work	Work	Work	Work	Work	Family time	Family time
5:30	Work	Work	Work	Work	Work	Family time	Family time
6	Work	Work	Work	Work	Work	Family time	Family time
6:30	Work	Work	Work	Work	Work	Family time	Family time
7	Work	Work	Work	Work	Work	Meal	Meal
7:30	Travel time	Travel time	Business develop	Travel time	Travel time	Meal	Meal
8	Travel time	Travel time	Business develop	Travel time	Travel time	Family time	Family time
8:30	Meal	Meal	Meal	Meal	Meal	Family time	Family time
9	Family time	Volunteer time	Family time	Volunteer time	Family time	Family time	Family time
9:30	Family time	Volunteer time	Family time	Volunteer time	Family time	Family time	Family time
10	Me time	Volunteer time	Travel time	Volunteer time	Me time	Me time	Me time
10:30	Me time	Volunteer time	Travel time	Volunteer time	Me time	Me time	Me time
11	Sleep	Me time	Me time	Me time	Sleep	Sleep	Sleep
11:30	Sleep	Sleep	Me time	Sleep	Sleep	Sleep	Sleep
12AM	Sleep	Sleep	Sleep	Sleep	Sleep	Sleep	Sleep
12:30	Sleep	Sleep	Sleep	Sleep	Sleep	Sleep	Sleep
1	Sleep	Sleep	Sleep	Sleep	Sleep	Sleep	Sleep
1:30	Sleep	Sleep	Sleep	Sleep	Sleep	Sleep	Sleep
2	Sleep	Sleep	Sleep	Sleep	Sleep	Sleep	Sleep
2:30	Sleep	Sleep	Sleep	Sleep	Sleep	Sleep	Sleep
3	Sleep	Sleep	Sleep	Sleep	Sleep	Sleep	Sleep
3:30	Sleep	Sleep	Sleep	Sleep	Sleep	Sleep	Sleep
4	Sleep	Sleep	Sleep	Sleep	Sleep	Sleep	Sleep
4:30	Sleep	Sleep	Sleep	Sleep	Sleep	Sleep	Sleep

and the two don't bleed into each other. If you choose to work this way, you can come home and, if you have younger kids who go to sleep early, see them off to bed. Then you watch TV or read. You have your family time on weekends. Because you've done your long hours during the week, you probably won't need to work on Saturday or Sunday. If you do, you keep the separation. You go to the office for a few hours and come home. You wouldn't squeeze work in during your children's nap time.

I found that most professional women with kids, however, choose to work differently. They choose to treat all tiles in the mosaic as fair game. When they do, we find some fascinating creations. Here are the most common strategies people used to make longer work hours, and personal time, fit into 168 hours, and how to apply these methods in your life, too.

1. Split Shifts

Williams's description of a fifty-five-hour week doesn't reflect how many women who work long hours actually clock that time. Rather than work these hours straight through, a woman might leave work at a reasonable hour during the week. The exact hour varies; it could be 4:30 or it could be 6:30. The point is that it's early enough to give you the evening for family or personal pursuits. Then, at least one weeknight per week, you go back to work after the kids go to bed. You work what I call a "split shift"—some work happens during the day, and some at night, too.

I saw this strategy or its cousin (working in the early morning hours before the kids wake up) on 45 percent of logs. Here's a log from a woman with a seven-year-old and a four-year-old, who put in 66.5 hours of work by splitting shifts (p. 60) and doing some weekend work.

This is an extremely long workweek, but these long hours haven't prevented this woman from seeing her kids. On this log, she's left work every day by 6:30 p.m., and twice by 4:00 p.m., to spend time with her kids after school hours: at lacrosse practice, taking them to the library, having dinner with them. As she told me, "I always try my best to make it to the boys' activities. I hope they will not grow up to remember how much their mom worked but rather that Mom came to watch me play. It is exhausting but much more important." (An important note: This was a busy-season

	MONDAY	TUESDAY	WEDNESDAY	THURSDAY	FRIDAY	SATURDAY	SUNDAY
5AM	Sleep	Sleep	Sleep	Sleep	Sleep	Sleep	Sleep
5:30	Sleep	Sleep	Sleep	Sleep	Sleep	Sleep	Sleep
6	Sleep	Sleep		Sleep	Sleep	Sleep	Sleep
6:30	Sleep	Sleep		Morning routine, including getting myself and kids ready for the day (including breakfast)	Sleep	Sleep	Sleep
7	Sleep	Morning routine, including getting myself and kids ready for the day (including breakfast)		Morning routine, including getting myself and kids ready for the day (including breakfast)	Morning routine, including getting myself and kids ready for the day (including breakfast)	Sleep	Sleep
7:30	Morning routine, including getting myself and kids ready for the day (including breakfast)	Morning routine, including getting myself and kids ready for the day (including breakfast)	Morning routine, including getting myself and kids ready for the day (including breakfast)	Dropping kids at school	Morning routine, including getting myself and kids ready for the day (including breakfast)	Sleep	Sleep
8	Morning routine, including getting myself and kids ready for the day (including breakfast)	Morning routine, including getting myself and kids ready for the day (including breakfast)	Morning routine, including getting myself and kids ready for the day (including breakfast)	Dropping kids at school	Driving/dropping kids at school	Morning routine, including getting myself and kids ready for the day (including breakfast)	Morning routine, including getting myself and kids ready for the day (including breakfast)
8:30	Driving/dropping kids at school	Meeting with teacher	Driving/dropping kids at school	Work	Work	Morning routine, including getting myself and kids ready for the day (including breakfast)	Morning routine, including getting myself and kids ready for the day (including breakfast)
9	Work	Meeting with teacher	Work	Work	Work	Driving	Family time

	MONDAY	TUESDAY	WEDNESDAY	THURSDAY	FRIDAY	SATURDAY	SUNDAY
9:30	Work	Meeting with teacher	Work	Work	Work	Work	Family time
10	Work	Meeting with teacher	Work	Work	Work	Work	Family time
10:30	Work	Work	Work	Work	Work	Work	Family time
11	Work	Work	Work	Work	Work	Work	Cooking
11:30	Work	Work	Work	Work	Work	Work	Cooking
12PM	Work	Work	Lunch with friend	Work	Work lunch	Work	Family potluck
12:30	Work	Work	Lunch with friend	Work	Work lunch	Work	Family potluck
1	Work	Work	Work	Work	Work	Work	Family time
1:30	Work	Work	Work	Work	Work	Work	Family time
2	Work	Work	Work	Work	Work	Work	Family time
2:30	Work	Work	Work	Work	Work	Work	Family time
3	Work	Work	Work	Work	Work	Work	Work
3:30	Work	Work	Work	Work	Work	Work	Work
4	Work	Work	Work	Driving/pick up kids	Work	Work	Work
4:30	Work	Work	Work	Driving/pick up kids	Work	Work	Powerskating
5	Work	Work	Work	Library with kids	Work	Work	Powerskating
5:30	Work	Driving/pick up kids	Work	Library with kids	Work	Work	Dinner
6	Driving/pick up kids from parents	Hockey	Work	Driving	Work	Dinner and visit	Dinner
6:30	Driving/pick up kids from parents	Hockey	Lacrosse	Dinner	Dinner	Dinner and visit	Family time
7	Swimming lessons	Hockey	Lacrosse		Dinner	Dinner and visit	Family time

	MONDAY	TUESDAY	WEDNESDAY	THURSDAY	FRIDAY	SATURDAY	SUNDAY
7:30	Swimming lessons	Family time	Dinner	Family time	Movie with family	Dinner and visit	Family time
8	Family time	Family time	Family time	Family time	Movie with family	Dinner and visit	Work
8:30	Making lunches	Making lunches	Making lunches	Making lunches	Movie with family	Dinner and visit	Work
9	Dinner	Dinner	Nighttime routine, including shower	Making lunches	Movie with family	Dinner and visit	Work
9:30	Nighttime routine, including shower	Nighttime routine, including shower	Nighttime routine, including shower	Nighttime routine, including shower	Movie with family	Nighttime routine, including shower	Nighttime routine, including shower
10	Work	Work	Work	Work	Nighttime routine, including shower	Nighttime routine, including shower	Work
10:30	Work	Work	Work	Work	Work	Work	Work
11	Work	Work	Work	Work	Watching TV	Watching TV	Work
11:30	Work	Work	Work	Work	Sleep	Work	Sleep
12AM	Work	Work	Sleep	Work	Sleep	Sleep	Sleep
12:30	Sleep	Sleep	Sleep	Sleep	Sleep	Sleep	Sleep
1	Sleep	Sleep	Sleep	Sleep	Sleep	Sleep	Sleep
1:30	Sleep	Sleep	Sleep	Sleep	Sleep	Sleep	Sleep
2	Sleep	Sleep	Sleep	Sleep	Sleep	Sleep	Sleep
2:30	Sleep	Sleep	Sleep	Sleep	Sleep	Sleep	Sleep
3	Sleep	Sleep	Sleep	Sleep	Sleep	Sleep	Sleep
3:30	Sleep	Sleep	Sleep	Sleep	Sleep	Sleep	Sleep
4	Sleep	Sleep	Sleep	Sleep	Sleep	Sleep	Sleep
4:30	Sleep	Sleep	Sleep	Sleep	Sleep	Sleep	Sleep

accountant, so "Thankfully," she said, "those work hours drop off a little May to October.")

Most people with split shifts worked far fewer than 66.5 hours. Here's a schedule of a woman with two school-age kids who works at a large tech company (p. 64). She logged 48 work hours during this week.

In her case, this schedule was driven by the need to work with customers in Asia during their office hours. The trade-off she made with her organization was that she would leave at three or four p.m. a reasonable proportion of days, given that she'd be logging late-night hours too.

There are downsides to splitting shifts. Working right before bed can hype you up, and staring at screens interferes with some people's ability to sleep. Many people did need to budget in time for decompression. If you intend to go back to work after your kids go to bed, be realistic and plan this shift as you'd plan your workday. You wouldn't expect to clear a one-thousand-e-mail backlog between 9:00 a.m. and 5:00 p.m., and you won't between 8:30 p.m. and 10:30 p.m. either. Create a priority list so you're disciplined about not trying to do *just one more thing* before shutting down for the night. In the log from the woman who works at the tech company, you'll see thirty to sixty minutes of personal time before bed. Depending on your energy level and ability to focus, you may have to be careful about which work you do during this time. I can edit documents and answer e-mails before bed, but I can't crank out intense rough drafts of new articles. I need to do that in the morning, when I'm fresh.

If your kids don't go to bed early, you might not need to work split shifts in order to see them. While I often do split shifts, my kids don't need much sleep. They never have. When Jasper was a baby, I'd hear of people racing home by 7:30 p.m. to put their children to sleep, and I'd ponder how much free time I would have if my kid went to bed then. For us, 8:30 p.m. is about as early as we've ever achieved. If your kids do go down early, though, split shifts can be the difference between having long stretches of time with them and not seeing them much in the evening. (You might still see them in the morning. This is real time that can truly be enjoyed. There's more on this in the "Be There" chapter.) Instead of working until 7:00, you work until 5:00, and then work at home from 7:30 to 9:30 p.m. It's the same number of hours, it's just worked in two chunks instead of one.

	MONDAY	TUESDAY	WEDNESDAY	THURSDAY	FRIDAY	SATURDAY	SUNDAY
5AM	Sleep	Sleep	Sleep	Sleep	Sleep	Sleep	Sleep
5:30	Sleep	Sleep	Sleep	Sleep	Sleep	Sleep	Sleep
6	Sleep	Sleep	Sleep	Sleep	Sleep	Sleep	Sleep
6:30	Up at 6:45	Up at 6:45	Drop 1st son to school	Up at 6:45	Sleep	Sleep	Sleep
7	Exercise till 7:10 Wake up 2nd son Prepare breakfast for him at 7:15 Pack his and my lunch	Exercise till 7:10 Wake up 2nd son Prepare breakfast for him at 7:15 Pack his and my lunch	Exercise Prepare breakfast for 2nd son	Prepare breakfast for 2nd son	Sleep	Sleep	Sleep
7:30	Take shower Leave home at 7:50	Take shower Leave home at 7:50	Shower Leave home and drop kid to school	Shower Leave home	Shower Leave home	Exercise	Sleep
8	Drop 2nd son to school Drive to work	Drop 2nd son to school Drive to work	Drop kid to school	Drop kid to school	Drop kid to school	Shower	Sleep
8:30	Come in to office Start meeting at 8:30	Come in to office and start on email	Come in to office and start on email and adjust schedule for the day	Meeting	Work	Take kids for chess tournament	Wake up and shower
9	Meeting	Meeting	Meeting	Work	Meeting	Work while waiting	Cook breakfast
9:30	Finish meeting at 9:30	Meeting	Meeting	Work	Meeting	Work while waiting	Housework
10	Scan and reply to emails Readjust the plan for the day	Work on my projects	Meeting	Meeting	Work	Work while waiting	Play tennis with kid
10:30	Work on my projects	Work on my projects	Work	Meeting	Work	Reading	Go to church

	MONDAY	TUESDAY	WEDNESDAY	THURSDAY	FRIDAY	SATURDAY	SUNDAY
11	Conversation with friend	Work on my projects	Work	Work	Work	Reading	Church
11:30	Back to work at 11:45	Coworker stops by discussing the project	Work	Work	Work	Reading	Church
12PM	Lunch, including 15-minute walk around the campus with a coworker	Lunch, including 15-minute walk around the campus with a coworker	Yoga	Work	Leave work and pick up kid, who has half day school	Take kids for lunch	Church
12:30	Lunch	Lunch	Yoga and lunch	Lunch	Lunch	Take kids for lunch	Church
1	Work on my projects	Work	Work	Meeting	Bring kid back to work	Drive home	Church
1:30	Work on my projects	Work	Leave office to pick up kid	Work	Meeting	Reach home and take nap	Home for lunch
2	Work on my projects	Work	Work from home	Meeting	Meeting	Reach home and take nap	Home for lunch
2:30	Meeting	Work	Work	Meeting	Meeting	Reach home and take nap	Exercise
3	Leave office to pick up 2nd son	Work	Work	Leave office and pick up kid for KUMON	Leave work and pick up other son	Reach home and take nap	Exercise
3:30	Drop him at KUMON	Work	Work	Work	Work	Housework	Housework
4	Continue to work from 3:30 on my projects while waiting for him	Leave office to pick up 2nd son	Work	Work	Work	Housework	Housework
4:30	Work on my projects while waiting for him	Reach home and start meeting	Pick up kid at 4:30	Work	Work	Housework	Housework

	MONDAY	TUESDAY	WEDNESDAY	THURSDAY	FRIDAY	SATURDAY	SUNDAY
5	Drop 2nd son for his piano class at 4:50 Pick up 1st son from school at 5 and drop him back home	Pick up 1st son exercise	Prepare dinner	Prepare dinner	Work	Go out for dinner	Housework
5:30	Pick up 2nd son at 5:45 Stop by Safeway for quick shopping for the item kid's school asked for	Exercise	Prepare dinner	Exercise	Exercise	Go out for dinner	Prepare dinner
6	Go back home, cooking	Dinner	Dinner	Dinner	Dinner	Go out for dinner	Dinner
6:30	Start meeting	Dinner	Dinner	Dinner	Dinner	Go out for dinner	Dinner
7	Finish meeting at 7	Work with 2nd son on homework and piano	Work with 2nd son on homework and piano	Work with 2nd son on homework and piano	Take kid for haircut	Exercise	Shower
7:30	Dinner and wash dishes	Work with 2nd son on homework and piano	Work with 2nd son on homework and piano	Work with 2nd son on homework and piano	Take kid for haircut	Shower	Watch TV with kids
8	Meeting	Work with 2nd son on homework and piano	Meeting	Meeting	Take kid for haircut	Play games with kids	Watch TV with kids
8:30	Meeting finished at 8:45, get chance to read book with 2nd son	Meeting	Meeting	Meeting	Play games with kids	Play games with kids	Kids nighttime routine
9	Meeting	Meeting	Work	Meeting	Play games with kids	Play games with kids	Kids nighttime routine
9:30	Meeting	Meeting	Work	Meeting	Play games with kids	Personal time	Work to prepare for next week

	MONDAY	TUESDAY	WEDNESDAY	THURSDAY	FRIDAY	SATURDAY	SUNDAY
10	Work	Meeting	Work	Work	Personal time	Personal time	Plan kids summer activities and vacations
10:30	Stop working at 10:30 Chat with my husband	Meeting	Work	Work and wrap up	Personal time	Personal time	Plan kids summer activities and vacations
11	Go to bed	Wrap up work	Personal time	Personal time	Personal time	Personal time	Personal time
11:30	Sleep	Go to bed	Personal time	Sleep	Personal time	Personal time	Personal time
12AM	Sleep	Sleep	Sleep	Sleep	Sleep	Sleep	Sleep
12:30	Sleep	Sleep	Sleep	Sleep	Sleep	Sleep	Sleep
1	Sleep	Sleep	Sleep	Sleep	Sleep	Sleep	Sleep
1:30	Sleep	Sleep	Sleep	Sleep	Sleep	Sleep	Sleep
2	Sleep	Sleep	Sleep	Sleep	Sleep	Sleep	Sleep
2:30	Sleep	Sleep	Sleep	Sleep	Sleep	Sleep	Sleep
3	Sleep	Sleep	Sleep	Sleep	Sleep	Sleep	Sleep
3:30	Sleep	Sleep	Sleep	Sleep	Sleep	Sleep	Sleep
4	Sleep	Sleep	Sleep	Sleep	Sleep	Sleep	Sleep
4:30	Sleep	Sleep	Sleep	Sleep	Sleep	Sleep	Sleep

2. Work Remotely

In early 2013, the business press lit up with the news that Yahoo!'s new CEO, Marissa Mayer, was nixing the company's telecommuting policies. As her head of human resources put it in a memo, "To become the absolute best place to work, communication and collaboration will be important, so we need to be working side-by-side." Yahoo!'s turnaround required everyone to work in the office, as "some of the best decisions and insights come from hallway and cafeteria discussions, meeting new people, and impromptu team meetings."

Most productivity experts cried foul and leapt to the defense of working from home. Jody Thompson and Cali Ressler, the former Best Buy executives who created that company's Results-Only Work Environment initiative, said in a statement that "Mayer has taken a giant leap backward . . . Instead of keeping great talent, she is going to find herself with a workplace full of people who are good at showing up and putting in time vs. a workforce that could most effectively and efficiently drive the business forward in the 21st century."

There is no doubt that most information work can be done anywhere, including from a home office, a coffee shop, a library, the sideline at a kid's soccer practice, a beach in Tahiti, etc. But while I agree with those who criticized Mayer's decision, I thought much of the defense of remote work missed a more interesting point. Yahoo! doesn't forbid working from home, in the sense that people's smartphones don't stop working when they leave the building. Yahoo! employees can work from home in the evenings and on weekends. It was not working from home per se that the powers that be objected to. It was working from home *during core business hours*, when Yahoo! employees were supposed to be coming up with innovations through spontaneous interactions when they were all in there together, inventing brilliant new products as they stood next to each other at the ladies' room sinks and the like.

I think the whole serendipity-in-person concept is oversold, but if you do believe in physical proximity during core work hours, then the mistake, in my mind, is thinking these core hours need to be Monday to Friday, nine to five. A more intriguing approach might be to have core work hours be Monday and Tuesday, perhaps, with Wednesday, Thursday, and Friday being potential buckle-down, work-from-home days if people wanted them. After all, offices can be distracting places. Eventually you need some quiet place to execute on all those innovations you come up with while waiting in line to pay for your salad. You do need interaction with your colleagues; this is true. But five days a week—Yahoo!'s requirement—is overkill.

Remote work need not be either/or. You do not need to only work from home (or a coffee shop, coworking space, etc.) or only work from the office. Working remotely on occasion was another common way Mosaic Project participants moved the tiles around to work long hours while having a life outside of work.* Particularly for those with a long commute, working from home one day a week, or maybe one half day a week if you've got a client meeting somewhere in the afternoon, frees up time and enables more family and personal time. You can eat lunch with your young children if they're home with a regular caregiver. You can meet an elementary school student's bus in the afternoon. You can possibly even work more hours with this strategy. Outside major metropolitan areas, most commutes are relatively short, but if you have a ten-minute trip to the train, a forty-minute train ride, and a ten-minute walk to your office, skipping that would give you an hour more to work and an hour more of personal time on the days you choose that option. That's a win on both fronts. Commutes also require energy. They have a funny tendency to make you feel like you've done something, even though all you've done is show up at work on time. Being able to devote that mental energy to work at least a few days per week may help you get more done before your first break than most people do all day.

While the most common option was to work from home one to two days per week, some people did work from home full-time. Most of these women were entrepreneurs, and while some worked out of standard issue home offices, a number whose revenue qualified them for the Mosaic Project had

---

* Technically, everyone who did a split shift also worked from home, as did the majority of people who did work on weekends, but in exploring this strategy, I'm talking about telecommuting during traditional work hours. An exact number is hard to produce; someone who stops by Starbucks to send a report in between client visits is technically doing remote work, but that's different from working in a home office from eight a.m. to five p.m. one day. Focusing on the "home" part misses much nuance of this work style.

graduated from that to more elaborate setups. Nika Stewart, owner of social media marketing company Ghost Tweeting, now has several employees visiting her home on occasion and other remote workers elsewhere. The varied nature of entrepreneurial businesses means it's sometimes unclear what constitutes a workplace anyway. A woman who owned and managed a number of rental properties traveled all over the place visiting her buildings. Not all people who worked from home full-time were entrepreneurs, though. One scientist in an administrative role worked four ten-hour days from her home in the Midwest for an employer located on the East Coast. One woman, who worked for a biotech firm, worked at home roughly three days a week, and traveled for two.

Many work/life tomes discuss how to negotiate a remote work arrangement, but I think there are a few problems with the usual approach. First, there's this word "negotiate." Negotiating implies giving something up. You are trading something you value in order to get this benefit from a company. To be sure, that's a common mind-set. Half the spam ads online promise "work from home" jobs without even saying what you'd be doing. The lack of a commute is considered the major selling point, not the work itself. But from an objective standpoint, most companies value both innovation and focused productivity. Working from home occasionally and the office occasionally gives you both. Especially with modern communication technology, and as a lot of office work involves calling and e-mailing people in other places, it's unclear what an organization loses by having people work elsewhere from time to time. It is clear that they're gaining a lot in terms of reduced real estate needs and fewer absences. Millennials especially don't seem to view location-independent work as a perk; it's the starting assumption. It's just another tool in the toolbox, there as an option when it snows or you have a doctor's appointment close to your house in the middle of the day. Indeed, a number of Mosaic Project participants didn't even mark on their logs that they were working from home on the day or two during their diary weeks that they did so. I'd see a conference call start at 8:30 a.m. or so, and not see any driving. When I'd ask, the person would mention, "Oh yeah, I worked from home on Thursday."

I also think that formal arrangements achieved via negotiation miss a big chunk of the magic that makes this form of flexibility helpful to people. You might reach an agreement with your company that allows you to work from home every Tuesday, then you find that you'd rather work from home on Wednesday this week because your meeting schedule is uncharacteristically lighter. Maybe the plumber can only come on Thursday. Or your kid is home sick from school and watching movies. Working from home when a family member is sick means that you're still providing something to your organization, even if you're not in the office. Or maybe you really just need to crank out a draft of a client proposal. Being able to work from home when you feel you need to do so is associated with being able to work much longer hours. One IBM/BYU study found that people able to work from home on occasion, and set their own hours, could work fifty-seven hours per week before a quarter of them reported that they were experiencing work/life conflict. Among those who had to be in an office at set hours, that point where a quarter experienced conflict occurred much sooner, at thirty-eight hours per week.

Rather than negotiating a formal agreement, a better approach might be to make sure you have the equipment you'd need to work remotely (laptop, cell phone), then look around and see if anyone else is working from home sometimes. If other people in your organization are already doing this, then just try working remotely on a day when there's a plausible reason to do so, like heavy traffic due to an accident on the freeway near your house. Turn in something huge that particular day, then go in the next day and rave about how productive you were. Hint about some upcoming project that will require a similar level of focus. That way, you've planted the idea with your manager or your direct reports that working from home is extremely productive for you. Then just shut up about it and work from home when you need to. It's the asking-for-forgiveness versus asking-for-permission mind-set. Life is a risk. Be bold.

I would suggest, though, that if you do need a formal work-from-home arrangement at your organization, you not automatically ask to work remotely on Fridays. Fridays may seem like the best day to request as they're quieter, there are fewer meetings, and they are probably the day a supervisor is most likely to approve as part of a regular schedule. The media executive profiled in the next section has Fridays as her work-from-home day, and the arrangement works for her. But consider this: some supervisors may assume that you're asking for Fridays so you can cut out around lunch for the weekend. If you work long days Monday through Thursday that may be the case, and your supervisor may sympathize. However, asking for a "peak" day shows you're making your request because you think you'll be more productive elsewhere, not because you want to work less. I like Wednesdays as work-from-home days. It breaks up the week well, and if you do have a brutal commute, you won't have to endure it more than two days in a row.

3. Think 168 Hours, Not 24

The third and perhaps most profound technique for taking charge of your time at work is to avoid what I call "the 24-Hour Trap."

When it comes to time, we often think that "balance" requires fitting all of our priorities into twenty-four hours. In particular, we want to fit those priorities into each of the twenty-four hours that constitute Monday, Tuesday, Wednesday, and Thursday. We act like these are the only four days that count. Indeed, when we lament the hard choices of long work hours or travel, we are often looking at what we are trading off during those four days.

But that's not the whole picture of time. Indeed, Monday through midday Thursday is exactly half the week. So is midday Thursday to Sunday. We have a funny tendency to think that work/life balance requires having a lot of personal time Monday through midday Thursday, but discount however much personal time (and relatively little work time) happens during midday Thursday to Sunday. Monday and Tuesday aren't balanced between work time and home time, but then again, neither are Saturday and Sunday, for the opposite reason. Why do we discount that?

As it is, it's possible to enjoy lots of family time, and personal time too, if you avoid the 24-Hour Trap, and take the whole week into account when assessing your life. Many women consciously chose to work longer some days, and less others. Any given 24 hours might not be balanced, but the 168-hour week as a whole can be.

Carolyn Polke is the chief operating officer for TheBlaze, Glenn Beck's media property. She lives in New Jersey and has an hour-plus commute by train into New York City, where her offices are based. That commuting and work commitment by itself wouldn't preclude family evenings, but in her organization, five to six p.m. is one of the busier hours of the day, which makes it tough to head out at a reasonable time.

Polke looked at her choices in figuring out how to work the hours she needed to work and also see her five- and two-year-old daughters. "I've experimented with it, with the kids' schedules, even catching an earlier train," she said. With an hour-long commute, however, "I don't make it home for any meaningful amount of time with them. My oldest daughter would be getting the last ten minutes of a book with Dad, and I'm all rushed." That rushing, and ten minutes of time with her kid, would require sacrifices at work because "I've left in the middle of things, or it feels that way."

So, after a while, Polke made the decision to release herself from the script that a good mother is there for dinner with her children and puts them to bed every night. This opened up other possibilities. She decided she could come into work a little later and have breakfast with her daughters every morning. Her husband, meanwhile, would start work early so that he could take the evening shift with the girls. Because her husband was there to feed the kids dinner and put them to bed, Polke could take the 7:25 p.m. train home, using the extra few hours to finish up work instead of racing out of the office in a frenzy while other people were still at their desks. She'd come home, hang out with her husband, and catch up on e-mails or relax. Then, on Friday, she could work from home and work a shorter day. She'd take her older daughter to school, and end the workday around 4:30 to do activities with the kids such as library trips. "I indulge in those things on Friday because I feel I can," she says.

Other Mosaic participants consciously chose to work quite late in the office—until 10:00 or 11:00 p.m.—a few nights during the week. If you have control of your time, but do need to work long hours on-site, you can have more family time overall by working past your children's bedtimes on Monday and Wednesday and coming home at 5:00 p.m. Tuesday, Thursday, and Friday, rather than coming home at 7:30 every night. Thinking you should do the bedtime ritual nightly falls into the 24-Hour Trap, and it limits your options. Looking at the "168-hour option" gets you both long work hours and time with your kids.

Women who traveled also tended to clock long hours when they were away from home, and then clocked reasonable ones when they returned. I saw this in particular with consultants in the Mosaic Project. One reason consulting skews male higher up the ranks is the perception that constant travel and the need to be always available to clients means you can't have a home life. Certainly some consultants seem to be plugged in or traveling all the time, but from studying logs, I've started to think this is more of a personal choice than an inevitable part of the work. The consultants in the Mosaic Project generally bifurcated their weeks, and so managed to be home a lot.

In the beginning years of consulting, you tend to work with one client, and spend big chunks of your workweek at that client's site. One woman a few years into her tenure at a consultancy, who was at the "engagement manager" level, lived in Texas and served a client in North Carolina. Every Monday she'd fly there, work fairly standard business hours at her client site during the week (eight a.m. to six p.m.), and would fly back home midday Thursday. Such a schedule meant she didn't see her young son in person on Monday, Tuesday, or Wednesday, although she did see him on video chat pretty much every night. However, she was home Thursday afternoon or evening. On Fridays, she worked from the local office and came home early, or worked from home. She did close to no work on Saturday and Sunday. The latter half of the week balanced the first half. One technique that helped with this lifestyle? If she wasn't catching up on work, she used her hotel time as me time and read or watched whatever shows she wanted to watch. This meant she could be more fully present as the "on" parent on weekends and hence give her husband, who didn't travel for work, a break.

As consultants rise up the ranks, they gain more control of their time and location, though the total work hours in this industry tended to the higher side, compared with the Mosaic Project average of 44 hours a week. I did notice, though, that most women concentrated these longer hours earlier in the week, and then preserved open time later on. Vanessa Chan, from chapter 1, worked 14.5 hours on Monday and 15.5 hours on Tuesday while she was traveling, but about 8 hours on Friday. If 60 hours is considered a decent workweek in that industry, then working 15 hours on Monday and Tuesday and 12 hours on Wednesday gets you most of the way there. Two 9-hour days on Thursday and Friday will do it. If you're willing to work 2 hours on the weekend, perhaps on Sunday night after the kids go to bed, you can work

8-hour days on Thursday and Friday and still hit 60. Since splitting shifts is a possibility too, you might work relatively shorter hours during the day on Thursday, and perhaps 2 to 3 hours at night. This is a schedule that allows for dropping kids off at school sometimes (as Chan did on her log) and being there for the evening shift about half the week, even while logging fairly extreme hours. Chan said this is how she consciously structured her weeks. "If I'm traveling, I may as well work," she said. "I'll schedule calls at night with people in Asia." But then, "when I'm home, I really try to unplug." It's balance over the whole week, rather than on any particular day.

4. Rethink Weekends

How best to spend one's weekends is a nuanced point, given what I said in the previous section. People with more traditional jobs often structure their lives to keep weekends free. Most Mosaic Project participants dialed things down on the weekends. Some 60 percent of logs featured zero work on Saturday, and 49 percent featured zero work on Sunday. Of course, that means that 40 percent of logs showed work on Saturday and more than half showed work on Sunday. Still, many women didn't work that much. Only 33 percent of logs showed more than half an hour of work on Saturdays; about 43 percent showed more than half an hour of work on Sundays. If I only count logs with more than an hour of work, 26 percent showed serious work on Saturdays, and 33 percent showed more than an hour on Sundays.

If you think that weekends should be sacred, that work is work and home is home, then these statistics—a third of high-earning mothers work more than an hour on Sundays!—could be cause for clucking. But I'd argue that this isn't the right conclusion. For starters, much of the Sunday work was done on Sunday night, and involved preparing for the week ahead. By Sunday night, many people are in workweek mode already. And second, while plenty of religions teach followers to treat one weekend day as sacred (and plenty of nonreligious people don't like the idea of working seven days straight either), they don't forbid work on *both* days. If you want a balanced, full life, there can be serious upsides to doing some work on weekends. Particularly for entrepreneurs and others with near complete control of their time, using the weekends makes a more limited schedule during the workweek possible.

Some women in the Mosaic Project consciously chose to limit their work hours to school hours during the week, or sometimes even take chunks of weekdays off. Then they'd work on weekends, sometimes up to a regular workday of hours, when the children could be with their other parent.

During the long winter of 2014, with many big storms in my part of Pennsylvania, we had a few weekends like this. They usually happened because I'd lost a workday earlier in the week when the kids' schools were closed due to snow and our nanny couldn't drive to the house safely, or because I saw snow in the forecast and anticipated losing a day in the coming week. On Sunday, March 16, I got up on the early side and worked for forty-five minutes before the kids got up. Then my husband, the boys, and my little brother (who was with us that weekend) all left to go skiing. Ruth stayed home with me. She watched cartoons for an hour while I worked. Then we went to the YMCA to go swimming, and came home for lunch. I put her down for a nap; the swimming tired her out, and she slept for a long time. I logged another three hours of work before she got up. Then the menfolk came home and my husband took the kids for the evening so I could continue working. The net result was a seven-hour workday, mostly making up for Monday the 10th, when I'd covered a snow day. I was also able to get a head start on my work for the 17th, as I saw the forecast called for snow *again*.

Working on Sunday didn't bother me. If I liked skiing, I might have been upset that the rest of my family was able to enjoy that activity, but I don't. Ruth spent Monday with me instead of in a backup care arrangement, and from her perspective, there wasn't anything that strange about Sunday either. It's not unusual to watch cartoons for an hour on the weekends, nor is it unusual to play with Dad. As for me, I just used the time to work instead of reading the paper or cleaning the house.

I do think it's good to take twenty-four hours off at some point to clear your head. That's the Sabbath concept, and that particular weekend, I did no work between 5:00 p.m. Friday and 7:30 a.m. Sunday. But look at it this way: if you're trying to work a certain number of hours, working five hours on the weekend translates to an hour less you need to work every weekday. If you have a hard stop on your weekdays, this can be the difference between working enough to make it feel like your career is moving forward, and feeling like it just can't work. As one woman who was generally responsible for day care pickup told me, "It helps me feel less stressed during the week to get a few extra hours in during the weekend." In the context of the whole mosaic, sometimes working on the weekend is less stressful than not working on the weekend. This isn't strange at all.

Time is highly elastic, and we found seven hours for me to work with just one hour of plopping one kid in front of the TV. It won't work for everyone, but done mindfully, weekend work can give each parent some solo time with the kids, and the kids more parental time overall.

The Personal Time Trade-off

These techniques have their drawbacks. A woman who left her tech company around the time school got out every day to shuttle her kids around, and who went back to work at night, described her split shift situation as "win-win." I agreed that it was a win for her kids and a win for her employer. As we looked at her log, though, we saw that it wasn't always a win for her. She had less personal time than she wanted, which was adding to her stress levels.

Some women go to profound lengths to maximize both kid time and work time. Em Hillier lives in the United Kingdom and runs two businesses, including the recently launched Cognibo, an education systems company offering online tools for teachers. Her time log from spring 2014 showed her functioning essentially as a stay-at-home mom for her young children from 7:00 a.m. to 7:00 p.m. Monday through Friday. She was the primary caregiver for her youngest child (the older ones were in school for a few hours a day) and she even watched friends' kids on occasion. She'd work on her business from 7:30 to 11:30 p.m. most nights, and for stretches of time on weekends while her husband cared for the kids. She logged about thirty hours of work this way.

This sounded tiring to me, and indeed, Hillier had the lowest sleep total in my study, averaging just over six hours a night. When I asked about her log, though, she told me, "I'm really, really happy with the way I spend my time. I love my life and all aspects of it." For one, she viewed neither her businesses nor caring for her children as "work." "They are so much fun," she said. "If you look at my schedule again in that light, it makes me seem like I have an enormous amount of leisure time!" She didn't require much sleep; even on vacations away from the kids, she wouldn't get much more sleep than she got on the log. She didn't like to watch TV, and her husband was happy to entertain himself in the evenings while she worked. They were good about spending at least one date night together each week, and one "admin night" in which they hashed out family schedules. While she did say she wanted more time with her husband and to schedule more regular exercise sessions, she also knew this situation wasn't going to be eternal. Her youngest would be in school soon and she'd do more daytime work then. Indeed, when I got back in touch in October 2014, her youngest had started attending preschool from nine a.m. to three p.m. two days per week. This gave Hillier those hours to accommodate her growing businesses while also giving her a little more downtime at night.

I think most people would find a schedule of being a primary caregiver all day and working for four hours per night hard to sustain—but if something works for you, it works. In less extreme versions, there are ways to protect leisure time, even if you are working long days or splitting shifts. These are discussed more in the last section of the book, but one option is to consciously carve out me time during the workday. Some women who worked at night took longer lunches. Others who worked at night left work a little earlier a day or two a week, and used that time for exercise or a quick coffee with a friend before picking their kids up. Even during a fifteen-hour workday, you can manage your energy, carving out time for work you really love as a reward for the things you have to do. If you plan to sleep seven hours on such a day, that leaves two hours for other things. It's not much, but it can be carefully stewarded for a favorite thirty-minute TV show and a brisk twenty-minute walk.

When you treat all 168 hours as your canvas, and don't hold to rigid assumptions of what must be work time, and what must be nonwork time, you can create some fascinating mosaics. For example, Ghost Tweeting owner Nika Stewart worked just over fifty hours during the week she logged, an identical quantity to the first log in this chapter with its straight M-F blocks. It took me a while to calculate this, though, because in her log (p. 80), work and personal time are so intertwined. She runs her social media management company, always needing to meet a payroll, with the urgency that entails. She worked at night and on the weekend. But in the context of her whole schedule, that doesn't make her seem unbalanced. Her log also revealed that she baked cookies with her daughter, went out to dinner with her husband, hung out with her friends, and picked her mom up from the airport in the middle of the day.

The upsides of this personalized schedule are why I'm not as enthusiastic as some other work/life pundits are about workplaces that tout their policies against late-night or weekend work, or occasionally proposed public policies that would prohibit such things. I know such policies make for good article fodder, and I've written about several companies over the years that make a point of such things. For a 2013 post for *Fast Company*'s Web site, I profiled Vynamic, a Philadelphia-based health care consulting company with a corporate policy—now called zzzMail—asking that e-mail not be sent after ten p.m. or before six a.m., or on weekends. At telecom company Bandwidth, CEO David Morken told me he walks the halls at six p.m. to make sure everyone's gone home.

The idea is that employees deserve to have a life. I agree. When companies can't keep workloads at a reasonable level, that's a management failure. By removing the option of forcing your employees to stay late, you light a fire under managers to keep things moving along. They learn to understand the opportunity cost of all decisions. Having a meeting at 4:30 p.m. is a choice that nothing else will get done after that meeting until the next morning. So is it worth it?

I understand this impulse, and yet I've pushed back a bit on this concept. I send and read e-mails all the time at 10:30 p.m., because it means I won't need to send e-mails at 3:00 p.m. when I've gone to a school program. Likewise, if an employee of Bandwidth wanted to work from 11:00 a.m. to 7:00 p.m. because she's training for a marathon and wants to do her long runs before work, true flexibility means she should be able to do that. Eileen Hiromura, a software engineer who is profiled in chapter 5, tells me she sometimes goes to bed early and wakes up on her own around 3:00 a.m. She works for ninety minutes to two hours, then goes back to sleep. This is not as crazy as it sounds; there is some evidence that this mimics the sleep schedule people had in pre-electric days. She likes that quiet middle-of-the-night time to work. She isn't sleep deprived. Indeed, she slept a perfect fifty-six hours

	MONDAY	TUESDAY	WEDNESDAY	THURSDAY	FRIDAY	SATURDAY	SUNDAY
5AM							
5:30		Went back to bed		Up to work on client web pages and PR			
6							
6:30	Made tea, cleaned desk, worked on documenting a system for upcoming employee training		Up, shower		6:45 got up		
7	E got up and came into office, asking me to stop working so I could play a game with her		Morning routine with E	Got dressed and did morning routine with E	Morning routine with E		
7:30	School delay: spent the morning making breakfast and playing games with daughter	Got up, another delayed school opening; played with E before call					
8	"	Phone consultation	Had breakfast & printed out last-minute forms for employee binders	Had coffee and worked on laptop in kitchen	Got dressed and prepared for radio interview with BBC	Got up to do some work, relaxed, got dressed	Got up to do some work on a client's account
8:30	"		Office manager arrived, set up the training room and got food prepared	Had breakfast while working on laptop in kitchen	Did a little work and more prep for interview		Had breakfast
9	"	Read with E until her bus came at 9:15. Met with team to plan day	9:20 employees arrived	Meeting with office manager - catch up, plan day and rest of week	Interview over phone		More client work

	MONDAY	TUESDAY	WEDNESDAY	THURSDAY	FRIDAY	SATURDAY	SUNDAY
9:30	Checked in with business group online, planned goal for the week	Handled emails Discussions with team about employee training	Begin Employee Training Day	Continued working on laptop in kitchen		Left to get E from sleepover	
10	Did a few urgent tasks (updating billing, returning emails)	Worked on more systems; documented, edited, printed, created manuals			Came into office to work with newest employees on Training Day 2	Dropped off E at friend's house for playdate	Got dressed to go out
10:30	Got dressed				Work with employees, and huddled in my office to work	Back home to do work, worked in kitchen on laptop	Went out with husband to do errands
11	Employees showed up, had breakfast, meetings with team to plan the day and week					Marketing and writing until 2:30	
11:30				Left for airport to pick up Mom			
12PM	General daily work tasks: big picture plans, sending outreach letters to potential clients	Worked with office manager, to plan/ set up the training room 12:15 call with BBC about potential interview	Break for lunch				
12:30		Spent the next 2½ hours on employee training manuals and phone calls with potential clients			Finally break for breakfast		Back home to unload car, then do a little work
1					More work in office		Back out to get kids and Mom

	MONDAY	TUESDAY	WEDNESDAY	THURSDAY	FRIDAY	SATURDAY	SUNDAY
1:30			End of Day 1 Training, back to my office to catch up on emails and work				Got kids ready to go out
2	Meeting with partner and office manager to plan Wednesday's employee training				"Personal shopper" came so I could choose pattern for a bag. Ordered bag		Out to mini golf and shopping with kids
2:30			Phone calls with potential clients	Dropped Mom at home, then drove home to do a little work, snack/lunch		Left to get E from friend's house	
3	E home Spent time doing quick office tasks while she got ready to do homework	Call with nonprofit to help create a Rock Kindness Day, created schedule for me and them to promote	E home, homework, snack, mommy work (printing out music sheets for E's classes)		Took E for playdate, so I could talk with friend about her new business ideas	Picked up E and did errands/got food & movie to prepare for cousins coming	
3:30	Homework with E	Homework with E		Pick up E from school	Talked with friend until 6:15		
4	Baked cookies with E	Out with E to stores to get food for tomorrow's Employee Training Day		Bring E to acting, and went home to do some office work			Drove everyone up to meet sister-in-law (1-hour drive)
4:30	Played a game with E		4:50 leave for voice lessons				
5	Went out with E to Staples for Post-it notes		Phone call with colleague while waiting for E			Got home, ordered pizza	

	MONDAY	TUESDAY	WEDNESDAY	THURSDAY	FRIDAY	SATURDAY	SUNDAY
5:30	Dropped off E at musical theater, and went home to do some work with husband		Took E to dinner in between classes	Picked up E from acting, and brought her to Grandma's house to surprise her		Mom brought over E's cousins for dinner	Stopped into rehab center to see sister-in-law's mom
6				Had dinner with E and Mom, talked and played	6:15, left E at friend's for sleepover	Hung out with Mom and husband in kitchen while kids played	
6:30		Got E ready for the night: fed her, showered, undressed	Dropped off E at "Glee" and hung out in lobby with other parents		Got home, got ready to go to dinner with hubby		Drove back home
7	Picked up E, came home, got her undressed and ready for bed	Worked on last-minute tasks for tomorrow			Dinner date with hubby, shopped for a new bed		Stopped in store to get dinner
7:30	Had dinner	Played games with E and cleaned the house	Brought E home, bedtime routine	Drove E home, bedtime routine		Drove kids and Mom back to her house	Drove Mom home
8	Got into bed with E to tell stories & talk about what we are grateful for today	Spent time with husband, had dinner	Quick phone call with colleague then into bed with family to watch TV and go to sleep	My own bedtime routine		Drove back home	Got home, got E undressed, had dinner
8:30		In bed with E, told stories	E asleep Stayed in bed working on social media	Got into bed exhausted		Got into bed to do some work on laptop	8:45 got E in bed
9	Got back up to work with husband on employee training	Talked with husband about tomorrow, hung out in bed talking		Heard friends show up, but was too tired to go down and see them	Back home, worked on some fun marketing ideas with hubby		Cleaned up

	MONDAY	TUESDAY	WEDNESDAY	THURSDAY	FRIDAY	SATURDAY	SUNDAY
9:30		Tried to relax and watch TV		Husband came up, told me I needed to come down—friends had exciting news			Got in bed with E to get her to sleep
10	Went to bed			Hanging out with friends in kitchen	In bed to watch TV and relax		In bed to relax
10:30			Sleep	Got back into bed	Sleep		
11							Sleep
11:30		Sleep				Sleep	
12AM							
12:30							
1						(time change)	
1:30							
2							
2:30							
3							
3:30	Got up to work on systems for Employee Training						
4							
4:30							

during her diary week. So why should an organization care if she sends e-mails in the wee hours?

Leaders of these companies have acknowledged my point, but indicated that their policies are mostly about establishing a culture of boundaries. The problem is that once an e-mail is sent, it's hard to control how others will react. Human nature dictates that people feel like they need to respond to their managers instantly. A manager can write NOT URGENT in the subject line until her fingers go numb, but if you've got competitive, driven employees, they won't think you mean it. So a manager with a schedule like Hiromura's would be welcome to write her e-mails, then save them as drafts, so the people who report to her don't start waking up at five a.m. to see what she's sent. Vynamic CEO Dan Calista also reminded me that a policy against e-mail isn't a policy against communication. Everyone has cell phones. If you truly need to know something urgently on Sunday night, you can pick up the phone and call.

Morken likewise notes that people at his company get broad leeway to figure out schedules that work for them. Many parents leave before six p.m., for instance, to pick up their kids at school. If they work later, they just don't do it at the office. Office core hours end by six p.m. in order to nip the face-time culture in the bud. I do see the point in that.

The Part-time Question

Companies can do a lot to encourage a reasonable workweek, and flexibility. When they do embrace flexibility, organizations often find that people will work *unreasonable* hours, and be quite happy about it. Some people, however, want something more officially limited. If you fall into that category, is negotiating a part-time schedule the way to go?

Part-time work remains a popular idea. Aside from the prospect of reduced hours (not always realized, but at least the prospect), the phrase "part-time" makes such a setup seem like the best of both worlds. I don't want to imply that work consumes my *full* life, so I don't want to work *full*-time. By working *part*-time, I show that work gets only *part* of me and my family gets *part* of me too.

In completely inflexible cultures, such concessions may be necessary to carve out space, though they still don't solve the problem of navigating work and life. You can take Tuesdays and Thursdays off, but your kid's school events won't always occur on Tuesdays and Thursdays. If you want to go to those, you'll have to take additional time off, or plan ahead to switch days, and this is where things go awry. Again, this is the nature of some jobs, though creative staffing can help. Building slack into a schedule means that people can cover for one another. Extra staffing also reduces profits, though, so there are forces working against this.

I agree that not all work is exciting compared with other amazing things you could be doing in your life. If you can afford it, and aren't ecstatic about your work, then by all means, work fewer hours. From my soapbox it's easy to say that you should go find a more scintillating job, but you may have valid reasons to stay put and take a reduced schedule. Looking at the logs, the handful of women on official reduced schedules in the Mosaic Project were *still earning more than $100,000 a year working part-time*. In the grand scheme of things, if you can pull that off, more power to you.

The big problem I saw with this option, though, is that officially going part-time does not always mean you will work significantly fewer hours. You might. If you're a lawyer with a billable hour target, then getting an 80 percent schedule means you will likely work about 20 percent less than you would otherwise. A woman at a New York City law firm with this arrangement told me that "I generally think of billable hours as a terrible thing, but here's a place where it's useful." Her log featured forty-three hours of work (p. 87).

Friday is her day off, and though you can see she did some work, it was only 1.5 hours. Beyond the hours alone, "I get to turn down the all-consuming matters," she says, such as working with clients who might expect her to be available around the clock. "Basically being part-time gives you the freedom to say no to that." (Mostly; you'll note on her log that she was at the office past eleven p.m. the night before she started tracking her time!)

That freedom, or at least partial freedom, played into others' decisions to take reduced schedules too, even in situations without billable hours. I had some women tell me that at their companies, going part-time and getting flexibility went hand in hand. It was assumed that people at their organizations worked 24/7, so if you wanted to do personal things at all, you needed

Time	FRIDAY	SATURDAY	SUNDAY	MONDAY	TUESDAY	WEDNESDAY	THURSDAY
5AM	Sleep	Sleep	Sleep	Sleep	Wake up at 5:15; eat protein bar, get ready for gym	Sleep	Sleep
5:30	Sleep	Sleep	Sleep	Sleep	Meet neighbor to walk to the YMCA	Wake up at 5:50	Sleep
6	Sleep	Sleep	Sleep	Sleep	Lift weights	Eat protein bar, get dressed; leave for TRX class 6:10	Sleep
6:30	Sleep	Wake up with E to let husband sleep; get E dressed	Sleep	Get up; shower and get dressed	Walk home; shower and get ready	TRX class	Sleep
7	Sleep	Make E and self breakfast and eat with him	Sleep	Shower and get dressed	Finish getting ready; E wakes up; get him dressed	TRX class	Sleep
7:30	Wake up (at work until 11:45 Thurs); check internet; greet E (son); breakfast	Wake up husband; get ready	Sleep	Make breakfast; see husband off; eat with E	Eat breakfast and pack E's lunch	Walk home; eat breakfast and hang out w/ Mom (who stayed over) and E	Wake up and eat; hang out with E
8	Shower and get dressed; blow-dry hair	Get ready; leave for volunteer shift at food pantry	Sleep	Hang out with E	Get E ready for preschool	Shower and get dressed	Shower and get ready
8:30	Work emails until 8:45; say goodbye to husband; get E dressed	Volunteer at food pantry	Sleep	Mom arrives (she watches E M-Th business hours)	E and husband leave for walk to preschool; read (fiction) for 15 min	Read with E; pack snacks for work	Hang out with E
9	Leave with E for Buy Buy Baby to buy baby gift for friend	Volunteer at food pantry	Wake up at 9:15 (daylight savings ended at 2am)	Leave for work	Leave for work; UPS store to ship clothing that doesn't fit	Mom arrives; leave for work	Mom arrives (no preschool for E today; lice outbreak); leave for work

	FRIDAY	SATURDAY	SUNDAY	MONDAY	TUESDAY	WEDNESDAY	THURSDAY
9:30	Shop at Buy Buy Baby and Whole Body (vitamins)	Volunteer at food pantry	Shower and get ready; play with E	Browse favorite Internet sites	Arrive at work; browse favorite Internet sites	Arrive at work; check favorite websites	Get off 1 stop early, walk 7 min.; arrive at 9:40
10	Arrive home; unpack purchases; fix E snack	Volunteer at food pantry	Hang out with E	Work	Work	Work	Work
10:30	Friend, B, arrives with her newborn for a visit	Volunteer at food pantry	Hang out with E	Work	Work	Work	Work
11	Visit with friend at our house	Volunteer at food pantry	Pilates class	Work	Work	Work	Work
11:30	Get E ready to go; leave with friend, baby, and E for diner	Volunteer at food pantry	Pilates class; leave for home	Work	Work	Work	Work
12PM	Eat at diner	Walk home; hang out with E	Return from pilates at 12:15	Work	Work	Work	Work
12:30	Eat at diner	Hang out with E	Eat lunch	Eat lunch	Lunch with coworker	Work	Work
1	Walk around with friend, baby, and E	Read with E	Work	Work	Back at desk at 1:10; work	Eat lunch	Work
1:30	Walk around with friend, baby, and E	Put E down for nap; take nap	Work	Work	Work	Leave for pro bono shift at family court	Go up to cafeteria and get lunch
2	Return home; visit with B at our house	Nap; wake up and eat lunch	Read (fiction) (husband has taken E out)	Work	Work	Pro bono	Work
2:30	Friend leaves with baby; babysitter for E arrives; read (fiction)	Read (fiction)	Read (fiction) (husband has taken E out)	Work	Work	Pro bono	Work

	FRIDAY	SATURDAY	SUNDAY	MONDAY	TUESDAY	WEDNESDAY	THURSDAY
3	Read (fiction)	Read (fiction)	Take walk with E and husband	Run to blood drive next door to donate (work slow)	Work	Pro bono	Work
3:30	Nap	E wakes up; get him ready for playdate	Take walk with E and husband	Give blood	Work	Pro bono	Work
4	Run errands (library and ATM)	Head to E's friend's for playdate	Go to supermarket	Give blood; return to office and work	Work	Pro bono	Work
4:30	Run errands (library and ATM)	Playdate	Go to supermarket	Work	Work	Pro bono	Work
5	Relieve babysitter; cook E dinner	Playdate	Unpack groceries; order dinner; play with E	Work	Work	Leave for home	Work
5:30	Sit with E while he eats dinner	Playdate (kids make and eat own pizza)	Read on couch while E plays; eat dinner with E and husband	Go home	Work	Arrive home; chat with Mom and sit with E while he finishes dinner	Work
6	Play with E	Playdate (help clean up)	Eat dinner with E and husband	Sit with E while he eats	Work event	Play with E	Leave work
6:30	Give E bath and get him ready for bed	Return home	Have E try on spring clothes that came via UPS yesterday	Bathe E	Work event	Bathe E	Arrive home, change into PJs; start E's bath
7	Read to E and put him to sleep	Work on computer	Internet browsing while husband gives E bath	Get E ready for bed	Work	Get E ready for bed	Get E ready for bed
7:30	Work on computer	Work on computer	Wash and blow-dry hair; laundry	Put E to bed at 7:45; work	Work	Put E to bed at 7:45; work	Put E to bed; eat dinner
8	Work on computer	Work on computer	Fold laundry	Work	Work	Work on computer	Work on computer

	FRIDAY	SATURDAY	SUNDAY	MONDAY	TUESDAY	WEDNESDAY	THURSDAY
8:30	Dinner (sushi delivery)	Work on computer	Work on computer	Work	Go home; arrive at 8:50 and eat	Work on computer	Work on computer
9	Watch TV with husband	Dinner w/ husband (takeout)	Work on computer	Eat dinner	Watch TV and talk with Mom and husband	Work on computer	Work on computer
9:30	Watch TV with husband	Dinner w/ husband (takeout)	Work on computer	Watch TV	Watch TV and talk with Mom and husband	Watch TV with husband	Work on computer
10	Watch TV with husband	Watch movie	Watch TV	Watch TV	Work emails	Watch TV with husband	Work on computer
10:30	Get ready for bed; go to bed	Watch movie	Get ready for bed; go to bed at 10:45	Get ready for bed; go to bed at 10:45	Get ready for bed; go to sleep at 10:45	Get ready for bed; go to bed at 10:50	Work on computer
11	Sleep	Watch movie	Sleep	Sleep	Sleep	Sleep	Put in mosaic data
11:30	Sleep	Get ready for bed; go to bed at 11:45	Sleep	Sleep	Sleep	Sleep	Get ready for bed
12AM	Sleep	Sleep	Sleep	Sleep	Sleep	Sleep	Go to sleep
12:30	Sleep	Sleep	Sleep	Sleep	Sleep	Sleep	Sleep
1	Sleep	Sleep	Sleep	Sleep	Sleep	Sleep	Sleep
1:30	Sleep	Sleep	Sleep	Sleep	Sleep	Sleep	Sleep
2	Sleep	N/A (daylight savings)	Sleep	Sleep	Sleep	Sleep	Sleep
2:30	Sleep	N/A (daylight savings)	Sleep	Sleep	Sleep	Sleep	Sleep
3	Sleep	Sleep	Sleep	Sleep	Sleep	Sleep	Sleep
3:30	Sleep	Sleep	Sleep	Sleep	Sleep	Sleep	Sleep
4	Sleep	Sleep	Sleep	Sleep	Sleep	Sleep	Sleep
4:30	Sleep	Sleep	Sleep	Sleep	Sleep	Sleep	Sleep

to go part-time. The problem is that when there's no check on hours, you can wind up working fairly similar hours on a part-time schedule as you would on a full-time one.

That's not a hypothetical possibility. One consultant in the Mosaic Project had an official part-time schedule, but during the two weeks she logged for me, she worked 53 hours and 47 hours. She had good explanations for both weeks. She'd just started a new project with new team members, and she had to get them up to speed. Indeed, when I circled back six months later, she reported that she had her schedule more under control, and it was working for her. But other consultants in the Mosaic Project logged similar hours on full-time, not part-time, schedules. A consultant who logged 43 hours one week on a full-time schedule said, "I let people think I work 60-plus hours and I let my work speak for itself." Sometimes people with part-time schedules had more flexibility during peak workdays than full-time employees. The consultant with a part-time schedule was able to go to a playground with her children on Monday morning. She didn't have to travel. On the other hand, people with full-time schedules didn't have zero flexibility either. The woman who worked 43 hours on a full-time schedule played with her son on Friday when she was working from home.

In any case, I found that "part-time" and "full-time" seemed to be fuzzy concepts in many industries. Since I bartered speeches for several companies in exchange for logs from employees, I could sometimes compare colleagues' logs. In at least one case, I saw a woman on a part-time schedule working more hours than a colleague on a full-time schedule.

It's hard to know exactly what's going on in any individual circumstance. Different people may face different requirements for their jobs or their level of responsibility. Regardless, I was struck by the differences in workweeks between colleagues, even when looking at people with full-time schedules. A ten-hour difference, which is two hours per weekday, was not unusual. That gap occurred in every organization from which I had more than one log. I have no doubt that a ten-hour gap corresponds to different career trajectories, but clearly "full-time" encompasses a host of lifestyle options.

What we do know is that going part-time almost always requires a pay cut. So is it worth it? Or does officially chopping a few hours from the week come at an extremely high marginal cost?

As we saw in the previous chapter, people generally work fewer hours than they think, especially in industries where people brag about their extreme work hours. If people who claim to work eighty hours a week are actually logging fifty-five to sixty hours, then taking a 50 percent pay cut and working fifty hours a week is not a great financial move. In particular, if there's no accountability for total hours, then taking a 20 percent pay cut to get an 80 percent schedule is a questionable tactic. In many fields, it's quite possible to get the same during-the-workweek time off that 80 percent would enable, without actually going to an 80 percent schedule. To be blunt, lots of people waste 20 percent of their work hours, and still get paid for this time they're not working. Why shouldn't you take advantage of this same margin?

I think some of the lure of part-time schedules is about being known as someone who plays by the rules. We all have to live with the decisions we make. One woman who had worked a part-time schedule at a tech company for several years told me that during a few intense projects, "I was working a lot more hours than I was getting paid for." However, she did this because "I wanted to be transparent for all of the people I work with. I didn't want to make it so that people would say, 'I can never get ahold of her, she's never here on Fridays, she's taking advantage of the situation.' It would be impacting other people more than if I just worked less five days a week." So she negotiated an 8:00 a.m. to 3:30 p.m. schedule, which, minus the lunch break and allowing for some during-the-day flexibility, comes out to thirty-two to thirty-five hours a week.

I asked if it would bother her if she found out colleagues were working thirty-five hours per week while getting paid for full-time work. "I've had people tell me, 'Why do you do this? You should go back to forty and do what you're doing,'" she says. Her boss has been very understanding, and if she asked to leave at 3:30 p.m. and do some work at night "she'd probably say fine, no problem." She sees colleagues go to the cafeteria to eat a leisurely breakfast daily while she avoids social media and other time wasters. "I could probably safely say I put in just as much or more time than they do even though I'm not in the office forty hours," she says. The problem with going to a full-time schedule and then slacking off is that she'd feel guilty, and so "I choose to do what I perceive to be the right thing."

I have a lot of respect for this woman and her level of integrity. However, as I look at the broader working world, I think there is a fine line between doing what you think is right and succumbing to the common female tendency to undervalue your work. It's easy to feel bad about setting boundaries, particularly in a culture where those boundaries are constantly tested. To assuage the guilt of saying no, we settle for less. We ask permission to set official boundaries and we pay the price. But what if others are advocating for their interests while still being confident enough to demand full fare? I think of someone like former Home Depot CEO Bob Nardelli. His company's stock was stagnant under his tenure, yet he negotiated compensation that hit $30 million a year and departed with a severance package estimated at $200 million plus. In the grand scheme of things, there's nothing wrong with being compensated like your colleagues if you're as productive as your colleagues. That's true even if you choose to leave by four p.m. Results matter more than hours, especially since many people aren't working nearly as many hours as they claim. Playing by the rules is good, but we should all play by the same rules. More people are working how they want than you think.

Maybe you should too.

.
.
.
.
.
.

CHAPTER 4

Make Success Possible

Perhaps it speaks to my secret wonkish side, but I knew who Lisa Camooso Miller was before she offered to keep a time log. The former communications director for the Republican National Committee, who is now a partner at Blueprint, a Washington, D.C., communications firm, appears regularly on Fox News, CNN, and other places.

Yet for all her fascinating political history, when she turned in her log, she told me, "I could be, maybe, the least interesting person on the planet." Certainly her days were regimented: up at five a.m. for CrossFit, ending precisely at ten p.m. on school nights. But here's something that was interesting: she spent a lot of her work hours grabbing coffee with people.

When I asked her about this caffeine habit, I learned it was a matter of strategy, not addiction. "A lot of working moms I know work a lot more hours than I do," she says, and indeed, unlike many Mosaic Project participants, she didn't split shifts or work on weekends during her diary week. So Miller makes sure the hours she works (she aims for forty per week) count. When she's at the office, she can hunker down when she needs to, cranking out pitches and proposals.

However, since it's her relationships with reporters and various political power players that open doors for her and her company, she doesn't just stay at the office. She invests time in these relationships whenever possible. Hence the coffees all over her schedule (p. 96). Miller watched an above-average amount of TV, and this too was for a reason: "So much of my business is having these stock things to talk about," she says. "When I go and meet with a reporter, I want to be having some understanding of pop culture, some sort of sense of the latest book. Those things tend to be easy pieces of conversations that open up doors." Small talk is the appetizer of any business relationship. People want to work with people they feel connected with. And so, "*House of Cards* is hot, and it's on the list." So are sports. "I try to figure that stuff out," she says, "so we can have a little bit of a conversation about something other than the business we have to do."

While I've been told many times that parents "can't" do happy hours, Miller has even figured out how to navigate the Republican strategist world, with its occasional required booziness, and get home at a reasonable hour. "I don't do dinners; I try to steer clear of that," she says. "But I do what I call 'mom o'clock.' I meet for a cocktail with a reporter at four thirty." Often, the reporter is happy for an excuse to leave work early. By 5:30 p.m., they've bonded and the reporter can then head off to his dinner and Miller can be home by 6:15.

The coffees and cocktails may not look like other people's schedules, but for Miller, it means she can have both a thriving family life and professional influence. "Especially here in D.C.," she says, "people are always looking for opportunities to connect."

•

If you want to have it all—a life that involves professional success and plenty of time for personal pursuits too—then you need to be strategic about how you spend your work hours. Invested well, work hours generate great returns. The problem is that when you have a full life outside of work, you often face the temptation to focus just on the work in front of you. Sometimes this is what you have to do. When kids are babies, life naturally involves some hunkering down. People often make big, life-changing decisions when they are in this survival mode, but if you hang on, eventually you can fathom the future. You can afford to realize that part of achieving happiness in both work and life is feeling like your career is going somewhere. You are improving at your craft. You are broadening your scope, one coffee at a time. There

	MONDAY	TUESDAY	WEDNESDAY	THURSDAY	FRIDAY	SATURDAY	SUNDAY
5AM	Wake up	Wake up	Wake up	Wake up	Wake up		
5:30	CrossFit	CrossFit	CrossFit	CrossFit	CrossFit		
6	CrossFit	CrossFit	CrossFit	CrossFit	CrossFit		
6:30	Make breakfast	Make breakfast	Make breakfast/walk dog	Make breakfast	Make breakfast/ walk dog		
7	Pack backpacks/ brush kids' teeth	Pack backpacks/ brush kids' teeth	Pack backpacks/ brush kids' teeth	Pack backpacks/ brush kids' teeth	Pack backpacks/ brush kids' teeth		
7:30							
8	Jump in shower	Jump in shower	Jump in shower	Jump in shower	Jump in shower	Wake up	Wake up
8:30	Dry hair	Get dressed	Dry hair	Get dressed	Dry hair	Make breakfast	Make breakfast
9	Head out the door	Head out the door	Head out the door	Head out the door	Head out the door	CrossFit	
9:30	Conference call	Conference call	Conference call	Conference call	Conference call	CrossFit	Watch morning shows with kids
10	Meeting downtown w/ client	Stop at Target for missed items on shopping list	Get to work	Get coffee w/ reporter	Get to work		
10:30		Get to work	Call w/ potential client			Shower	
11	Coffee with mutual friend/possible work resource			Return to office			
11:30			Check Twitter		Check Twitter	Take kids to park	
12PM	Lunch with partners	Lunch at desk	Lunch w/ partners	Lunch w/ colleague			
12:30					Lunch at son's school		Meet kids for son's birthday

	MONDAY	TUESDAY	WEDNESDAY	THURSDAY	FRIDAY	SATURDAY	SUNDAY
1		Check Twitter		Meet at potential client's offices		Return from park for lunch	Movie birthday party for son
1:30	Check Twitter		Conference call with reporter	Commence pitch for business	Check Twitter/ FB		
2		Write proposal for work		Finish up pitch		Pack up kids and run errands	
2:30			Finish work on proposal	Back to office	Grab coffee with colleague		Movie ends
3	Office meeting	Travel downtown for coffee w/ reporter					Take kids to park
3:30			Research kids' summer camp options	Schedule kids' summer camps	Finish up end of the week projects	Return home/ walk dog	
4	Finish up daily work/ check email	Finish up coffee/ return to office					Leave kids with husband, to supermarket
4:30			Head out the door			Start dinner with husband	
5	Head out the door	Head out the door		Head out the door	Head out the door		Finish groceries and head home
5:30	Home	Home	Take son to hockey	Home	Home		
6					Movie night with kids	Movie night w/ kids	Serve kids dinner
6:30	Homework w/ kids	Homework w/ kids	Return home	Homework w/ kids			
7			Serve dinner				Kids in shower
7:30		Kids in shower		Kids in shower			Dinner with hubby/kids watch TV
8	Kids to bed	Kids to bed	Kids to bed	Kids to bed	Kids to bed	Kids to bed	Kids to bed

	MONDAY	TUESDAY	WEDNESDAY	THURSDAY	FRIDAY	SATURDAY	SUNDAY
8:30	Watch TV w/ hubby	Watch TV w/ hubby	Watch TV w/ hubby	Watch TV alone (hubby biking)	Watch TV w/ hubby		
9							Watch TV w/ hubby
9:30	Read book	Read book	Read book	Read book			
10	Off to bed	Off to bed	Off to bed	Off to bed	Read book		Read book (*Goldfinch*)
10:30					Off to bed		Off to bed
11							
11:30							
12AM							
12:30							
1							
1:30							
2							
2:30							
3							
3:30							
4							
4:30							

is great power in small wins. Small wins are sustainable, and sustainable growth over the years is what makes success possible.

Achieving such growth requires a balance between hard-nosed efficiency and a more abundant perspective on time. For many of us, this is a work in progress. When I told people about this project, they'd ask if the logs showed that successful women used every minute well. The answer is . . . no. I found plenty of wasted time. People even labeled it as such: "Horrible unproductive hour of Internet time warp" showed up on one log. Then there were less obvious inefficiencies: A woman drove thirty minutes to her office and stayed there for all of two hours, during which she was on the phone, before leaving for a midday obligation. Phone calls can be taken from anywhere, and less driving means more time available for deeper work; that might have been a morning to work from home. I also saw logs with seven to eight hours of meetings per day. Meetings look like work, but even if you're in management, eight hours of formal meetings per day will limit your ability to seize new opportunities or deal with problems that arise. You don't have the space to get back to people in a timely fashion. I'd argue that's not an efficient use of that work time.

As I studied the logs, though, I saw many ways that people like Miller consciously designed their work lives to make success possible while working reasonable hours. In particular, I found five strategies that helped people choose the tiles of their work lives to create sustainable patterns, focusing on what matters and minimizing what doesn't.

Strategy 1: Look Forward

Write about productivity for long enough, and some fascinating statistics cross your desk. One recent one: According to a 2013 survey by Accountemps, Tuesday is the most productive day of the week, chosen by 39 percent of HR professionals surveyed about their offices, with Monday lagging a reasonable distance behind at 26 percent. (For what it's worth, Mosaic women worked more on Tuesdays than Mondays: 8.8 hours versus 8.0 hours.)

As a proud member of Team Monday myself, I wasn't quite sure why this was, so I talked to office sorts to figure it out. First, I learned that people tend to have a lot of meetings on the first day of the week. Indeed, the Monday morning staff meeting is a fixture in many offices, and if Mondays are packed with meetings, you can't start "real" work until Tuesdays. Second, because people slack off later in the week (only 3 percent of HR people called Thursday or Friday the most productive day in their workplaces), Monday becomes a catch-up day. You tackle last week's to-dos that didn't get done. And finally, the worst problem is that people wait until Monday to figure out what they should do on Monday and for the rest of the week. One woman who does temp placements told me that "A client will always call me on Monday saying 'I need extra help.' Rarely do they call me on Friday"—timing that would allow her to get someone there Monday.

All this points to a missed opportunity. We tend to structure our lives in weeks, and since Friday is the end of the workweek for most people, they're naturally in wind-down mode by then, working fewer hours than other days, and often working less effectively during these hours. If you don't seize Mondays, then you're left with just three days to knuckle down at work. Making success possible while working reasonable hours, like the forty-four hours a week the average Mosaic participant works, means you need to optimize the hours available to you.

Fortunately, it is quite possible to seize Mondays, and to plan for staying focused at work even when life gets a little chaotic. A key breakthrough is realizing that time management is like chess. The masters always think a few moves ahead.

This works on a micro level: ideally, you plan the week before you're in it. I used to do my planning on Sunday nights, but after interviewing productivity expert David Allen, and hearing his offhand remark that many clients do this planning on Fridays, I decided to switch. I am a big fan. Friday planning turns unproductive Friday afternoons into useful planning and thinking time. My brain isn't willing to start on a big new project, but it is willing to think about what those projects should be, and when I should block in time over the next week to do them. I think through my professional and personal priorities, and block these into my days. If I need to meet or talk with people, I can send e-mails on Friday afternoon and often hear back in time to set the week's schedule before I quit for the evening. Plus, knowing there's a plan for Monday keeps those Monday worries from taking over the weekend, an issue that keeps many people from enjoying their free time.

Planning ahead of time also means you allocate time for your goals. In the rush of daily to-dos, it's easy to let the important-but-not-urgent stuff slide. You don't *have* to work on finding new clients, so you don't. You deal with the ones clamoring for attention currently . . . which is fine until they disappear and you need new ones and suddenly you're scrambling. You can look at important tasks already on the calendar and figure out what prep or planning you need to do. In Nika Stewart's log in the previous chapter, there's an entry, "prepared for radio interview with BBC." If you do a lot of media spots, as she does, you can wing such things, but it's almost always better not to.

Perhaps the biggest reason to think ahead, though, is that life doesn't go as planned. This may sound paradoxical, that we are planning because of the futility of plans, but even if some parts of life are unknowable, planning lets us make allowances for, as Donald Rumsfeld might put it, the "known unknowns."

I don't like to miss deadlines. It's likely my daily journalist's training, but I tend to think of a deadline as a commitment I've made to the people I'm working with. I can renegotiate, and I have, but I don't like to, especially if I can foresee and plan around any issues. I turned in the manuscript of a previous book a few days after giving birth to my second child. Some people think this sounds crazy, but it's not like I wrote the book in the hospital. I had nine months of fair warning about both the book and the baby. I finished the substance of the work far enough ahead of my due date that the odds were against my going into labor prior, and I left the polishing for the last month, which I knew could be interrupted at any point. I wouldn't have made my deadline if I'd been dealt unknown unknowns like big complications for either of us, but with my normal, low-risk pregnancy, my son's birthday was simply a known unknown. I could plan for it.

Looking forward lets you deal with all sorts of other known unknowns. February and March 2014 were among the snowiest months in recent history on the East Coast. And so, by March, I started to see this entry on time logs: "prep for snow day." If you look at a week and see that a giant blizzard is headed your way, you can assume school might be canceled. You can make the appropriate plans. You move lower-priority things to a different week, and you tackle high-priority items first, before the snow starts falling.

Even if you don't have kids, or if your partner is responsible for all things kid-related, this mind-set helps make progress possible. Lots of things can go wrong, and something almost assuredly will. Here are some more known unknowns: Some proportion of your employees will get the flu during the winter. You don't know what that proportion is, but you can be pretty sure it won't be zero, even if you're paying for flu shots. Someone will be out for a week with a family emergency, or a personal health crisis. One reason strong organizations don't get too dependent on any individual is that they need the flexibility to deal with these realities.

Planning ahead means all of this is less daunting. Life can still be daunting, but some progress can be made. Ahlia Kitwana has two daughters and works in Rochester, New York. She had just started a new job before she kept a time log for me in January. The snow days were piling up thick. On Monday night, an entry read "Found out school is closed tomorrow, initial plan to bring girls to my mom's house while we go to work." She got up early and drove to the gym, but by the time she emerged, things had deteriorated: "At 7:45 head home, roads are treacherous, at a red light, unable to stop, so I ran it. At that point resolved not to take girls to my mom's. When I got home, asked husband if we could split the day with the girls." She worked the first shift. The main roads to her office were better than those to her mom's, so she drove there and, upon arriving at work, her entry described shifting meetings and getting set up to work from home: moving files, printing documents, and prepping for calls. She also came up with a strategy for being productive at home during the latter half of that day, despite having no child care. She made plans for the girls to watch a movie while she took a conference call. That one happened, though with everyone else discombobulated by the snow, too, her second call of the day didn't. What's interesting to me, though, is that Kitwana—the working mother of two young kids dealing with a snow day while making sure her husband got a chance to work too—was ready for that call. It's other people who weren't.

The chess master knows what she's doing.

Strategy 2: Do Real Work

Perhaps this has happened to you. You describe your job to someone and it sounds incredibly cool. Yet when you look at how you spend your days, you seem to devote precious little time to the cool stuff. Other work is always crowding the cool stuff out, and these auxiliary tasks can inspire much angst and soul-searching about whether your life is going in the right direction. An academic medical researcher who kept a log for me wrote of this problem, which had manifested itself as "slacking off"—a development that surprised her. In her overachieving life, that wasn't something she did. Her first thought was to blame the tiredness that ensues from having two little kids, but eventually she realized that "the underlying reason for my lack of drive is that I don't love what I'm doing these days."

She loved the science, "but I haven't even been doing science. I've been dealing with administrative BS, [institutional review boards] and budgets and monitoring boards and deciding which of 50 different blood collection tubes I need to buy and so on. I like the medicine involved in my new clinical program, but not the enormous amount of behind-the-scenes work and sweet-talking I have to do to set up the clinic space, and the computer system, and make sure the schedulers understand my plan, and get all my collaborators on board. The countless meetings and more emails and more phone calls. It's not easy to get caught up in the flow of this kind of work, the same way I can with writing grants or analyzing data."

She resolved to plan her weeks and "make sure that plan includes at least *some* amount of actual 'science' each week," be that data analysis, actual experiments, reviewing new literature, or discussing results with colleagues. She needed "something that will inspire me to want to keep doing what I'm doing."

Many people experience this drift. Some administrative and support work is necessary, but if you do too much, then work no longer feels compelling. In extreme cases, you might go and find a new job, which will solve the problem for a while. If the underlying issue is one of prioritization, though, then eventually you'll experience the exact same malaise.

Another option? Try to fall in love with your job all over again. If it sounds awesome to other people, it can be awesome for you too—if you make time to do *real work*. As the medical researcher wrote me a few months later, "I've been blocking out time in my week to work on each project—and when there isn't any hard data to analyze or emails to keep up with related to that project, I spend that time reviewing the literature for new updates, talking to my coworkers about possible collaborations, and playing around with data in less efficient but more creative ways." This deep work, this real science, is why she chose her career in the first place.

Chances are there's a reason you chose your career too, and it probably comes down to finding some aspect fascinating and *fun*. I have never understood the curmudgeonly admonition on professional pursuits that "You're not supposed to enjoy it! That's why they call it work!" That would be a dreary way to go through life, writing off so many hours as a source of happiness—and not just the fleeting happiness of a smile at the watercooler. Deep happiness comes when we are so completely absorbed in our work that time seems to stand still. We are doing something difficult but manageable. We can see progress, and find the work pleasurable for its own sake. For me, editing book drafts has always felt like this. I willingly shove everything else aside and stay up later than I should playing with my sentences until they come out right. For others, like the medical researcher, it's about experimenting with numbers and patterns. A designer tries out combinations of colors and shapes. For managers, it's about creating time to think and strategize.

DeLene Bane works for her family business selling John Deere construction equipment. She manages a number of people, and wants to be available to them. Her time log showed an admirable number of conversations through the day (p. 105). But she also told me she wanted to make time for concentrated thinking. I noticed that on Monday, Wednesday, and Friday, when she was not responsible for the morning school run, she got to work at the crack of dawn. "I get in between six thirty and seven, and I'm not sure what happens," she says. Her time log suggests e-mail, which is the normal way we start work. Yet e-mail is perhaps not the best way to use quiet early hours. At one point Bane recalled looking at her inbox and realizing "this is just a lost cause." So I suggested going somewhere else for a bit. Even an hour focused on thinking, perhaps in a coffee shop from 6:30 a.m. to 7:30 a.m., would give her quiet time to ponder strategy without taking away from her in-office visibility.

Morning hours are great for getting things done, but doing first things first is really about doing them when you have the most energy and willpower. You should match your most important work to your most productive hours. Move other things around, and pack them together rather than

	TUESDAY	WEDNESDAY	THURSDAY	FRIDAY	SATURDAY	SUNDAY	MONDAY
5AM	5 wake up; 10 yoga	5 wake up; 10 yoga	Wake up and talk with husband	5 wake up; 10 yoga	Sleep	Sleep	Groom
5:15	Dinner prep	Shower and groom	Yoga	Shower and groom			"
5:30	"	"	Shower and groom	"			"
5:45	Shower and groom	Breakfast and make kids' lunch	"	"			Prep for the day
6:00	"	Groom	"	"			Commute to work
6:15	"	"	Laundry and prep for	Talk with B	5 wake up; 10 yoga		"
6:30	"	Commute to work	the day	Commute to work			Settle in and email
6:45	Breakfast with kids	"	Breakfast with kids	"	Shower and groom		Fill in time from weekend
7:00	"	Settle in and email	"	Settle in and email	"	Time change	Customer requirements
7:15	Get kids ready and	Employee convo	Get kids ready and	Customer requirements	"	lost an hour	Regular work
7:30	finish myself	Project work	finish myself	"	"		Problem work
7:45	Leave, drop off kids	"	Leave, drop off kids	Employee convo	Commute to work	"	"
8:00	and drive to work	Employee convo	and drive to work	"	with Dad	Wake up and read news	"
8:15	Settle in and email	Regular work	Settle in and email	Customer requirements	Settle in and email	on Internet	"
8:30	Employee convo	Email and response	Regular work	"	Email and response	Hang out with the kids	Employee convo
8:45	Email	Regular work	Employee convo	Email	Problem work	Laundry	"
9:00	Problem work	Personnel convo with	Problem work	Problem work	"	Make breakfast and eat	"

	TUESDAY	WEDNESDAY	THURSDAY	FRIDAY	SATURDAY	SUNDAY	MONDAY
9:15	"	HR Mgr	"	Organize	"	"	Problem Work
9:30	"	"	Employee convo	Mtg with HR	Regular work	Relax with husband and make grocery list	"
9:45	"	Regular work	Problem work	"	"	Shower and groom	Employee convo
10:00	Project work	"	"	"	"	"	Problem work
10:15	"	Employee convo	Employee convo	Strategy work	Customer requirements	"	"
10:30	Email	Regular work	Customer requirements	"	Problem work	Deal with daughter's biography catastrophe and	Email and response
10:45	"	"	"	Email and response	"	son's homework	Problem work
11:00	Personnel issues	Problem work	Email and response	Customer requirements	Project work	Get kids ready and finish	"
11:15	"	Regular work	"	"	Organize and work through	myself and laundry	"
11:30	Lunch (sit with Dad and	"	Problem work	"	paperwork and prep for	Commute to grandparents	"
11:45	after go over work)	Lunch (sit with Dad and	Problem work	Employee convo	Monday		Lunch while
12PM	Email	after go over work)	Lunch (went over some	Lunch (sit with Dad and	Commute		working
12:15	Problem work	Problem work	issues with Dad)	after go over work)	"		Problem work
12:30	"	"	Problem work	Customer requirements	Lunch and clean up		"
12:45	"	Regular work	Problem work	Employee convo	"		"
1:00	"	Personal tasks	Customer requirements	Strategy work	Down time with husband and	Family gettogether	Email and response

	TUESDAY	WEDNESDAY	THURSDAY	FRIDAY	SATURDAY	SUNDAY	MONDAY
1:15	"	Regular work	"	"	kids	"	Employee convo
1:30	Project work		"	Personal convo	Read magazine and start to	"	Problem work
1:45	"	Problem work	"	Employee convo	organize dinners for week	"	"
2:00	Problem work	"	Email and response	Problem work	Gym (10 min commute)	"	"
2:15	Email	Customer requirements	Customer requirements	Problem work	Cardio and strength training	"	"
2:30	Regular work	"	"	Employee convo	"	"	Employee convo
2:45	"	"	"	Customer requirements	"	"	Employee convo
3:00	"	Email and response	"	Problem work	"	"	Customer requirements
3:15	"	Regular work	Project work	"	Commute home	Commute home	"
3:30	"	"	Wrap up	Wrap up	Laundry		"
3:45	Commute	Email and response	Employee convo	Husband picked me up and	Kids' homework		"
4:00	"	Customer requirements	Customer requirements	we left for a date night			Employee convo
4:15	Dinner and prep for	Employee convo	Employee convo	"	Take kids shopping	Get ready to go to store	"
4:30	dance	Organize	Customer requirements	"	"	Take daughter to grocery	Customer requirements
4:45	Commute	Commute		"	"	store	Wrap up day
5:00	Dance (daughter)	Pick up kids from Spanish	Commute	"	"	"	Commute

	TUESDAY	WEDNESDAY	THURSDAY	FRIDAY	SATURDAY	SUNDAY	MONDAY
5:15	Work while watching	Commute	"	"	"	"	"
5:30	(45 min of email and	Dinner prep and prep for	Dinner prep, laundry,	"	"	"	Dinner prep, prep for
5:45	prep for Wed)	Thurs.	and house pickup	"	"	Put groceries away and	Tues. dinner, and laundry
6:00	Adult tap class	"		"	"	dinner prep and laundry	"
6:15	"	Dinner	Dinner	"	Make dinner and eat	Eat dinner and clean up	Eat Dinner
6:30	(45 min of reviewing	"	"	"	"	"	"
6:45	notes from store visits	Dishes, laundry, and	Kitchen pickup	"			Clean up and finish prep
7:00	and actions to take)	house pickup	Read with son	"	Kitchen cleanup	House pickup and prep for	For Tues. dinner
7:15	"	"	"	"	Read with son and listen	Mon.	Laundry and pickup and prep
7:30	Commute	Read with son	Pickup and prep for Fri.	"	to him play drums	Go through work email	For Tuesday
7:45	Prep for Wed. dinner	"	"	"	Bedtime groom	Laundry	"
8:00	and for Wednesday	Bedtime groom	Bedtime groom	"	Watch movie with kids	Stretch	Read news article
8:15	Kids' bedtime routine	Kids' bedtime routine	Kids' bedtime routine	"	"	Kids' bedtime routine	Kids' bedtime routine
8:30	Prep for Wed.	Laundry	Laundry, dishes, and	"	"	Prep for Mon.	Bedtime groom
8:45	Visit with friend	Relax with husband (searched	house pickup	"	"	Bedtime groom	Talk with husband

	TUESDAY	WEDNESDAY	THURSDAY	FRIDAY	SATURDAY	SUNDAY	MONDAY
9:00	"	Internet)	Relax (search Internet	"	"	Relax (read Internet news as	Personal Emails
9:15	Bedtime groom	Sleep	and read)	"	"	husband watches TV)	Relax (read news on
9:30	Relax		Sleep	"	"	Sleep	Internet and book)
9:45	Sleep			Picked up kids	Kids' bedtime routine		Sleep
10:00				Kids' bedtime routine	Relax in bed and read		
10:15				Bedtime groom	"		
10:30				Relax (stretch and read	Sleep		
10:45				news on Internet)			
11:00				Sleep			
11:15							
11:30							
11:45							
12:00 AM							
12:15							
12:30							
12:45							
1:00							
1:15							
1:30							
1:45							

	TUESDAY	WEDNESDAY	THURSDAY	FRIDAY	SATURDAY	SUNDAY	MONDAY
2:00							
2:15							
2:30							
2:45							
3:00							
3:15							
3:30							
3:45							
4:00							
4:15							
4:30						10 wake up 5 yoga	
4:45						Shower and groom	

consigning real work to the scraps of time left when all auxiliary work is finished. That is a recipe for feeling like life, or at least the work part of life, is no fun.

Of course, when you have a family, you may not have automatic access to your most productive hours. Ahlia Kitwana's log contained this little gem one afternoon: "Notice I hit a serious stride after 4 p.m., which is when I usually have to start wrapping up to pick up girls and start dinner." Day cares and after-school programs have hard stops that don't easily allow for a 4:00 p.m. to 7:00 p.m. state of "flow." You can encounter this problem on the other side of the day, too. If 6:30 a.m. to 8:30 a.m. is your most productive time, but you are responsible for getting the younger members of your household on the bus or off to school, you may not start work until after this window.

We shouldn't blame this all on families. Plenty of supervisors schedule pointless meetings during some team member's most productive time. If it is a family issue, however, and in Kitwana's case it was, then it's important not to fall into the same 24-Hour Trap that stymies people in their attempts to create schedules that combine work and a personal life. Just because you can't use your most productive hours *every day* doesn't mean you can *never* use them. Kitwana's office was closer to the girls than her husband's was, so it usually made sense from a time and gas usage perspective for her to pick them up after school. But when I asked about her four p.m. discovery, she told me that she'd figured out how to solve this problem two days per week. "My husband picks up the girls on Wednesdays because of my [evening] triathlon training, so I can stay until about six on Wednesdays," she noted. "On Fridays, I pick the girls up at three p.m. and drop them off at my mom's house, then I can go back to work and stay until six or later if I choose. Right now that gives me two days a week with those sweet hours to work without worries." Two days a week isn't five, but it's not zero either. That's worth acknowledging and reveling in, rather than grumping that it "never" happens.

Strategy 3: Invest in People

Many women in the Mosaic Project worked in management. If you're in management, you know it involves a lot of meetings, both as you supervise projects and as you develop the talents of the people who work with you. This is the nature of the job: you're going to spend a lot of time with other people. You *want* to spend time with other people. But formal meetings also have a downside. They suck energy out of a schedule. You're thinking about them before they begin, and you don't tackle anything major as you're waiting for them to start. They rise in the hierarchy of people's days, sometimes far beyond their actual importance, because they happen at specific times and involve commitments to other people. You could be on the verge of solving your most vexing business issue, but if your calendar says you have a phone call to fix some slightly off numbers for a presentation you're giving next week, you will stop thinking about that vexing issue and prepare to dial in. After all, the calendar decrees it, and others are expecting you.

That's how we're used to working, but it's not insurmountable. If possible, it might be better to save formal meetings for things that require a lot of prep and will result in big decisions. Then, instead of scheduling yourself to the hilt, you invest in people by looking for creative ways to build one-on-one time into your life.

Maureen Sullivan, president of AOL.com and its lifestyle brands and mother of a toddler, told me she has power walks with team members as they go between the two buildings in New York City where they work. These mini-meetings have become a great time to catch up—and don't require a thirty-minute slot that might cut into other meaningful work. DeLene Bane works with her father, and her log shows them having lunch together as a way of nurturing their relationship on a personal and professional level. People at one tech company where I spoke and collected logs took strolls with colleagues on the walking trails near the corporate campus. I won't say "never eat alone" because if you're an introvert dealing with meetings all day, sometimes that's your best chance to decompress. However, asking people to grab a cup of coffee with you on the days you're working in the office can be a good way to chat and accomplish whatever you'd accomplish in a formal meeting with a lot less mental overhead.

Incidentally, these little one-on-ones are great ways to mentor, which, along with exercising and reading, is an activity people claim they'd like to do *if only I had the time!*

Laurie Glimcher, an immunologist and dean of the Weill Cornell Medical College in New York, has a reputation for making time for all kinds of people.

When I interviewed her for a *Fast Company* post, she told me that she considered mentoring "my most important job." She believes that now as she's trying to nurture young physicians, but says she also felt this way decades ago when she had young kids at home and was building a research lab at Harvard, activities that, combined, sound like they might push mentoring off someone's to-do list.

Her biggest realization was that *mentoring is not a charitable act.* None of us has so fully arrived that we cannot be helped by other people. This is even true for late-career professionals. But if you're going to choose a season of life to mentor people, it's more effective to do this early in your career, because the people you mentor as you're also fairly new in your career may wind up being most helpful. We all rise at different speeds, and these mentees are starting just a few years behind you. In Glimcher's case, the young scientists she mentored early on went on to become rock stars who wanted to coauthor papers with her later. In business, an entrepreneur you advise when she's still figuring things out can cash out for a billion dollars and want to invest in the company you decide to start.

Time is limited, so you have to be strategic. In *Lean In*, Sheryl Sandberg notes that smart mentors "select protégés based on performance and potential." She believes that this means we're sending the wrong message to young people. "We need to stop telling them, 'Get a mentor and you will excel.' Instead we need to tell them, 'Excel and you will get a mentor.'" It's okay to play favorites. Indeed, because time is absolutely limited, you have to play favorites. If someone is so brilliant and hardworking that you cannot imagine losing her from your field, spend all the time you want with her. You might check in with her every week or two to see how things are going. If you don't mind losing her? That's a different matter. Make a list of answers to frequently asked questions that you can send to people you're not as sure about who ask to take you out for coffee or (that horrible image) to "pick your brain." If someone comes back with specific and intelligent follow-up questions (most people won't), you could reevaluate, and schedule a phone call.

You can also mentor as you manage. Hopefully, many people you want to mentor are your direct reports, because you've hired awesome people whose careers you can't wait to watch. In this case, mentoring can be part of your normal working life, as long as you're not trying to manage too many people.

One Leadership IQ poll of thirty-two thousand people found that employees are most engaged and motivated when they spend six hours per week interacting with their bosses. Even allowing for group meetings, that means it's pretty difficult to manage more than seven people effectively. Glimcher knows this firsthand. "Having a medium-sized lab rather than a large lab was best for my style," she says. "My style was and still is to meet with everyone in the lab one-on-one." She'd review experiments and plan the next weeks with team members. "When things were not going well, I let them know they had my emotional and intellectual support. I couldn't do that with a huge lab."

As long as you figure out how to carve out quiet time when you need it, maybe by coming in early some mornings, working from home occasionally, or (a suggestion from time management expert Laura Stack) wearing a funny hat that colleagues know is your "thinking cap," you don't need to fear accessibility. Let mentees know that they should feel free to drop by. You want them to share exciting new results or challenges with you. Glimcher won people's loyalty by being easy to reach. "You have your scheduled appointments," she'd tell them, "but don't hesitate to pop your head in the door." A lot of mentoring can happen in quick spurts, not just formal sessions. I'd see this on logs: a fifteen-minute coffee break with a direct report or a professor's ten-minute chat with a grad student. It can happen outside of work, too. Have a few people over for a casual backyard barbecue. If you've got kids the same ages, you can have them over to play. Whatever you do, make time for people, and the investment will come back to reward you down the line.

Strategy 4: Be Strategically Seen

When it comes to the soft side of careers, many of us aren't like Lisa Camooso Miller with her coffee dates and early happy hours. We fall into the trap of thinking either/or. *I'm a working parent and therefore I can't go to networking events.* But you don't have to go to postwork events every night. No one wants to spend every night away from home, even if all you're caring for is houseplants. If you keep such interactions as a possibility, though, people will still ask you. You will stay in the loop.

This can be a tricky thing to handle. If you negotiate a schedule that allows you to leave at four p.m., but you stick around until six p.m. some days shooting the breeze with people and going out with them for happy hour, you signal to your colleagues that staying late is a possibility. That means that you might be asked to stay on nights you don't want to stay late. There isn't a good way around this, which is why working for a manager who's generally flexible is usually better than negotiating a formal schedule. In many offices, though, Mosaic Project participants told me that no one was tracking the times they came in and left. If you want to leave at four, you can, except when you don't want to. Sometimes, you might strategically choose to leave later.

It's the same if you work at home, or remotely. Brandy Hebert lives in Maine and works remotely for a major consumer products company in the Midwest. She travels there one week out of every four, and so she sent me two logs, from a travel week and a nontravel week. During her travel week, her log showed her socializing or working late every night she was at company headquarters, putting in enough time to keep those relationships strong. There is no huge difference in the quality of relationships you will build going to work dinners or networking events once or twice a month as opposed to once a week. You also don't lose much time with your family by going out with professional colleagues once or twice a month. "Never" is a rather defeatist strategy, just as sticking around the office until ten p.m. nightly for the face time might be.

It's easy to underinvest in the "be strategically seen" part of a career, and it's an area an unfortunate number of women, in particular, get tripped up on. It's not just about the higher-ups seeing you so that you are at the front of their minds, adding a dollop of visibility on top of work performance in a way that can help you score a promotion. Even after you reach management levels, teams can interpret efficient, no-nonsense instruction as coldness if it's not tempered with the occasional relaxed get-together. Is that fair? No. But if your upward feedback is terrible, it can hurt your career anyway.

Efficiency is great, but business is never just business. People who make success possible recognize this and structure their lives and worldviews accordingly. One outcome of tracking time (discussed in the next chapter) is that many women discover they are spending far more hours with their kids than they thought. Knowing that, they realize that they can join their teams for dinner on occasion, and they don't have to race out after the appetizers. Keeping some potential evening or overnight child care arrangement on backup means that neither parent has to forgo dinners or bigger networking events like conferences if there's a conflict. While the handful of Mosaic women who went to conferences during their diary weeks mostly relied on their partners' caring for their children, not all women have this as a ready option, either because they don't have partners, or because their partners travel frequently too. One single mom told me she was struggling to figure this out, because "in a few years, I'd like to be able to have the capacity to travel a few times a year."

If you're in this situation of trying to figure out overnight sitters and extended family coverage, then you become quite focused on whether any individual conference is worth it. And the truth is, not all are, though as I've asked veteran conference goers about this topic, I've realized that making a good return on investment is partly about being smart in your approach.

First, to get more out of a conference, go with a goal. Figure out what you hope to get out of a conference before you sign up. Maybe you want to leave with a solid lead on a new client, or meet three people you only know virtually. Knowing why you're going keeps you focused. It also keeps you from wasting time and money on a conference you've outgrown.

Second, don't rely on serendipity. Find out who will be attending that you know virtually and would like to get to know better. Invite people for a small gathering early on, like a dinner on the first night when there's nothing formally planned. That way, no matter what else happens, you make sure to meet these people you want to meet. Chances are, at least one of them will ask to invite someone else along to your initial dinner. Say yes. This is a good sign you've got a thoughtful connector on your hands who's already figuring out who else you should know. If people can't come to your dinner, make appointments for breakfast, coffee, or drinks.

Third, spend more time in the halls saying hello to people, and less time attending the panels. Panels can be enlightening, but my sense is that they primarily serve as a way to expand the number of big-name people asked to attend the conference. Racing up to the stage afterward to meet these people is not a good strategy for connecting. They'll be trying to talk to a line of people. A better approach might be to volunteer with the conference organizing team. That way you get to meet anyone you want.

Fourth, be open to new experiences. Say yes to the invitation to go clubbing. Say hello and introduce yourself to people who look intriguing. Amanda Steinberg, founder of DailyWorth, a financial Web site for women (and a mom of two kids who play with mine), told me that she raised venture capital from Google chairman Eric Schmidt because she introduced herself to the person she later learned was his fund manager at a conference.

And finally, realize that conferences are partly about deepening relationships with people you already know, like members of your own team. Getting out of the office together is great for cohesion. While bored at SXSW in Austin, Steinberg and the DailyWorth team all decided to get tattoos together. This was "all by choice and all with enthusiasm," she assures me, but it was definitely a memorable bonding experience.

Strategy 5: Build In Slack

Human beings have human bodies. Because humans have human bodies that cannot run perpetually, we take breaks whether we consciously schedule them or not. When you don't take real breaks, you take fake ones that involve cruising to Facebook or checking your stocks. We get lost in transition. And that's a shame because breaks are a great opportunity to nurture yourself and to shape work culture, too. Take Kimberli Jeter for instance, profiled in the next chapter, who works with international teams, including one in Mozambique. During one logged day, one of her colleagues prepared a lunch of food from Mozambique. This offered everyone both some needed decompression time and an opportunity to feel more connected to the work they were doing.

Building in space isn't just about taking breaks, however. It's also about building unclaimed time into your life, particularly into your work life, both for sanity and so you can seize new opportunities without life falling apart.

In their 2013 book, *Scarcity*, Sendhil Mullainathan and Eldar Shafir use the term "slack" to describe this unclaimed space. Time and money are both ultimately limited, requiring choices, but some choices are made in more constrained situations than others. Someone on a limited budget going to a grocery store faces tough decisions. If the price of milk has gone up, the money to purchase milk has to come from something else that our shopper probably wanted, like fresh produce, and may have really needed, like diapers.

On the other hand, if you are a multimillionaire, going to the grocery store does not involve stressful choices. Your decision to pay extra for the steak you want instead of the ground beef you don't may result in your third-generation heirs purchasing one less gold-plated faucet down the line, but you really don't care.

We all have the same 168 hours in a week, but having slack in your schedule can make you feel like the millionaire at Safeway. You don't face the hard choice of getting off the phone with a client who really wants to talk because you're already late to your next appointment, which you've rescheduled three times. A too-busy schedule precludes new opportunities. If you're pushed up hard against a deadline and a radio station wants to interview you about an area in which you're hoping to become a thought leader, you can't give it your all. If you have slack in your schedule, you can.

Creating such slack in your schedule isn't easy, particularly if you have lots of people asking for your attention. Sometimes you just have to put your foot down about your own limits. If you fly overnight to Europe, tell your teams there that you cannot take meetings the second you land. You might build in time to shower, take a one-hour nap, or go to the gym. You're still traveling, but it's more sustainable. One reason I still use a small (3⅝-inch by 6⅛-inch) weekly paper calendar is that it provides a visual signal that a day is getting too full. Electronic calendars can let you load up a day with something every fifteen minutes, but I run out of lines to write appointments and phone numbers after I commit to five or six things. When I find myself scribbling items in the margins, that's a sign I need to look for time on a different day.

Some women told me they took drastic measures to build slack into their working lives. When Crystal Paine started the Web site Money Saving Mom several years ago during the economic crisis, it took off fast. For a while, the Web site was crashing daily and new advertisers and potential affiliate entities, not to mention conference organizers and publications, kept asking for her time. Since she had no staff, and was homeschooling her young children, this didn't work. "I remember that, so many nights, it would be ten o'clock, and I'd look at all I had left to do," she told me in an interview for *Fast Company*. "It was so not healthy. I pulled all-nighters. Or I'd be up until three and have to get up in the morning again." You get to the point where "your body forgets how to relax and sleep, you're running on so much adrenaline." She kept thinking she'd get through the next project and then she'd have more breathing room, but "that's never how it is with a start-up. There's always something more you need to be doing. It took me months to finally realize that it's never going to get better. I have to step back and make better choices if I want this thing to run for the long haul."

Her solution? She said no to pretty much everything for six months. She hired help in bits and pieces, figuring out what she could efficiently outsource. Then, slowly, she began thinking about where she wanted her business to go, and whom she should be reaching out to, rather than seeing who was reaching out to her. "Being very careful about saying yes helped me a lot," she says.

This is a fine balance, to be sure. We often lament women's tendency to say yes to everything from running the nursery school silent auction to leading the Girl Scout troop. Countless articles have been written advising women how to say no, and there's something to this. But I have also found that when it comes to work, we're facing different headwinds, and sometimes we say no too easily. When I heard Wendy Clark, senior vice president of Coca-Cola's Global Sparkling Brand Center, speak at the MAKERS Conference in California, she said that when Coke had called her up, she'd figured she couldn't take the opportunity. She was a busy mom of three young kids! How could she take such a big job? Her family wouldn't want that, right? Then she tried actually asking her family what they thought. Her husband told her to reconsider. She took the job, and she made it work.

Saying yes to big things like a new job is sometimes wise. It's saying yes to too many little things that forces one's hand. You get overwhelmed, so you don't take on the big stuff, because when you're overwhelmed, it's hard to see that the little stuff just doesn't matter. *I can't take on this high-profile project that gives me access to the CEO because I won't have any time to format my department newsletter!* You do not have to fill every minute. If something is merely a good use of your time, rather than a great use of your time, it might not be worth doing.

How to Chuck the Rest

There's a reason I started this chapter on productivity at work with what I think people should spend more time doing, rather than on micro fixes like using keyboard shortcuts in Outlook. I think a lot of the time management advice people seek out at work is misguided. It doesn't get at the root of our time management woes. Some things will expand to fill all available space. In the white-collar working world, e-mail and meetings serve this role. The key to handling these tools is not to aim for more organization or efficiency. It's to change your mind-set.

That's not to say there aren't some efficiency breakthroughs that can really make a difference in your work life. Some of the best strategies I've picked up on how to manage meetings came from a book that wasn't about managing meetings at all. It was Doug Lemov's *Teach Like a Champion*, and it looked at how the most effective teachers keep students engaged and coax out their best work. The insights work well with adults, too. In the classroom version, every class session needs to have an objective. A good teacher lets students know what information or skills they'll learn. Sure, the kids have to be there, but sharing the objective honors students' time, and keeps them focused. Second, master teachers plan their lessons extensively—both what they'll do and what their students will do with every minute they have together. Third, master teachers do not let anyone disengage. They'll cold-call on children to make it very clear that the teacher controls the classroom, and to keep everyone's thoughts whirring.

Likewise, all meetings need an objective. Why are people there? There's no point in meeting if nothing in the world will change as a result. Smart meeting facilitators think through what everyone in that meeting will do with every minute they'll be sitting in that conference room. If you're giving a presentation, you obviously think through what you'll do, but it's just as important to let everyone else know what you want them to be thinking and doing. Should they shoot holes in your argument? Would you like them to offer feedback on your style because you'll give the presentation again tomorrow? Do you want them to come up with new ideas to add to your slides? This double planning keeps people from wasting time. And finally, cold-calling on participants, like with students, is a great option for meetings, too. Asking, "Does anyone have any questions?" means the same people who always speak up will speak up and say exactly what they always say. Ask people who don't speak up what they think. It's probably just as interesting. As a side note, calling on people randomly cuts down on under-the-table e-mail checking.

As for e-mail, that other massive work time suck, there are various defensive strategies you can use, such as unsubscribing frequently from any lists you find yourself on, or reading only the most recent installment in a thread. But I'd warn against investing too much energy in any organizing system aimed at processing everything in your inbox. For starters, it will take a lot of time. Helen Fox was the director of marine science at the World Wildlife Fund when she kept a time log for me in June 2013. During this week, she had attempted to achieve that allegedly mind-calming state of Inbox Zero. She kept her log in fifteen-minute increments, and so I saw line after line of "IBZ" and a number. When she started the log on a Wednesday, she was at IBZ (~450). On Thursday she hit 400. On Friday she hit 275. On Monday she was back up in the 300s. She got this all the way down to IBZ (~20!) before, as inevitably happens, people responded to all the responses she sent in one giant deluge, and she was back up to IBZ (~50) the next day and couldn't make headway from there.

There was a lot of other great stuff going on in Fox's life. She made a quilt for a baby shower, she did yoga, and she went on a date with her husband in addition to her scientific work. I don't want to make too much of her quest for Inbox Zero. Nonetheless, processing her e-mail did take ten of the thirty-nine hours she worked that week.

When I caught up with her a year later, she told me that she had "completely given up" on getting through all her messages. "It's not how I'm going to spend my time." It had been a long journey, but after keeping the log, and working with a career coach, she'd decided that she would manage her work life in a way that was not e-mail based. Instead, she'd look at other markers of productivity and efficiency: "What are my big projects? What are my objectives for the week?" Achieving these objectives "does still entail writing e-mails, but it's me setting the agenda rather than the overflowing inbox." She'd been telling herself that "once I get on top of it once, I'll stay on top of it—but that never happened." In the meantime, she was skimping on the science and people management that drew her to her career in the first place.

When it comes to e-mail, most of us, like Fox in 2013, are operating from a faulty mind-set. Because much useful information does come in via e-mail, we're tempted to treat the inbox as a task list, to be processed the way a dishwasher must be emptied. But this impulse is misguided because, unlike a dishwasher, an inbox has no meaningful space limit, and can be useful whether it's emptied or not. In the case of this particular dishwasher, people are also loading it up with things you don't care about, or need, or that are interesting but will resolve themselves without your input. Constantly emptying this sort of dishwasher will keep you from ever starting dinner.

I try to work from this premise: *you will never reach the bottom of your inbox.* Better to realize that anything you haven't gotten to after a week or so will have either gone away or been thrust back upon you by follow-up messages or calls. You can probably stop thinking about it. Earth will not crash into the sun.

There is no virtue in being productive toward ends that don't matter. Indeed, there's an opportunity cost. If you want to be productive, the best question to ask is not whether anything's lurking in your inbox. It's the question Fox learned to ask: Am I making progress toward things that are important to me? Am I solving the problems I want to solve? Am I doing my research on coral reefs, or writing the papers I want to write?

E-mail is a wonderful tool, just as meetings are wonderful tools to accomplish things as a group. Before I compose too mournful a lament about the time office workers spend on e-mail, I recall learning to report before e-mail existed. I had to play phone tag with sources all day.

That said, e-mail is just a tool, not an end in itself. Since e-mail expands to fill the available space, true inbox management means choosing to make space for meaningful things first, and trusting that e-mail will fill in around the edges. When you face a choice of whether to strategize about your career, do deep work, mentor a colleague, or even enjoy some slack in your schedule, or whether to spend an hour cleaning out your inbox, just remember that your inbox will fill up again, but you'll never get that hour back.

You don't build the life you want by saving time. You build the life you want, and then time saves itself. Recognizing that is what makes success possible.

·
·
·
·
·
·

HOME

·
·
·
·
·
·

. . . .

CHAPTER 5

Be There

O f all the work/life narratives out there, the most insidious is this: success in the larger world requires painful trade-offs at home. As essayist Caitlin Flanagan, author of *To Hell with All That: Loving and Loathing Our Inner Housewife*, summed it up, "When a mother works, something is lost." It is the dichotomy from chapter 1: on one side we find paychecks; on the other side, hugs and dandelions. A side effect of a more-than-full-time job is you risk "never" seeing your kids.

We don't question this narrative—until we look at our time. For many Mosaic Project participants, one unexpected outcome of keeping a time log was realizing that even if they worked a lot, they spent *a lot* of time around their families too. As one woman put it, "I used to have guilt. I don't have guilt anymore." To be sure, a stay-at-home mother of a toddler probably spends more hours around her child than a parent who works outside the home, but most working parents rack up a reasonable number of hours in the presence of their children, too. A woman gone from 8:00 a.m. to 6:00 p.m. Monday through Friday could easily spend an hour before work and two hours after with her young kids, and ten hours on each weekend day. That adds up to thirty-five hours per week, the equivalent of a full-time job. Many women consciously arranged their schedules to leave work earlier than that. If you pick up your kids at 5:00 p.m. and are with them until their 8:00 or 8:30 p.m. bedtime most days, you could hit forty hours per week spent together if you add in morning and weekend time. People who spend forty hours per week at their jobs don't lament that they "never" see their workplaces.

That said, I know that being *around* family, and really being *with* family, aren't the same things. This is true no matter how many hours we spend together. Indeed, time diary data show that parents who are both in and out of the workforce don't spend copious hours interacting with their offspring. When I was conducting time makeovers for a previous book, a homeschooling mom of young children told me that she hoped I would help her figure out how to spend more time with her kids. When I expressed surprise at this desire, she admitted it was a strange request, but "When I say I want more time with the boys, I am wanting more time where they have my undivided attention. I guess because I stay at home and homeschool, we are technically together 24/7 but seldom do they get all of me." Like many of us, "I multitask way too much, and too often at the end of the day I am disappointed in myself that I didn't carve out time for each boy independently where my phone was put away, laptop closed, TV off, and where I wasn't switching loads of laundry or cleaning one mess or another up."

While I didn't have any homeschooling parents keep time logs for this project, this issue of kid time being copious enough to be treated carelessly did play out to a lesser degree. One woman who arranged her work schedule to pick her son up at three p.m. told me, "I love being able to have the four- to five-hour block of time with my son in the afternoon, but at the same time some days it can feel like I am counting down the hours until my husband gets home, until dinnertime, until bedtime." I know this feeling, too, of waiting for time to pass. When you know that time is finite, wanting it to pass can feel like a miserable bargain. With no plan for these giant blocks of time, "I end up frittering that away doing dishes or tidying up and not really getting much done," she said.

This clock watching also stems from another reality: kids aren't always the easiest people to interact with. In the usual narrative, time with family is supposed to be a meaningful respite from the larger world. It can be. It can also be soul-crushing when, on a rainy Saturday, you've got multiple children screaming and scratching each other at once. As for one's partner, over the years it becomes easy to simply inhabit the house together, crashing together on the couch at the end of the day. We accept this as the natural softening of intimacy over time. Date night is contrived, not to mention a hassle to arrange.

Yet we still hope for transcendent moments. In between mealtime tantrums and bedtime battles, how do we create tiles in our mosaics that stand out and shine?

This isn't the old quantity/quality time question, because the two aren't independent variables. Being with your family for large chunks of time creates space for transcendent moments. Jackie Woodside, who runs a coaching and consulting firm in Massachusetts, spends a lot of time shuttling her eight-year-old son from activity to activity. On one day, she sent him out to play with friends on the playground from 3:00 to 3:30 as she did a phone consultation in the car. It started snowing, and as Woodside and her son drove home, conditions worsened. On her log, she wrote that they "stopped to help a high school kid who had just totaled his car by sliding into two trees with the front and rear of his car." They waited with the distraught young man until his mother could get there; Woodside noted that she and her son had a rather vivid conversation about "the perils of driving too fast in the snow." It was a chance "to teach my son how to be a good citizen and help strangers." Most days, they enjoy talking, but nothing major comes out of their time in the car. On this day, the space allowed her to impart her values.

That said, some decisions we make about our time increase the chances that meaningful moments can emerge, and I don't just mean meaningful for children. Parents deserve to enjoy life too. When we're spending too much time checking e-mail outside piano lessons, and hustling kids through the evening routine, life can feel like a forced march. The joy isn't there.

Fortunately, being mindful of family time—making a commitment to be there physically and mentally and enjoy life while doing so—makes memories possible. We control a lot less about our children's outcomes in life than we think. They are their own people. But one thing parents do shape is whether kids remember their childhoods as happy. Creating a happy home is a conscious choice, as is creating a happy marriage. This chapter is about how people craft their lives to make that happen.

Be There, Part 1

The Ten Secrets of Happier Parenting

The mosaic metaphor is that life consists of many tiles. Some tiles are stressful and some are wonderful. Of all the activities we do, parenting presents these tiles in starkest relief. As I studied the Mosaic logs, though, I did see strategies that increased the highs while mitigating the lows. These ten secrets of happier parenting make life with little ones more enjoyable, not only in the haze of memory where everything looks rosy, but even in the midst of busy days themselves.

1. THINK THROUGH YOUR WEEKDAY EVENINGS. The usual rhythm of dual-income family life involves everyone descending on the house at some point. Then what? People are tired, and these hours need to contain dinner, and homework, and bedtime routines. So we discount this as usable time. If you had a similar three-hour stretch at work, however, you would at least think through how you wanted to spend it. You aren't going to plan your evenings in fifteen-minute increments, as you would with work, or send calendar invites for dinner. Still, home life deserves the same intention as work, and there is a lot of space between planning every minute and complete mindlessness.

Diana Hobbs, a San Antonio–based project manager, showed this mindfulness on her log (p. 130). On Monday evening, she, her husband, and kids, ages four and six, went for a family walk with the dog. Then, she and her husband made dinner using vegetables from their garden. On Wednesday, she visited with her brother. On Thursday, she picked strawberries and jumped rope with the kids, and on Friday, they went out for ice cream. There was work in there too, after the kids went to sleep, but her nights didn't conform to the march of dinner, bath, and bed that you often see with young kids.

When I asked her about her routine, she told me that she had always been cognizant of her evenings. "I used to go to night school after work," she told me. "You can pack in a lot after work. You can get a whole degree!"

These days, she usually calls her husband while riding home on the bus. "We talk about what we might do," she says. "If you come home and you're tired and you don't know what you're going to do, then surprises wear you out." Instead, she and her husband brainstorm their evening plans so they can mentally prepare themselves. It only takes five minutes, but if she's thought, "I'd like to play a board game with the kids tonight," then she can walk in and be excited as she talks about this with her family. Given that the kids are little, they're often willing to play along. Planning a little bit means "we're not just going straight from work to staring at the TV to bed. That feels like being on a hamster wheel."

Many of Hobbs's weekday activities didn't involve leaving the neighborhood. If you've been running around all day, that may be the way to go. There are plenty of fun things you can do at home. Stories don't have to happen just before bed; you can spend the postdinner hour reading chapters aloud. You can bake cookies together or attempt craft projects.

Your evenings can involve excursions too. Summer evening trips to a playground or a community pool can be nice. My husband or I usually covered Jasper's weeknight soccer practice during the fall of 2014, but when we were both traveling and one of our longtime sitters took him, she remarked how quickly the evening went with the little ones climbing on the nearby playground as he played. Being outside at twilight feels special; you're sneaking in minutes of pleasure that might otherwise disappear. Wintertime requires more creativity, but some libraries have evening hours, and school-age children might enjoy local sports events too. If you go out to eat every night, it loses its charm, but if you usually eat at home, going out to a diner can be a once-every-few-weeks treat. The point is to recognize that evening family time deserves some thought. Even if you want to do nothing, when you have young kids, *it's impossible to do nothing*. You'll do something, but it may not be a something any of you enjoy. A little intention goes a long way.

2. THINK THROUGH YOUR MORNINGS. In chapter 3, I mentioned an assertion that mothers won't work fifty-five hours a week because once you add on a commute, you're gone from 8:30 a.m. to 8:30 p.m. each weekday, and mothers want to see their children awake. It is true that most parents choose not to work like this. Even if you did, however, there's a good chance you'd

	MONDAY	TUESDAY	WEDNESDAY	THURSDAY	FRIDAY	SATURDAY	SUNDAY
5AM	Sleep	Sleep	Sleep	Sleep	Sleep	Sleep	Sleep
5:30	Sleep	Sleep	Sleep	Sleep	Sleep	Sleep	Sleep
6	Snooze for 10, get dressed, hair and makeup	Get dressed, hair and makeup, make breakfast	Snooze for 10, get dressed, hair and makeup	Get dressed, hair and makeup	Sleep	Sleep	Sleep
6:30	Breakfast with the kids	Personal emails, then eat with the kids, and fit in a little crochet afterward	Breakfast with the kids	Breakfast with the kids	Get ready	Sleep	Sleep
7	Drive to the bus stop, singing my favorite songs; read while waiting for the bus	Drive to the bus stop, singing my favorite songs; read while waiting for the bus	Drive to the bus stop, listen to NPR	Drive to the bus stop, singing my favorite songs; read while waiting for the bus	Get kids ready/ walk oldest son to school with husband and youngest son	Sleep	Sleep
7:30	Bus ride - read and talk with other rider who loves to read	Bus ride - catch up on weekly and daily planning	Bus ride - read	Bus ride - listened to music and worked on my flower garden quilt	Get kids ready/ walk oldest son to school with husband and youngest son	Sleep	Sleep
8	Weekly project schedule review	Weekly status reporting - project reviews	Project status reporting	Prepare for the day	Clean up	Get dressed, hair and makeup	Sleep
8:30	Weekly project schedule review	Weekly status reporting - project reviews	Was told to clear my calendar of all meetings today to assist with the Quarterly Business Report. Moved all meetings to Thursday and delegated all that I could	Prj. 2 - pilot follow-up call	Quilt	Laundry and make a large family breakfast	We skip church and Sunday school and lounge instead - it was worth it after working last weekend on a project install. That is the reason for the compensation day off

	MONDAY	TUESDAY	WEDNESDAY	THURSDAY	FRIDAY	SATURDAY	SUNDAY
9	Work with project manager to prepare for Project 1 meeting	Weekly status reporting - project reviews		Followed up with CIO on Quarterly Business Review to see if anything was needed	Purchase flowers for my mom and drop them off at my parents house	Head to the zoo	
9:30	Work with project manager to prepare for Project 1 meeting	Weekly status reporting - project reviews		Followed up with CIO on Quarterly Business Review to see if anything was needed	Off to the zoo with our youngest son	Zoo	Breakfast
10	Update Prj. 1 meeting materials	Prj. 1 - testing review		Prepared for Prj. 1 status meeting/	Zoo beyond crowded so we go to Lego store	Zoo	
10:30	Prj. 1 - testing review	Prj. 1 - budget work	Was told to clear my calendar of all meetings today to assist with the Quarterly Business Report. Moved all meetings to Thursday and delegated all that I could	processed emails related to Prj. 1	Played at tiny tot playground	Zoo	
11	Finish Prj. 1 meeting materials	Prj. 1 - budget work		Direct report 1x1	New shoe shopping for youngest son	Zoo	
11:30	Prj. 1 - CIO meeting	Snack and read through email		Direct report 1x1	Lunch at a restaurant	Zoo	
12PM	Prj. 1 - CIO meeting	Gym - walked and jogged, then called my husband to see how his day was going		Went out to eat with coworker	Lunch at a restaurant	Zoo	Laundry and housework mixed in with sporadic crocheting and quilting
12:30	Prj. 1 - update budget based on CIO meeting	Gym - walked and jogged, then called my husband to see how his day was going		Went out to eat with coworker	Nap	Zoo	
1	Update Prj. 1 budget and eat part of my lunch	Eat lunch, process emails		Finished preparing status materials for Prj. 1	Nap	Drive home	
1:30	Prj. 2 - pilot status meeting	Prj. 1 conference call		Met with team to develop approach for managing Prj. 3	Nap	Eat lunch	

	MONDAY	TUESDAY	WEDNESDAY	THURSDAY	FRIDAY	SATURDAY	SUNDAY
2	Resume Prj. 1 budget work	Prj. 1 - testing review		Met with team to develop approach for managing Prj. 3	Walk to school with husband and youngest son to pick up oldest son	Eat lunch	Laundry and housework mixed in with sporadic crocheting and quilting
2:30	Resume Prj. 1 budget work	Prj. 1 - server strategy meeting		Business status meeting for Prj. 1	Family car wash - my husband's car was beyond filthy	Garden with my brother and the kids	
3	Resume Prj. 1 budget work	Recap Prj. 2 pilot meeting and scheduled follow-up	Was told to clear my calendar today to assist with the Quarterly Business Report. Moved all meetings to Thursday and delegated all that I could	Business status meeting for Prj. 1	Family car wash - my husband's car was beyond filthy	Run errands with my brother	
3:30	Met with PM to delegate work effort	Process email and knock out a few action items		Go/No Go decision meeting for Project 4	Family car wash - my husband's car was beyond filthy	Run errands with my brother	Finished crocheting baby blanket for my friend's baby shower/watched kids run around playing Batman, and then my youngest son crawled on the couch and fell asleep next to me while my other son did his reading homework
4	Eat the other half of my lunch and catch up with my husband	Prj. 1 - testing review		Go/No Go decision meeting for Project 4	Quilt	Run errands with my brother	
4:30	Prj. 1 - testing review	Prj. 1 meeting on communication materials		Process invoices and email check	Figure out dinner and decide on ice cream!	Run errands with my brother	
5	Clean up desk and head out to the bus stop	Clean up desk and head out to the bus stop		Pack bags and out of office preparation	Go out for ice cream	Pick spinach from the garden for making pesto	

	MONDAY	TUESDAY	WEDNESDAY	THURSDAY	FRIDAY	SATURDAY	SUNDAY
5:30	Bus ride - call husband and discuss our day	Bus ride - audio book and nap	Caught the bus, talked to husband for a bit, and then closed my eyes and relaxed	Catch the bus and send out a few emails	Go out for ice cream	Make pesto	
6	Bus ride/drive from the bus stop and sing out loud at the top of my lungs	Bus ride/drive from the bus stop and catch up on NPR	Bus ride/drive from the bus stop and catch up on NPR	Bus ride - listen to music and rest	Clean up	Family dinner	
6:30	Family walk with the dog	Dinner and hangout with the family	Wrap up business review work at the kitchen table	Bus ride/drive from the bus stop and sing out loud at the top of my lungs	Check out the garden with the kids	Family dinner	Make dinner
7	Help husband prepare dinner - pull vegetables from the garden	Dinner and hangout with the family	Eat dinner	Jumped rope and picked strawberries with the kids	Check out the garden with the kids	Clean up around the house and make cookies	Eat dinner
7:30	Eat as a family	Work email, status reporting, low-effort tasks	Visit with my brother who came over earlier to work in the garden	Write in my journal and fall asleep	Watch TV with my husband and crochet	Clean up around the house and make cookies	Eat dinner
8	Baths, homework, and crochet	Work email, status reporting, low-effort tasks	Visit with my brother who came over earlier to work in the garden	Sleep	Hang out with the kids	Hang out with the family	Kids' shower and bed
8:30	Kids to bed, make lunch, watch a little TV	Spend time with husband	Kids to bed	Sleep	Hang out with the kids	Hang out with the family	Kids' shower and bed
9	Process notes from work, develop plan for tomorrow, check emails, and shower	Wrap up work	Spent time with my husband	Sleep	Watch TV with my husband and crochet	Drive my brother home with youngest son	Get clothes and bag ready for tomorrow

	MONDAY	TUESDAY	WEDNESDAY	THURSDAY	FRIDAY	SATURDAY	SUNDAY
9:30	Process notes from work, develop plan for tomorrow, check emails, and shower	Shower and prepare outfit and bag for tomorrow	Called my mom to see how surgery went	Eat Dinner	Watch TV with my husband and crochet	Drive my brother home with youngest son	Shower
10	Spend time with my husband	Journaling	Called my mom to see how surgery went	Talk with my husband	Shower	Kids to bed	Sleep
10:30	Spend time with my husband	Sleep	Showered and went to bed	Talk with my husband	Sleep	Clean up/talk with husband	Sleep
11	Sleep	Sleep	Sleep	Quilt and watch TV	Sleep	Sleep	Sleep
11:30	Sleep	Sleep	Sleep	Quilt and watch TV	Sleep	Sleep	Sleep
12AM	Sleep	Sleep	Sleep	Sleep	Sleep	Sleep	Sleep
12:30	Sleep	Sleep	Sleep	Sleep	Sleep	Sleep	Sleep
1	Sleep	Sleep	Sleep	Sleep	Sleep	Sleep	Sleep
1:30	Sleep	Sleep	Sleep	Sleep	Sleep	Sleep	Sleep
2	Sleep	Sleep	Sleep	Sleep	Sleep	Sleep	Sleep
2:30	Sleep	Sleep	Sleep	Sleep	Sleep	Sleep	Sleep
3	Sleep	Sleep	Sleep	Sleep	Sleep	Sleep	Sleep
3:30	Sleep	Sleep	Sleep	Sleep	Sleep	Sleep	Sleep
4	Sleep	Sleep	Sleep	Sleep	Sleep	Sleep	Sleep
4:30	Sleep	Sleep	Sleep	Sleep	Sleep	Sleep	Sleep

see your kids for a reasonable amount of time during the week because 8:30 a.m. isn't all that early. Young children often wake at the crack of dawn. Indeed, some of the toughest moments of parenthood involve a little voice calling, "Is it breakfast time?" at six o'clock on a Saturday morning. (Smart couples learn to trade off weekend mornings, so each parent gets to sleep in once. Single parents have it tougher, but that's true of many things.)

You can lament this or, on weekday mornings at least, you can look at this as time you can have together with your children. You can spend time with them *first*, before the rest of life gets in the way. True, everyone's trying to get ready for the day ahead, but there is always stuff to be done, and as with evenings, must-dos need not occupy every minute. On summer days when it's light out early, you can load little ones in the stroller and go for a walk. On dark winter mornings, you can read, do a craft, or make elaborate breakfasts (more on that on p. 144). Most of the low-key activities that work for evenings work for mornings too. Eventually you'll need to focus on the end point of getting out the door, but it's a mistake to be so focused on the end point that you miss all the time passing. You can set an alarm for the moment when you need to get ready, and relax until then. Kids may also be willing to sit and chat while you're doing your hair or makeup. One of my favorite observations in Tina Fey's *Bossypants* is how she experiences genuine bonding time with her daughter while cutting the little girl's fingernails in the morning. She may be holding a pile of fingernail clippings "like a Santeria priestess," but mindfulness turns what could be nothing time into something much more profound.

3. PLAY. For many parents, time with kids—and weekend time in particular—feels amorphous for a simple reason: it is constantly multitasked with housework. When I go into the basement with the kids, they become engrossed in projects, and I commence the eternal process of picking up toys. It feels productive, and kids don't need to interact with their parents constantly. Yet when I do play—doing puzzles, building with Legos, coloring, running through homemade obstacle courses outside—I remember that much of this stuff is intrinsically fun. At least it's more fun than putting toys away. That's why kids prefer to do these things rather than cleaning up.

Most of us could stand to increase the fun in our lives. Doing so just requires a different mind-set, and that mind-set was evident on Eileen Hiromura's log.

She works for Google in California and has two young children. She told me she was "amazed by how little cleaning I do in a week," with much of that week's 4.5 hours of housekeeping and errands involving a party (see p. 137). She wasn't confessing some dark secret; that e-mailed observation was accompanied by a smiley face. Despite her tough work schedule and long commute, "I was happy with how much family time I got in," she says. That's what happens when you use your nonworking time to really play and do projects with your kids.

Legos are a self-explanatory log entry, occupying a full two hours on Sunday. I don't think I could swing that level of focus, but then again, Hiromura's the engineer. I was more intrigued by the weekday evening entry of "color stained glass pictures with kids." Hiromura explained that "Santa brought the kids these stained glass coloring books—it's like a coloring book on wax paper. If you hang them on the window it looks like stained glass." The kids really liked them, so Hiromura bought more, covering content including Greek mythology and mythological creatures. "It's what we do at night," she says. "They're getting pretty good at coloring in the lines, but stained glass is forgiving. The black lines are thicker." The sheer volume of artistic output has been impressive, and has slowly taken over the decor of Hiromura's house. "We have French doors all around the living room, and have room for about one hundred stained glass windows. We're at around sixty right now!" In life, happy memories are more likely to stem from drawing with your kids than from spending hours on the super-responsible parts of parenting, like ensuring that the pantry always has an adequate supply of garbage bags. Yes, you need garbage bags. But you can fit that around the playing, rather than the other way around.

4. SHARE A FAMILY MEAL (NOT NECESSARILY DINNER). Family dinner has become a sacred concept in modern life. In conversations, it becomes prima facie evidence of good parenting and the sign of a functioning family. To be sure, some research has found that children who eat dinner with their families frequently do engage in fewer risky behaviors, though other analyses find that this is more correlative than anything else. People who've got their act together enough to schedule and cook dinner regularly have other things going for them that boost their children's prospects in life

	THURSDAY (1/2)	FRIDAY (1/3)	SATURDAY (1/4)	SUNDAY (1/5)	MONDAY (1/6)	TUESDAY (1/7)	WEDNESDAY (1/8)
5AM	Woke up - snuggled with my daughter	Woke up - snuggled with my daughter	Sleep	Sleep	Sleep	Sleep	Work
5:30	Snuggled with my sleeping daughter and read tech news and headlines on my iPhone	Snuggled with my sleeping daughter and read tech news and headlines on my iPhone	Sleep	Sleep	Sleep	Sleep	Sleep
6	Got dressed, then 6:15 - 7, running w/ dog	My son woke up early and wanted to snuggle. Snuggled with him and fell back to sleep	My son woke up early and wanted to snuggle. Snuggled with him and fell back to sleep	Sleep	Sleep	Sleep	Sleep
6:30	Running	Sleep	Sleep	Sleep	Sleep	Sleep	Get dressed
7	Breakfast with my son	Had breakfast with my son	Sleep	Sleep	Snuggled with my son	Had breakfast with my son	Wake up kids and get them ready for school
7:30	Played games and snuggled with my son, gave him a back massage	Cleaned up kitchen from party	Personal email	Sleep	Had breakfast with the kids	Get dressed	Leave house for pediatric dentist visit
8	Got dressed for work	Cleaned up kitchen from party	Bought new stained glass coloring books for the kids on Amazon	Sleep	Get dressed	Drive to work/ check email	Stop at Starbucks for coffee

	THURSDAY (1/2)	FRIDAY (1/3)	SATURDAY (1/4)	SUNDAY (1/5)	MONDAY (1/6)	TUESDAY (1/7)	WEDNESDAY (1/8)
8:30	Daughter woke up - changed her bedsheets (oops), helped her get dressed. 8:45: supervised both kids clean up the playroom mess and the art room mess from yesterday's cousin playdate	Sat in bed with my husband and shopped for new wheels/rims for our Acura	Eat breakfast with family	Had breakfast/ helped my son with his new Lego set	Drive to work	Work: meeting	Pediatric dentist visit (both kids' teeth cleaning)
9	Drove to work/bought 2 towel racks on Amazon	Got dressed	Shopped for valentine crafts, planned next month's party	Lego building	Work: interviews	Work: meeting	Pediatric dentist visit (both kids' teeth cleaning)
9:30	Work: coffee, email	Drove to work/ made kids' dentist appointment	Helped kids get ready, checked that they did their chores	Read the news	Work: interviews	Work: meeting	Pediatric dentist visit (both kids' teeth cleaning)
10	Work: leadership survey response for team member	Work: coffee, email	Got dressed	Read the news	Work: interviews	Work: meeting	Drive to work 10:15 - work
10:30	Work: meeting	Work: email	Cleaned up house	Tennis lesson	Work: interviews	Work: meeting	Work
11	Work: meeting	Work: meeting	Left house with 2 kids (driving)	Tennis lesson	Work: interviews	Work: meeting	Work
11:30	Work: dig out from under holiday email avalanche	Work: meeting	Returned 2 gifts at Toys R Us and bought a birthday present	Get dressed	Work: interviews	Work: meeting	Work
12PM	Lunch	Work: prioritize/ kill new feature requests for my product	Toys R Us shopping with kids	Lunch with family	Lunch	Work: meeting	Work

	THURSDAY (1/2)	FRIDAY (1/3)	SATURDAY (1/4)	SUNDAY (1/5)	MONDAY (1/6)	TUESDAY (1/7)	WEDNESDAY (1/8)
12:30	Prioritize/kill new feature requests for my product	Eat lunch at office with kids and husband	Lunch with my 2 kids at a Chinese restaurant	Lunch with family	Walk to Starbucks with team members	Work: meeting	Work
1	Work: make time: designed new feature	Give kids an office tour	Took kids to 4th birthday party of a friend at Color Me Mine	Clean up kitchen	Work: interviews	Lunch	Work
1:30	Work: meeting	Work: meeting: personal research	Party	Start reading for book club *Do Androids Dream of Electric Sheep?*	Work: interviews	Work: meeting	Work
2	Work: make time: designed new feature	Work: meeting: support feature requests	Party	Reading	Work: interviews	Work: meeting	Work
2:30	Work: make time: designed new feature	Work: schedule new meetings for new year	Party	Take a nap	Work: interviews	Work: meeting	Work
3	Teatime with colleague	Work: prioritize/ kill new feature requests for my product	Picked up husband at home to drive to LA for 2 more parties	Take a nap	Snack	Work	Work
3:30	Work	Work: prioritize/ kill new feature requests for my product	Work: email on the way to LA	Take a nap	Work: interviews	Work: meeting	Work
4	Work	Work: email	Took kids to 3rd birthday party of cousin at My Gym	Help son with homework	Work: interviews	Work: meeting	Work

	THURSDAY (1/2)	FRIDAY (1/3)	SATURDAY (1/4)	SUNDAY (1/5)	MONDAY (1/6)	TUESDAY (1/7)	WEDNESDAY (1/8)
4:30	Work: prioritize/kill new feature requests for my product	Work: email	Party	Help son with homework	Work: interviews	Work: meeting	Work
5	5:15: leave work early to drive home	Work: email	Party	Build Legos	Work: interviews	Work: meeting	Work
5:30	Shop at Ross to pick up a present for the gift exchange	Drive home/plan Valentine's party for the kids and their friends	Party	Build Legos	Meeting	Work	Work
6	Clean the house	Order sushi/play with the kids	Drove to 20th wedding anniversary party at my sister-in-law's house	Look for/order a movie for the kids, get them set up for the night	Leave work, drop off colleague at airport	Work	Work
6:30	Host a book club/supper club New Year's Eve party for 12 women at my house	Turn on movie for movie night (*Super Buddies*) and pick up sushi	Party	Go on a date with my husband	Get home, catch up with kids on school day	Drive home	Drive home/catch up with friend
7	Party . . .	Dinner	Party	Stop for a drink at a bar	Dinner	Eat dinner with kids	Dinner with family
7:30	Party . . .	Watch the end of *Super Buddies* movie with the family and snuggle on couch	Party	Watch movie: *Catching Fire*	Color stained glass pictures with kids	Watch funny YouTube videos with kids	Color stained glass pictures with kids
8	Party . . .	Get kids ready for bed	Party	Watch movie: *Catching Fire*	Color stained glass pictures with kids	Snuggle with my son	Get kids in bed

	THURSDAY (1/2)	FRIDAY (1/3)	SATURDAY (1/4)	SUNDAY (1/5)	MONDAY (1/6)	TUESDAY (1/7)	WEDNESDAY (1/8)
8:30	Party . . .	Put away laundry	Party	Watch movie: Catching Fire	Get kids in bed	Snuggle with my daughter	Email (work)
9	Party . . .	Organized closet	Party	Watch movie: Catching Fire	Sleep	Sleep	Sleep
9:30	Party . . .	Played video games/Facebook	Drove back home	Watch movie: Catching Fire	Sleep	Sleep	Sleep
10	Party . . .	Created playdate event for Sat 2/8 and invited guests Looked on Pinterest for craft ideas	Drove back home	Play video games/Facebook	Sleep	Sleep	Sleep
10:30	Party . . .	Sleep	Put sleeping kids in bed/got dressed	Sleep	Sleep	Sleep	Sleep
11	Party . . .	Sleep	Played video games/Facebook	Sleep	Sleep	Sleep	Sleep
11:30	Sleep	Sleep	Sleep	Sleep	Sleep	Sleep	Sleep
12AM	Sleep	Sleep	Sleep	Sleep	Sleep	Sleep	Sleep
12:30	Sleep	Sleep	Sleep	Sleep	Sleep	Sleep	Sleep
1	Sleep	Sleep	Sleep	Sleep	Work: check work email	Sleep	Take care of sick kids
1:30	Sleep	Sleep	Sleep	Sleep	Read news	Sleep	Take care of sick kids
2	Sleep	Sleep	Sleep	Sleep	Sleep	Sleep	Sleep

	THURSDAY (1/2)	FRIDAY (1/3)	SATURDAY (1/4)	SUNDAY (1/5)	MONDAY (1/6)	TUESDAY (1/7)	WEDNESDAY (1/8)
2:30	Sleep	Sleep	Sleep	Sleep	Sleep	Sleep	Sleep
3	Sleep	Sleep	Sleep	Sleep	Sleep	Wake up, book flights and arrange business trip for Friday	Sleep
3:30	Sleep	Sleep	Sleep	Sleep	Sleep	Email (work)	Take care of sick kids
4	Sleep	Sleep	Sleep	Sleep	Sleep	Work	Sleep
4:30	Sleep	Sleep	Sleep	Sleep	Sleep	Work	Sleep

as well; it's not dinner itself that's working the magic. One attempt to find a causal relationship looked at what happened when families changed the frequency with which they ate dinner together from year to year. The answer was not much; rates of delinquency and drug and alcohol abuse didn't change.

Here's another reason to keep family dinners in perspective: as with most socially desirable activities, people exaggerate its frequency. One survey found that more than 50 percent of U.S. families claimed to almost always have dinner together. But an anthropological study of dual-income Los Angeles families, done by a team from UCLA and involving hours of video footage, found that only 17 percent of families had dinner together every night. About 60 percent did semiregularly, but these dinners tended to be fragmented in a way that would make it hard to pose for a Norman Rockwell painting. "Family members eat sequentially or in different rooms," the researchers reported. "Children often start the cascade of staggered eating by pleading to eat different foods when they do not like the main dish. Contestations over what to eat often result in different main dishes for children that may not be ready at the same time as what parents eat. Busy schedules also intrude. Meals are eaten when and where children and the non-cooking parent find it convenient, sometimes near TVs in the living room or bedroom." I am pretty sure that when people exalt family dinner, they are not talking about a situation in which one parent is sitting at the table eating, the other is heating up something else in the microwave, and the kids have drifted over to the living room with their chicken nuggets to watch *Power Rangers*.

Given that working parents often compare themselves to a mythical ideal, I was surprised how many women in the Mosaic Project engaged in contortions to come together for family dinners more frequently than the average American household. One, an accountant who worked 63.5 hours during the week she logged, was home for dinner six out of seven nights (she worked a lengthy split shift to make that possible).

If sitting down together for dinner every night is a strongly held value for you and your family, even during busy season, then by all means, make it happen. Having time to focus on each other can build relationships over time. I would push back, though, on the sanctity of *dinner* as the important family meal. If you do breakfast with the kids six out of seven days, I think that deserves just as much recognition as sitting down for dinner together. For many families, precisely because little children wake up early, breakfast is an easier option than dinner. Work schedules and activities can complicate evenings. Breakfast food can be low-key and is often kid-friendly; strawberries and waffles inspire less arguing than chicken and broccoli. That's not to say you shouldn't push the broccoli in the evenings, but it's nice to have at least one meal in which the focus can be on conversation, rather than on which foods each meal participant likes and doesn't like. Where many families use dinnertime to talk through what happened that day, at breakfast, you can talk through what's ahead of you. You can strategize before the day happens.

If you work from home and have young kids, family lunch can be an option too. A few Mosaic families had weekend dim sum brunches. The main point is simply to have family meals frequently. If you can do Friday dinner and Saturday and Sunday lunch and Sunday dinner together, that's four meals right there. Throw in two sit-down breakfasts during the week and you're making family dining a regular feature of your life. It may not be a daily six p.m. sit-down to a traditional roast, but it doesn't have to be. Since it turns out many people are lying about their achievement of that ideal anyway, do what works for you.

5. LET THE KIDS KNOW WHAT YOU DO ALL DAY. Beyond the playtime, another highlight from Hiromura's log was the time her kids spent with her at her office. On Friday, her kids came to visit her for an hour. They ate Google's famous food and toured the campus.

Because parents go to the office all the time, we sometimes forget that just seeing the desks and riding in elevators can be an adventure for kids. If your work is more adventurous than most people's, that would be fun to share with kids, too. Helen Fox, whom we met in the previous chapter, was the director of marine science at the World Wildlife Fund when she kept her log. She brought her seven- and eleven-year-old daughters to Indonesia for the summer of 2014 while she was working on projects there. This extended version of Take Our Daughters to Work Day is about "making it possible to do the work and not be away from the kids as long," she says. She did this years ago when they were nursing babies, and they're enjoying it now that they're older and can learn about Indonesian culture. She has built friendships over the years in this part of the world, so she knows people who can watch the girls. Her husband banks overtime while they're gone so they can have more family time later on.

Just as parents enjoy seeing their kids' lives when we get to visit their schools, kids like to see what their parents do. Given that we spend a lot of time working, it's a way our children get to know us as people. You can share your passions and provide context to the usual discussions of "How was your day?" You can talk about your successes and challenges. You don't want to burden children with matters that aren't fair to let them worry about (such as impending layoffs), but you can show that challenges are not things to be feared. They are surmountable with the right combination of hard work and strategy. This is an important lesson to teach, whether you're in Indonesia or in a regular old cube.

6. CHAPERONE KID EXCURSIONS. Many Mosaic logs showed school-related volunteering. Kathryn Truax, who works at Wells Fargo Advisors, told me that her log (printed later in this chapter) clocked in on the low side for work because that Friday was her turn to be the parent helper for her son's school.

That said, regular during-the-day volunteering is often tough for working parents. Fortunately, there are ways to be strategic about this. Volunteering for specific events lets you be part of a memorable experience in your kid's life, while recognizing the limits to what you can take on. My favorite option is to chaperone school field trips. Yes, you may need to take a day off from work, though not necessarily. Lots of people have flexibility at work. You may be able to make up the time at other points during the day or week.

Kimberli Jeter, the chief learning and partnerships officer at PYXERA Global, chaperoned her fourth grader's field trip to the Colorado state capitol in Denver during one of the weeks she logged. "That's something I've been trying to do more of this year," she says. At one point, she thought she shouldn't take advantage of her work flexibility, but "all these things were self-imposed expectations." Better to figure out what's important and "get it done, and everything else works around it. I did a phone call while on the bus, and a few little things at night and the next day. But the kids are growing quickly. I know that pretty soon they're not going to want me to come chaperone." A trip is not only fun in its own right, you spend time with your kid and your kid's friends while they're doing something more exciting than sitting in history class. Plus, it only takes a few hours.

You can also invest more time in your kids' activities. Meg Stout, who lives near Washington, D.C., and works with the navy, used to take a week off from work to volunteer at the camp her now mostly grown daughters attended, driving campers around and the like. While not all camps are amenable to this, Stout traveled a lot with her job while her husband did primary parenting duty. Taking that week off to help at camp meant "we shared that experience," she says. Church day camps in particular often need additional help, as do church youth groups. Chaperoning the youth group mission trip to Belize is a great use of a vacation week: sharing your values, spending time with your teenage child and her friends, and seeing a part of the world you won't go to on a package tour. That's a lot of upside for 168 hours.

7. GO ONE-ON-ONE WHEN YOU CAN. Some of my happiest parenting moments happen when my children play peaceably together. They have their own bonds that don't involve me. They have their own secrets and games I will never understand. As the brood grows, life becomes a constant playdate: bicycle riding while waiting for the bus in the morning, Pokémon cards before bedtime. I fantasize about their vacationing together decades hence, sharing the closeness being bred in shared hours now.

Then I wake up because someone has smacked someone else in the head with a Melissa & Doug wooden toy frying pan. The smacked child, seeking solace, climbs on my lap only to have yet another child scream and try to yank him off. Sibling rivalry, alas, accounts for the most agonizing moments of parenting. Seeing two people you love quarreling is traumatic with adults. It is equally traumatic when it happens with children, even though it happens *all the time.*

There is no good way around this. We train children, over the long run, in rules of civility, but developing the self-discipline to stay calm when someone else gets something you want is a long process. Mommy's attention is a desired commodity. It is not infinite. However, I do know that when each child gets my whole attention regularly, it increases the odds that he or she will be well behaved. I also know this gets difficult in larger families, but since two is the modal number for children in American households (and in the Mosaic Project; the mean was 1.8), it's doable for many people.

Some parents did "dates" with their kids. One woman took her daughter to a chocolate class at a local candy store. Another joined a mother-daughter book club, saying it "has given me some pretty cool insight into my daughter." The four pairs of moms and preteens got together every six weeks or so to discuss a book they'd all read, like *Wonder*, *Ungifted*, and *Rump*, and they did activities related to the books. "The girls have fun together and because of the different books we have read we really get to discuss some interesting subjects, like bullying, independence, sibling relationships, etc."

Errands can be an opportunity for one-on-one time if the other kid is occupied, and they're less painful when you're not chasing two children (or three, or four) through Target. On one log, a woman took one daughter shopping while the other was at a slumber party. They had a leisurely day together, chatting as they worked through the shopping list. In general, people spend more time than necessary on errands, but if they're done with interaction as the primary goal, they can be good options.

All of this is easier if you have a partner to occupy the other children, but it's possible even if you don't. Kathryn Truax is widowed, and on her log, you can see times when she's focused on one kid (daughter "I" or son "D") (p. 148). On Monday, she picked up her son at school, chatted with his playmates, and spent one-on-one time with him. She picked up her daughter a little later. Her daughter goes to bed later than her son, so Truax spends this time helping her with homework, and doing their bedtime routine together with no little brother involved. Recognizing that even the mundane tasks of daily life can be special one-on-one time elevates this time, and makes the kids think it is special, too.

8. BE ACTIVE TOGETHER. Exercise is a well-known mood booster, which means that moving together makes for happiness together. That's why generations of dads have played catch with their sons, and why moms should try it with their sons and daughters too. You can kick a soccer ball around and shoot hoops. I saw lots of family bike rides on logs, though loading three

	MONDAY	TUESDAY	WEDNESDAY	THURSDAY	FRIDAY	SATURDAY	SUNDAY
5AM							
5:30				Wake/shower			Wake/shower
6	Wake/shower	Wake/shower	Wake/shower	Prep kids for the day	Wake/shower		Wake kids/breakfast
6:30	Prep kids for the day	Prep kids for the day	Prep kids for the day	Leave for meeting	Prep kids for the day	Wake/shower	Wake kids/breakfast
7	Wake kids/breakfast	Wake kids/breakfast	Wake kids/breakfast	Meeting	Wake kids/breakfast	Clean living room	Leave for skiing
7:30	Wake kids/breakfast	Go to home office for call	Go to home office for call	Meeting	Email clients	Clean living room	Skiing
8	Wake kids/breakfast	Client call at home	Email clients	Meeting	Email clients	Read newspaper	Skiing
8:30	Walk I to school	Client call at home	Email clients	Coffee w/ prospect	Monitor client accts	Declutter house	Skiing
9	Play with D	Client call at home	Call clients	Coffee w/ prospect	Monitor client accts	Breakfast	Skiing
9:30	Take D to school	Dress for work and leave	Call clients	D school event	Parent helper at D's school	Homework w/ I	Skiing
10	Check work email	Arrive at office/email	Call clients	D school event	Parent helper at D's school	Homework w/ I	Skiing
10:30	Check work email	Monitor client accts	Call clients	Drive to work	Parent helper at D's school	Play w/ kids	Skiing
11	Work on client portfolios	Monitor client accts	Call clients	Email clients	Parent helper at D's school	Play w/ kids	Skiing
11:30	Work on client portfolios	Lunch	Lunch	Lunch	Parent helper at D's school	Play w/ kids	Skiing
12PM	Client calls in	Lunch	Lunch	Email clients	Parent helper at D's school	Play w/ kids	Skiing
12:30	Lunch/personal organize	Organize Client Mailing	Lunch	Monitor client accts	Parent helper at D's school	Lunch	Skiing

	MONDAY	TUESDAY	WEDNESDAY	THURSDAY	FRIDAY	SATURDAY	SUNDAY
1	Client calls in	Organize client mailing	Monitor client accts	Monitor client accts	Take D home sick	Lunch	Skiing
1:30	Pick up D/play at school	Email clients	Monitor client accts	Call clients	Sit w/ D	Declutter house	Skiing
2	Chat w/ D's playmates	Email clients	Email clients	Call clients	Sit w/ D	Declutter house	Skiing
2:30	Organize office	Call clients	Email clients	Call clients	Sit w/ D	Pack for mountains	Skiing
3	Pick up I from school	Call clients	Call clients	Call clients	Pick up I from school	Pack for mountains	Skiing
3:30	I and D playtime	Call clients	Call clients	Monitor client accts	Kids' playtime/ declutter kitchen	Read book	Drive back to condo
4	Take I to RE	Leave for home	Call clients	Plan for the next week	Kids' playtime/ declutter kitchen	Read book	Grocery store
4:30	Play with D	Home/change/ pack	Call clients	Leave for home	Sit w/ D	Declutter house	Snack/TV
5	Play with D	Leave for dance class	Leave for home	Homework w/ I	Sit w/ D	Leave for dinner	Snack/TV
5:30	Make dinner	Head home from dance class	Send I to skating fun	Make dinner	Make dinner	Dinner	Make dinner
6	Dinner	Dinner	Make dinner/eat dinner	Dinner	Dinner	Leave for mountains	Dinner
6:30	Homework w/ I	Play with D	Play with D	Homework w/ I	Organize office	Leave for mountains	TV
7	Homework w/ I	Play with D	Play with D	Homework w/ I	Organize office	Leave for mountains	TV
7:30	D bedtime	D bedtime	D bedtime	D bedtime	Play w/ kids	Unpack at mountains	TV
8	Homework w/ I	Homework w/ I	Call clients	Homework w/ I	D bedtime	Kids' bedtime	D Bedtime
8:30	Homework w/ I	Homework w/ I	Homework w/ I	Homework w/ I	Play w/ kids	Read book	I Bedtime

	MONDAY	TUESDAY	WEDNESDAY	THURSDAY	FRIDAY	SATURDAY	SUNDAY
9	I Bedtime	I Bedtime	I Bedtime	I Bedtime	I Bedtime	Pay bills	TV
9:30	Declutter dishes/ house	Declutter dishes/ house	Declutter dishes/ house	Declutter dishes/ house	Watch a movie	Pay bills	TV
10	Go to sleep/read	Go to sleep/read	Go to sleep/read	Go to sleep/read	Watch a movie	Go to sleep/read	Go to sleep/read
10:30	Fall asleep	Fall asleep	Fall asleep	Fall asleep	Watch a movie	Fall asleep	Fall asleep
11					Watch a movie		
11:30					Fall asleep		
12 AM							
12:30							
1					Wake w/ sick D		
1:30					Wake w/ sick D		
2					Wake w/ sick D		
2:30					Wake w/ sick D		
3							
3:30							
4							
4:30							

bikes, a tag-along, and a kid carrier on the car is quite an undertaking. Some more interesting family activities I saw included paddleboarding and numerous weekend ski trips in more snowy climes. Truax and her kids headed into the mountains for the weekend and spent 7.5 hours skiing, which was a great way to bond and be outside together.

Another approach is to double down on the time you already spend shuttling kids to practices and cheering on the sidelines by volunteering to coach a team (or at least volunteering to be an assistant coach if you can't guarantee attendance). Coaching can be enjoyable for the same reason that chaperoning kid excursions has a lot going for it. If you pick a sport you like, you may boost your skills too, and sharing victories and defeats has much in common with sharing your approaches to work challenges. You're teaching resilience, which is the ability to bounce back from losses and keep going forward. It's a skill most of us would like to encourage in our children and, frankly, learn ourselves.

9. PLAN ADVENTURES. Time passes whether we choose what to do with it or not. With kid time, it's always easier not to do things, and sometimes that's fine. Some kids are bigger homebodies than others, and even with outgoing sorts, there are times when everyone just wants to snuggle on the couch watching TV, or play games on the iPad. Screen time is not evil. The kids will be fine.

However, creating memories is often about creating the opportunities for memories, and sitting on the couch in front of the TV creates fewer opportunities than using the same time for "beach and marshmallow roast," as one woman wrote on her log, a four-word phrase that by itself conjures up summer memories for me.

In general, to have meaningful experiences in our lives, we need to think about what we'd like those experiences to be. When I do workshops, I encourage people to make something called a "List of 100 Dreams," which is an exercise shared with me by career coach Caroline Ceniza-Levine years ago. It's an unedited bucket list of anything you'd like to do or have more of in your life. The more specific the items, the better. Over the years, my list has grown to include visiting the Netherlands during tulip time, writing a novel, and owning a bicycle, among many other things. But this sort of list need not be a list of solo dreams. It can be a list of family dreams, anything you and the people you are closest to would like to experience.

Melanie Nelson, who worked as a project manager at a San Diego biotech before launching her own company in 2014, began creating a similar annual Family Fun List in early 2013 when she realized that "I should be enjoying life more."

Nelson, her husband, and their two young girls each contributed three items to the twelve-item list. The goal was to schedule roughly one adventure per month. In 2013, they decided to:

ride a surrey bike
go to the aquarium
go to the "dinosaur museum" (aka the San Diego Natural History Museum)
hike to the top of a hill or mountain
visit "Mimi and Boppa" in Arizona
go to New Zealand to see Nelson's husband's family
take a family trip to Orange County
pick a day and watch TV all day long
go to the San Diego Zoo Safari Park
go to Legoland
go camping
explore a new neighborhood in San Diego

By year's end, they were nine for twelve on their list, with a few substitutions and recalculations (SeaWorld for Legoland; they didn't watch TV all day because Nelson confesses that she didn't go out of her way to remind the daughter who'd requested it about this bit of sloth). They explored new parts of San Diego, and even made it to New Zealand, which definitely qualified as an adventure. Inspired by that success, they made another list for 2014. Sweetly enough, because two of Nelson's husband's items didn't get done (hiking to the top of a mountain and camping), Nelson's eldest daughter chose those for *her* contribution to the 2014 list.

Having an official list allows you to anticipate your fun beforehand, and recognize that something special is happening. Thanks to keeping a family fun list, "we remember to do the things that will build the memories we want," says Nelson.

If you make a list of adventures like this, you'll never lack for weekend ideas. Or you can piggyback on others' ideas. "People who participate in religious communities have an easier time because there's already, typically, activities," says Meg Stout. Family-friendly houses of worship plan full calendars of family volunteering options, spaghetti suppers, Advent calendar–making workshops, and the like. Some even have nursery care for little ones so parents can participate in activities with older kids. It can get to the point that "we're not going to do everything that somebody has put on a plate for us to do," says Stout, but one adventure per weekend can make for a compelling mosaic.

10. GIVE YOURSELF CREDIT. To have family adventures, you need to get up and do them. If you work long hours, you may get to what could be family time and think, "I'm tired." And you are. But to me, another secret of happier parenting is to realize that with small children, *I will always be tired.* So what? I can be tired lying on the couch while the children whine, or I can be tired driving them to a nearby creek where they can distract themselves from the whining by tossing pebbles in the water. At least in the latter case I'm outside in the fresh air. I also draw energy from meaningful things. So I need some way to nudge myself to do meaningful things, trusting that eventually the intrinsically energizing aspects of these activities will kick in.

I've read much literature about the power of nudges, but I became more personally aware of their impact when, for his seventh birthday, Jasper asked for a Fitbit step counter. I got him the Fitbit Zip (the cheapest version) and after I saw how he enjoyed racing around the house to load up on steps, I bought one for myself. It took all of twenty-four hours for the obsessive side of my personality to kick in. I do not want to go a day without hitting ten thousand steps, and ideally hitting fifteen thousand steps or more. I would haul my pregnant self out to run, to go up and down the stairs, to pace around my bedroom at night if I was three hundred steps under the daily target. Obviously there are many intrinsically good reasons to be active, but sometimes it's hard to get motivated. The Fitbit helped with that because I was getting credit for doing the right thing. I'd come home from a run and quickly sync the Fitbit just to make sure I got credit for my forty-five "very active minutes."

With parenting, we often have things we'd like to do, and we know that doing them would make us happy or energized, but it's similarly difficult to get moving. Maybe you'd like to read more with your kids. You like to read and your kids like stories, but it's always easier to putter than sit down and pick up a book. That's human nature, so the smart approach is to figure out how to give yourself credit for what you'd like to do but aren't doing. In the simplest version, you put "read with kids for twenty minutes" on your daily to-do list and cross it off when you're done. In a more elaborate version, you could create a whole merit badge system for parenting. Maybe the reading badge requires reading to the kids for twenty minutes, five times a week, for three months. You visit the library every other week. You research and find a new chapter book series you'd all enjoy. You listen to an audiobook on a family car trip. You go to a bookstore event featuring a favorite children's book author. You write a story together. When you do all that, you can sew yourself a patch if you like, or even just draw a book and a smiley face on a scrap of paper and post it on your bathroom mirror. You'll have made all this reading a habit long before the ninety days are up, but checking off the criteria will motivate you along the way. You're giving yourself credit. Parenting is a tough job. Anything that nudges you toward feeling better about it is probably a good thing.

Be There, Part 2

How to Nurture Your Romantic Life

When I asked Mosaic Project participants what they wanted to do more of with their time, spending adults-only time with their husbands or partners (or attempting to find partners on Match.com) came up a lot. In some cases, people expressed this desire with resignation. One woman told me that she was "actually pleasantly surprised" at how much time she spent with her twenty-two-month-old. As for the father of that twenty-two-month-old, "I should spend more time with my husband but I already knew that."

To be sure, spouse time did happen, and while some instances turned out to be tamer than they first seemed ("sat in bed with my husband and shopped for new wheel/rims"), after studying a few logs, I realized I was seeing a variety of euphemisms for sex.

Time use researchers know that most people don't mention sex in their time logs. Partly that's a privacy consideration, and partly it's because it's not nearly as substantial a proportion of people's time as we might wish it were. So I was interested to see that at least a handful of women did write down when they had sex, and labeled it as such. More often, it showed up as "relations," "private time," "husband time," or "with husband, then shower," or "went to bed with husband" two nights per week when the other nights just said "went to bed."

On the logs, I saw that with intimacy, the key is making it a priority and being creative with timing. The traditional before-bedtime approach is great if it works, but "relations" showed up during early-morning hours on time logs, too. You can put the kids in front of cartoons on weekend mornings and sneak back upstairs, or "nap" together while the kids nap in the afternoon. If you both work from home on Fridays, you can build in a simultaneous break.

As for romantic excursions that might lead to "husband time," I did see date nights—movies, bowling, dinner out—which is heartening, though I suspect some of the frequency may be a function of people keeping track of their time. The act of observing changes the thing being observed, and because you are sharing your time, you think about how you are spending it. If you know that date night is something you want to make happen, you might get your act together during a recorded week and do it. As far as when these date nights happened, some people chose to have a babysitter come after their children went to bed. It may be a struggle to stay awake for a nine p.m. dinner reservation, but that way you don't miss any time with the kids. It's also relatively easy to get a sitter if she's just getting paid to watch TV. On the other hand, if you are doing the bedtime routine every night, part of the fun of date night might be getting out of it for an evening.

For many people, date night didn't require a sitter. Some couples chose to cook a late dinner together after the kids went down or watch a movie together. Those normally working a "split shift" might choose one weeknight not to work or watch TV, but to sit out on the porch together enjoying a glass of wine. I once saw a "baby swap" on a log: two couples with similarly aged babies traded off Friday evenings. The kids were good sleepers, down by eight p.m., who wouldn't freak out about being transferred into their own beds late at night. The setup meant that, each week, one couple got an opportunity to go out with no sitter fare, and the other could do an in-home date night after lights out. A big upside of having family nearby is the ability to drop the kids off at Grandma's for free overnight babysitting, and then go out as a couple and possibly even *sleep in the next morning*.

Date night also doesn't have to be at night. Several women who worked near their husbands got together with them for lunch once a week. Date breakfast might work as well. Drop the kids off at day care, then hit a diner together. Or get up before they do. One woman with teen and preteen kids got up at 3:30 every weekday morning to have coffee with her husband before he left for work around 5:00. While most people wouldn't want to do that, she liked having the time with him, and she liked getting a workout in by the time she started work at 7:00 or 7:30. Since she went to bed around 8:30 most nights, the early rising time didn't require sleep deprivation. This somewhat strange schedule guaranteed her a daily date, which is more than most people can say.

It's definitely more than I can say. When you have young children, the tendency is either to trade off, so each parent gets work or leisure time, or to all be together. Nurturing a partnership isn't the default. You have to consciously choose to do it, to schedule romantic time together and even just administrative time together—which is not a bad idea to schedule separately, if you can. Otherwise you'll spend all of date night talking about who needs to pick up the kids on Thursday.

Melanie Nelson and her husband have beers together every Friday night after the kids go to bed. They use this time to plan the weekend and to discuss anything that might be on their minds. The beers keep things light and friendly, so they can hash out the married couple grievances that tend to fester, like Nelson's habit of never washing the components of her husband's espresso maker when it's her night to do dishes. ("They didn't even register with me! They're not over by the dishes they're over by the espresso machine," she says. "That just came up in our Friday night beers.") One woman's time log showed a Saturday morning date with her husband while both their girls had piano lessons. The two of them snuck out for coffee and conversation while the kids were at the studio taking lessons simultaneously from different teachers. It was a brilliant feat of planning that made life much nicer than the usual setup: one parent shuttling both girls to back-to-back lessons with the same teacher during the week.

Be There, Part 3

Go All In

With both partners and children, being there comes down to two skills.

First, we need to seize the opportunities that always exist, even in the craziest lives. No one is so busy that she can't devote a few minutes to morning snuggles when a small child creeps into her bed. No one is so busy that she can't give her partner a real hug and kiss before she takes off for work (even at the risk of this leading to "husband time" later on, or right then, if it's that sort of morning).

When Eileen Haley, who works for a financial firm, first kept a time log for me, she had a tight morning schedule. She got her boys ready by 7:00 a.m., but then, rather than rushing them out the door, she made a conscious decision to play with them for a few minutes. They'd tickle, hug, make faces. Then they'd load the car at precisely 7:10 a.m. Ten minutes may not sound like much, but it's not nothing. According to the American Time Use Survey, the average mother of kids under age six spends a mere thirty-six minutes per day playing with them. Ten minutes in the morning gets you almost a third of the way there, and sends the kids off with a little levity rather than stress.

You can also try to think of other ways to work bits of joy into your days. A family trip to a playground can be extended with a visit to the ice cream truck. A boring car ride can be made more entertaining with a drive through the car wash. One woman, doing errands with her young son, elected to sit in the parking lot for a while as he sat on her lap and "drove." She could have quickly ended the fun, strapped him into his car seat, and pursued the rest of her day. Instead, she decided to wait and let him play and giggle for a few minutes.

Second, we need to savor moments as they come. A lot of time and life management is mental. The human brain easily wanders and it wanders more to worries than to happy musings on what a blessed life you have. Such ruminations steal happiness. If a small child wants to snuggle with you, it is madness to ponder the laundry that needs to be done and all the work necessary to get everyone out the door. You can think of that later. Nothing need exist but those little pajama-clad arms wrapped around your neck.

Cultivating such focus is a skill, and like all skills, it can be learned and practiced. You can leave the phone in a different room for a while to lessen its pull. You can get in the habit of listing good things that happened during the day—amazing moments, sweet moments, poignant moments—in a journal at night. Over time, as you record such things, you start to look for them, so you'll have something to write down. You pause to pay attention to a child's cute exhortations ("Mommy, I'm eating my lunch now with no whining!") because you want to remember them for the nightly list.

This conscious decision to hunt for the positive can help combat the common tendency to focus on dark moments, the sort that lead us to stormy conclusions about whether life with a big career and a family is doable. Sometimes things looks bleak, but life is not all black-and-white.

I was reminded of this during a summer weekend when my family elected to drive to the New Jersey shore for the day. There's a little restaurant near Cape May we like to visit. We can eat lobster outside by the boats and then head to the Wildwood beaches and boardwalk after.

If I wanted a drumbeat of evidence that this trip was a disaster, I could create quite a crescendo. We got stuck in a traffic jam that turned a one-hour-and-forty-five-minute trip into a four-hour ordeal. The weather turned rainy and almost cold on the way there. A seagull stole our dessert while we were eating. The kids got out of control on the beach and sent each other sprawling into the sand. As we were eating pizza in a boardwalk restaurant, Sam started to complain that he felt bad, and soon enough, he was vomiting into my hastily constructed container of paper plates. We tried to get everyone to the car but the kids had been promised Skee-Ball at the arcade, and weren't about to leave. So I cleaned Sam up, and we went into the arcade, which was fine until he had to throw up again. Then I was out amid the boardwalk crowds, holding my kid over the trash can. As we headed toward the car, Ruth ran away from me. I found her and we loaded them all up only to realize that her pacifier had gone missing. So despite its being eight o'clock, she wouldn't be sleeping on the trip home, and she let us know how unhappy she was, as her brother kept throwing up into the bags I'd found.

This certainly sounds like a disaster. But what if I didn't try to put a conclusion on the day? What if I looked at it moment by moment instead? In this mosaic of time, there were awful moments to be sure—but they were not all awful. The kids had slept in that fateful morning until almost eight a.m. As we sat in the traffic jam, we had some fun family conversations about what we'd like to name the new baby brother who'd be arriving that winter. My lobster, scallop, and shrimp lunch tasted fantastic. The clouds cleared as soon as we hit the beach, and we enjoyed gorgeous sunshine—cheery, but not too hot. The kids fought some, but played well enough that I could relax on my towel for five-minute stretches. Even on the car ride home, there were some blessed moments when no one was screaming or throwing up.

In life, and particularly in a life with little ones, happiness is a choice. I can choose how to remember our day at the beach. It's not that the stressful moments don't happen; it's just that they are not the only moments that happen. In the narrative format, the light moments are forgotten in the march to our conclusion. In the mosaic, they are there too.

Life is stressful and life is wonderful. There is no contradiction here. These facts exist side by side. We simply need to learn to see them as they are. Indeed, many Mosaic Project participants told me that the act of recording their time helped them appreciate the transcendent tiles already there in their lives, just waiting to be noticed. It's one reason some chose to keep tracking time after the week they sent me. Observation breeds mindfulness. Being there spreads joy into even unlikely corners.

CHAPTER 6

Make Life Easier

Lynda Bascelli has what could be a stressful life. She's the medical director at a center for the homeless, and spends her days treating people living in traumatic situations. Her husband works full-time as well, and together they care for three school-age children with activities and sick days and other needs that can make parents crazed.

Yet when I looked at her log, I didn't see constant stress (p. 162). She read poetry. Her mornings featured journaling, yoga, and time on the elliptical trainer. She played the guitar at night. While seeing patients for ten hours straight was tough ("I didn't even eat on Friday!" she told me), I didn't get the sense of battling time that I saw on some logs that featured morning household to-do lists and frantic rushing out the door. Bascelli took wintry two-hour school delays in stride. She woke up without her alarm on Thursday and Friday, possibly because she slept fifty-nine hours over the course of the week. For all she had on her plate, she managed to get enough sleep.

How was this possible? It was a combination of strategies, of thoughtfully enlisting help and maintaining a relaxed approach to life. Bascelli's husband's schedule is more flexible than her patient schedule, and he does plenty to keep the household running along. Her kids are incredibly independent. "They grab their own food," she says, and one child walks himself to the bus stop. Just as Bascelli manages her own job, the children are responsible for theirs as students: "I don't check homework. We don't have homework struggles," she says. They have a family friend, a college student, who's living with them right now, and though that can create its own occasional issues (such as the night Bascelli came home to find her kids hanging out on the roof with their fun but perhaps too-adventurous older brother figure), having an extra adult around who can drive kids to after-school activities helps. They're strategic about activities too. All of her children take music lessons at the same time, which condenses their activities into one trip. Finally, "we let a lot of stuff go." Her seven-year-old "goes to school in whatever she chooses to put on." It can be completely mismatched, but Bascelli views this as a victory: "She's just a little mess but she gets herself ready."

Talking to Bascelli, I learned that her low-key mind-set had been partially cultivated over time, in years of parenting three children—a feat that tends to mellow all but the most stubborn of perfectionists—and realizing that she could make life harder, or she could choose differently. It also stems from her work. The patients she sees have problems that make freaking out over household logistics seem stupid. "People run out of money, they run out of food stamps, they're cold," she says. Patients die from complications of drug and alcohol abuse. But, as she says, "nobody ever died of 'going-to-school-in-the-same-shirt-as-yesterday disease.'" So much of what people worry about in life is "so not important. When I first started working there, the kids got that. This person doesn't have any food to eat, so don't complain about what's on your plate." If you've got food, a bed, and a healthy family, there's really no reason to make life harder than it needs to be. The laundry can wait. Contentment shouldn't.

•

I found Bascelli's attitude refreshing as I studied the Mosaic logs, and particularly as I thought about how people managed the logistics of running their households. We make many choices in our lives, sometimes without thinking about them, and some of these play out in ways that have profound effects on day-to-day existence.

Mosaic Project participants worked different hours and slept different amounts, but time devoted to kid shuttling, household management, housework,

	MONDAY	TUESDAY	WEDNESDAY	THURSDAY	FRIDAY	SATURDAY	SUNDAY
5AM	Awake in bed, phone call from school: snow day						
5:30	Got up, coffee, bathroom, looking at recipes online				Wake up without alarm, get coffee		
6	Journaling	Phone call—2hr weather delay for school	Phone call—2 hr delay/awake, coffee	Wake without alarm, coffee, bathroom, read news	Bathroom, online surfing for recipes, news		
6:30	Showering	Woke up, coffee, bathroom	Bathroom/internet (news, vegan food blogs)	Exercise/elliptical trainer	Quick workout Physique 57	Wake up, have coffee and surf online, bathroom	Wake up, coffee, sit with husband
7	Getting dressed, hugging kids goodbye	Journaling	Yoga	Exercise/elliptical trainer	Shower, getting ready to go to work		Still relaxing, deciding on workout for the day
7:30	Driving to work, listening to audiobook	Exercise/elliptical trainer	Yoga	Hang out with kids before school, eat breakfast	In car, drive to work, listen to music	Shower and driving to get haircut	Making breakfast, doing laundry, emptying dishwasher, delegating tasks
8	Work—seeing patients	Exercise/elliptical trainer	Breakfast, hang with kids	Shower	Work—seeing patients	Haircut, buy bagels for breakfast	
8:30	Work—seeing patients	Make breakfast for kids, hang out with them	Fold laundry	Drive to work, get more coffee on the way	Work—seeing patients	Breakfast at home with everyone	Get ready for yoga class
9	Work—seeing patients	Shower	Shower, get ready for work	Catch up with admin staff/meeting re grant opportunity	Work—seeing patients	Getting daughter ready for ballet/ drive to ballet	Driving to yoga

	MONDAY	TUESDAY	WEDNESDAY	THURSDAY	FRIDAY	SATURDAY	SUNDAY
9:30	Work—seeing patients	Leave house, drop J at bus stop, drive to work	Help kids get ready for school	Meeting re grant opportunity	Work—seeing patients	While daughter is in ballet, get gas for the car, get cash from bank	Yoga class
10	Front desk huddle	Work—seeing patients	Make lunch to bring to work, hang with kids	Wrap up meeting, talk with CEO and other mgmt staff	Work—seeing patients	Back to dance class, return emails from car while waiting for her to be done	Yoga class
10:30	Work—seeing patients	Work—seeing patients	Drive kids to school/to work	Drive to next meeting	Work—seeing patients	Drive to music lesson, drop daughter off, rest of the family is there already for lessons	Yoga class/ drive home
11	Work—seeing patients	Work—seeing patients	Arrive at work, prep for a few hours of admin work	Meet with Camden Coalition re Housing First, discuss integration	Work—seeing patients	Run to the store to pick up a pink shirt for work event Monday	Arrive home, tend to a little more laundry and get ready for baby shower
11:30	Work—seeing patients	Work—seeing patients (shovel food in mouth)	Admin/patient paper work/email	Meet with Camden Coalition re Housing First, discuss integration	Work—seeing patients	Back to music school; my guitar lesson	Getting ready for shower
12PM	Work—seeing patients	Work—seeing patients	Admin/patient paper work/email	Drive back to admin office	Work—seeing patients	Guitar lesson until 12:15, then drive home	Driving to sister's house for shower
12:30	Eating lunch	Work—seeing patients	Admin/patient paper work/email	Walk across street to get lunch/eat lunch	Work—seeing patients	Rest of family out getting lunch, running errands—I eat lunch at home in the quiet	Driving to sister's house for shower

	MONDAY	TUESDAY	WEDNESDAY	THURSDAY	FRIDAY	SATURDAY	SUNDAY
1	Work—seeing patients	Work—seeing patients	Case management meeting	PCMH meeting	Work—seeing patients	Digest, family home, put away groceries, get ready for afternoon run with husband	Arrive at shower, talking with friends and family
1:30	Work—seeing patients	Work—seeing patients	Addictions treatment meeting	PCMH meeting	Work—seeing patients	Impatiently waiting for husband to get ready for run	Friends and family
2	Conference call (Healthcare for the Homeless)	Work—seeing patients	Work—seeing patients	PCMH meeting	Work—seeing patients	Running	Friends and family
2:30	Work—seeing patients	Work—seeing patients	Work—seeing patients	PCMH meeting	Work—seeing patients	Running	Friends and family
3	Work—seeing patients	Work—seeing patients (and texting sister)	Work—seeing patients	PCMH meeting	Work—seeing patients	Running	Friends and family
3:30	Driving home—out early due to snow day	Work—seeing patients	Work—seeing patients	Try to assess what tasks I can get done in time period	Work—seeing patients	Running	Getting in car to drive home
4	Acclimate to home, hello to husband, kids; snack	Work—seeing patients	Work—seeing patients	End up leaving to come home early	Work—seeing patients	Home, resting after run, kids playing with friends, deciding on evening plans for date night	Driving home
4:30	Pilates	Work—seeing patients	Work—seeing patients	Arrive home, kids are doing homework, sit down with them	Work—seeing patients	Shower	Arrive home
5	Pilates	10 minutes for dinner, then right back to patients	Work—seeing patients	Make dinner	Work—seeing patients	Laundry, dishes, clean up—prep dinner for kids	Start dinner

	MONDAY	TUESDAY	WEDNESDAY	THURSDAY	FRIDAY	SATURDAY	SUNDAY
5:30	Start dinner	Work—seeing patients	Work—seeing patients	Dinner and clean up	Work—seeing patients/ wrap up	Drive to Philadelphia	Decide to rearrange furniture in our "library"—school work, work-at-home space
6	Cooking	Work—seeing patients	Wrap up at work, drive home, audiobook	Cleaning up	Work—seeing patients/ wrap up	Arrive and park car—walk to restaurant via Penn campus	Cleaning after the furniture move
6:30	Dinner	Work—seeing patients	Walk in house, get everyone mobilized to clean up/prep for cleaning service	Drive kids to piano lesson	Driving home, listening to music	Order, sit and relax, and eat	Dinner ready, at table eating, whole family
7	Clean up	Work—seeing patients	Making stand-up dinner, everyone in the house standing in kitchen talking	Work on computer while kids are in piano lessons	Arrive home, find children outside (on the roof—with our sitter! And then have a meltdown)	Eating, sitting, talking	Clean up, beginning to prep for work week (did not feel I got enough done)
7:30	Practice guitar, everyone hanging around	Work—seeing patients	Practice guitar	Work on computer while kids are in piano lessons	Come inside, make dinner and drink a glass of wine	Walking back to car leisurely	Still cleaning, distracted by the TV
8	Scoop ice cream for kids, looking at pile of work	Done! Drive home, listen to audiobook	Practice guitar, read	Drive home	Eat dinner, waiting for husband to get home, kids playing and helping with chores like dishes	Driving home	Sit on couch with kids and watch TV (Vegucated)

	MONDAY	TUESDAY	WEDNESDAY	THURSDAY	FRIDAY	SATURDAY	SUNDAY
8:30	Getting kids ready for bed	Arrive home, home alone! Eat snack	Read, surf the internet	Getting kids ready for bed	Husband gets home, talk with kids about behavior. Read new poetry book on the couch	Run an errand for the next day—shop for baby shower gift	TV
9	Fall asleep on couch with pile of family	Practice guitar	Get kids ready for bed	Kids to bed, struggle to stay awake while husband does bedtime routine	Up to bed and fall asleep within minutes	Arrive home, getting kids ready for bed, hanging out with them	Everyone getting ready for bed, everyone in bed, reading
9:30	Up to bed	Kids to bed, cuddle with daughter	Kids to bed, cuddle with daughter, fall asleep in her bed	Bed		In bed	Lights out
10		Read food blogs, NPR, Dooce					
10:30		Turn off light					
11							
11:30							
12AM							
12:30							
1							
1:30							
2			Get up and get into my own bed				
2:30							
3							
3:30							
4							
4:30							

and errands showed more vast proportional differences. The average total for housework (cooking, cleaning, laundry) and errands (grocery shopping, Target runs, etc.) was about ten hours per week—which is roughly what Bascelli logged—but this spanned a range from two hours per week to more than twenty-five hours per week. In some families, whole weekend days disappeared into chores.

Few people truly want to spend this kind of time on maintenance, especially if they've got big careers and kids. Consequently, when people tell me they want help with time management, they often say they'd like to be more organized about household tasks and routine child care activities such as making lunches. Such organization tips are staples of women's magazines and books on how to make it all work. I recall a feature in *Real Simple* a few years ago in which writer Stephanie Booth profiled seven busy women, who explained "how they reclaimed their a.m. hours and—yes—their sanity." Exhibit A? Christine Bolzan, a career coach and mom of three young girls who was usually getting her kids ready for the week solo. Her strategy: "Every Sunday, after checking an online weekly weather forecast and a list of school activities she has posted in the older girls' closets, Christine helps Caitlin and Fiona choose an outfit for each weekday; Christine makes the selection for AnnaSophia. The girls place each ensemble, plus anything else they might need, such as gym pants or a Girl Scout uniform, on a shelf of a hanging sweater organizer, which is labeled with the days of the week." Most of the work, however, happened nightly after the girls went to bed. Bolzan emptied the dishwasher, set the table for breakfast, lined up the lunch boxes, packed napkins and drinks. She checked the girls' backpacks for homework folders, and lined up jackets and shoes, "leaving nothing to chance." She even untied and loosened the shoelaces on their sneakers: "One stubborn double knot can throw a wrench into the works."

Mosaic Project participants read these stories like everyone else, and it seems many took notes. Partly because such tips are staples of time management literature, I sometimes found in phone conversations that people wanted to compare time-saving techniques, and many assumed I had hanging sweater organizers labeled with the days of the week and the like. No one mentioned checking shoelaces, but I saw logs featuring a level of household organization that would win gold stars from any Homemaking Board of Review, if there were such a thing.

Some women slept less than the overall sample average partly because they got up early to complete various household rituals. On Monday, a woman with one young child wrote, "Alarm set 5 a.m.—get up at 5:15; work on morning to do list:—one load laundry, unload dishwasher, respond to personal emails, paint nails, write tasks for nanny, details on lunch, etc."

If one wanted to construct a narrative of being starved for time, waking up at 5:15 a.m. to do laundry would fit with that. After seeing a few of these logs, though, I started to ponder the larger question of how we manage our lives. How could Bascelli, with her stressful job and three children, spend her mornings journaling, doing yoga, and hanging out with the kids—with just one weekday laundry-related entry on Wednesday—while many people seemed to be soldiering through?

I came to see that using time well, so that you enjoy time, rather than battle it, is often *not* about being more organized in the running of a household. It is about changing your mind-set and recognizing that much of what fills our time is a choice. We can choose to make life easier on the housework, child care, and overall logistics fronts if we want. While this is certainly more doable for some people than others, depending on finances, partners, and the nature of one's work, it's just as likely to be a matter of questioning what is a deeply held value, and what is merely a script memorized long ago. Sometimes life is hard for a good reason. Sometimes narratives serve no purpose beyond keeping you from the life you want.

A Tale of Two Camps

Let's start with what making life easier is not about. It is not about giving up things you want to do. In contrast with the usual assumptions about women with big jobs, the Mosaic logs featured plenty of domestic diversions. People quilted and crocheted (see Diana Hobbs's log in the previous chapter for an example of weaving crafts into a busy life). They gardened. They baked. They perused decorating books and did elaborate home improvement projects. A leisurely trip to the farmer's market on a Saturday morning may count as an errand, but it's probably done as much for fun as anything else. A few participants with the highest housework totals had good explanations for all this work: an elaborate dinner party, for example, that involved hours of prep, but brought people together. Socializing is among the most pleasant activities we do, and parties are probably worth the cleanup (or you can hire a catering service, which is an option worth looking into, too).

Not all domestic work fell into these categories, though. I was also intrigued by the volume of time many women spent on core household tasks. A number packed lunches and did laundry daily. People ran errands and planned and cooked the week's meals from lunch until dinner on Sunday. Some even clipped coupons, which on one level is surprising, but on another isn't, since one Nielsen survey found that households earning more than $100,000 a year made up a higher proportion of coupon "enthusiasts" than those earning in the various categories under $30,000.

A number of families had outsourced the major cleaning tasks such as vacuuming and mopping floors to a cleaning professional. Still, I'd sometimes see this on the logs: "spend time cleaning before cleaning service came." (Even Bascelli did this, though at least she made the rest of the family participate, according to her Wednesday 6:30 p.m. log entry.)

As I crunched the numbers, I began to notice something. The people who spent the *most* time on housework often had seemingly good systems for keeping tasks such as cooking or laundry from stacking up. On the logs, the folks in what I started calling the "Organized Camp" showed recognizable routines. They did chores regularly as part of their mornings and evenings. They completed major tasks at what they told me were appointed times, like shopping on Saturday and cooking a week's entrées on Sunday.

If you ask busy parents for their secrets, many will swear by routines just like these. This is why *Real Simple* and other women's magazines are able to run stories like Booth's monthly. When you plan meals, you don't face the six o'clock madness of coming home starving but unsure what you're going to eat. You can make economical choices at the supermarket based on what's on sale. Cooking on weekends means you can make different dishes from those you might make on weekday nights. Doing laundry and dishes every morning ensures they don't pile up, and you don't come home to a stack in the sink. As for cleaning before the cleaning service comes? That's about picking things up so floors can be swept and vacuumed.

Except here's the thing: the time logs showing daily cleaning rituals tend to show a lot of this activity on weekends as well. People are in their homes more on weekends, usually, and they make messes—and organized people don't like messes, so they spend time cleaning then, too. People who cooked on weekends still cooked during the week, because they decided to make side dishes for those prepared entrées. If you make a habit of doing laundry daily, you'll spend time on laundry daily, whether it really needs to be done or not.

Housework expands to fill the available space, particularly if you sub-scribe to the belief, even unconsciously, that busying yourself around the house is just what a good household manager does. And so, the time logs that showed admirable organization—morning cleaning rituals, weekend meal planning—were also the logs with the highest total number of hours spent on household tasks. I have come to believe that such systems, lauded in most literature on how to manage a job and a family, actually contribute to the feeling that we have no free time at all.

On the other hand, people in what I'll call the "Good Enough Camp"—and I would include myself in this—just have a different attitude about chores in general. We outsource what we can depending on our budgets and prefer-ences, and we've also realized that we're not participating in some game show that gives us points for having empty clothes hampers. There is no daily eleven p.m. home inspection, with someone coming into our homes and not-ing whether all the toys are put away. Remember: the toys will just come out again the next morning, whereas you'll never get that time back. Consciously choosing to spend less time on things you don't enjoy leaves more space for things you do. The difference between spending fourteen hours per week on chores and seven hours per week is an hour a day to advance your career, or do something more enjoyable like reading with your kids or taking a nap.

So how can you beat the organization trap? As I studied the logs, I iden-tified a few strategies from the women with the lowest housework and errand totals:

If you're going to outsource housekeeping, really outsource it. Lots of people with above-average hours devoted to household tasks told me they had hired cleaning services to come weekly or every other week. They may have had more pristine houses than they otherwise would, but they didn't really lighten their loads, both because they prepped for the service and because they still did the recurring tasks such as laundry and dishes that much housekeeping entails. Because these tasks need to be done so frequently, they tend to matter more from an overall time perspective than the vacuuming and floor mopping a service will do. Other families realized that these frequent tasks can be negotiated as part of hiring someone specifically to clean, or perhaps can even be negotiated as part of a sitter's job description (particularly if the sitter is watching older kids, or those who take long naps). In our family, we looked at the options and decided we were better off hiring an on-the-books housekeeper to come twice a week rather than finding a commercial service that would come once a week. The twice-a-week frequency is more convenient; our housekeeper does the laundry and cleans the kitchen when she's here, two tasks that need to be done almost constantly. Outsourcing this way saves us time in a way that having a service vacuum carpets every other week would not.

Of course, you can also "outsource" tasks to family members, particularly children. They can often handle more than we think. Helen Fox's husband, who normally does the laundry in their house, has been teaching their eleven-year-old daughter how to do it. "She's doing all right," Fox says. "She's getting there." The girls understand that the money they save by not outsourcing housekeeping goes to other family priorities, like their Indonesian trips. That's a trade-off they're willing to make.

You can stop going to stores for most household items. Several women had their weekly groceries delivered. One told me she used a concierge service run by a neighbor to take this chore off her plate. Some asked nannies to do errands if they had time with only one child in their care. Another frequently mentioned strategy? Signing up for Amazon Prime to nix the need to shop for incidentals, or once-a-month purchases such as diapers. Even at $99 a year (up from the previous $79), it's a bargain to get free two-day shipping on things such as birthday presents or costumes for a school event that might otherwise send you scurrying off to random stores, hunting for items that the stores might not carry anyway. Sometimes Amazon's prices are higher, but time is valuable too, and weekends are too precious to spend them driving around just to save a few bucks. Even outside the Amazon universe, online shopping tends to be a good deal. You can use the ten minutes before a conference call starts to knock a household to-do off your list, like buying your kids clothing. Most of my kids' clothes now come from OldNavy.com. Mine, increasingly, come from Stitch Fix, an online personal shopping service that sends you five items at a time to try on at home. Add shoes from Zappos and my shopping trips become more about entertainment than anything else (such as the Thursday afternoon trip with a friend in my time log from chapter 1).

Some people love to shop, and if you love pushing a cart around Costco as me time, go for it. I think many of us have more mixed feelings about it. An adults-only afternoon perusing new arrivals at a favorite boutique is fun; a rushed postwork trip through Walmart necessitated because your kid needs poster board and scissors for a school project next week is not. Making life easier is about figuring out ways to avoid the second scenario even if you indulge in the first.

You do not have to make your kids' lunches. I grant that if they are four years old and attending a preschool without a cafeteria, making your kids' lunches may be part of the deal. But once children are in elementary school, they can learn to add items to the grocery list and be responsible for preparing their own lunches. Or they can bring lunch money on occasion, or even every day. This is what Jasper elected to do when he started first grade and weighed the options of helping to pack his own lunch or purchasing the cafeteria fare. I weighed the options too, even writing an article on school lunch fare for *City Journal* that included visiting cafeterias and interviewing numerous food service directors and the Department of Agriculture undersecretary responsible for the national school lunch program.

While program quality does vary, these days most school cafeterias have to meet strict nutritional standards for lunch, such as ensuring that fewer than 10 percent of calories come from saturated fat, and offering legumes and dark green vegetables on a regular basis. Most brown bag lunches are not this balanced or conscientious. If the school cafeteria serves pizza, it's usually got a whole grain crust and low fat cheese, and it's served with fruits and vegetables. If lunch is a corn dog, it belongs in an entirely different food group from what's served at the Minnesota State Fair. Just because the food is kid-friendly doesn't mean it's unhealthy, nor is it worse than the bologna sandwiches and gummy snacks people bring from home. Fun fact: when the new nutritional standards went into effect, the average number of daily paid lunches dropped precipitously. The idea that families want healthy food and schools are resisting has it *exactly backward*. My son recently came home and reported that the food service workers in his school had the kids taste-test arugula. I have never managed to get him to eat any leafy green, so chalk one up for peer pressure and the school cafeteria.

To be sure, if you're already packing your own lunch, then making an extra doesn't add much time. If you've got ten thousand people following your photos of amazing bento box lunches on Pinterest, then we've crossed into the realm of hobbies, which have their own inherent pleasures. Some parents like the idea of sending something with children to school to remind them of home, and reap real enjoyment from doing so. But if it's just a task, then it need not be inevitable. You can always pack a note in a backpack telling your child you love her, even if you don't pack a lunch.

You can eat well without eating up time. When it comes to food, there's a narrative out there that modern women have become too busy to cook, and this is the root of all our social ills. Or we want to cook, but life doesn't allow it. In many a Recitation of Dark Moments from can't-have-it-all literature, the heroine confesses that she rushes to cook dinner during a TV show. Such twenty-two-minute creations are taken as a sign that she has a harried, unsustainable life.

I respectfully disagree with this assessment. I do agree that cooking (and related ventures, such as gardening, or subscribing to a CSA) can be enjoyable. One recent Harris poll found that 79 percent of Americans claim to at least enjoy cooking, including 30 percent who love it. For many people, cooking is an important part of their identities, and people like tapping their creativity to make special dishes that require elaborate steps. Some admit to "stress baking"—kneading dough to knead out tension.

Given the usual narrative of how starved we are for time, I was fascinated to see how many women with big jobs defied all stereotypes and allowed their cooking to stretch far beyond the confines of a twenty-two-minute episode of *Dora the Explorer*. Amy Kellestine lives in Edmonton, Canada, and works as a manager in learning and development for a construction management company. She has a two-year-old son with cystic fibrosis. She recently decided that she wanted the family to eat more gluten-free, vegan meals, a lifestyle change that has required much prepping and learning new recipes.

When I interviewed her, she told me she had a Band-Aid on her finger because her son had tried to climb on her while she chopped onions and garlic. "I do find it challenging," she says. Sometimes he'll watch cartoons, and sometimes he'll play with things in the sink, but other times, like all two-year-olds, he wants Mommy's attention *right now*. Cooking with a two-year-old in the kitchen is often stressful. But Kellestine is committed enough to their eating habits that "it's a conscious adoption of stress," she says. The payoff is that her son has become a very healthy eater, willingly devouring broccoli and Swiss chard alongside the cookies all two-year-olds request.

Values are worth the time. On the other hand, if your point is to get a tasty, healthy meal ready quickly, you can make good options with little trouble. The key is developing a basic competence around the kitchen and around ingredients, then keeping lots of staples around, so you're able to pull dinner together quickly (no meal planning required). In my house, for instance, my husband figured out how to whip up a breaded eggplant dish for a late "date night" dinner in the time it took me to get the three kids to bed. Steak grilled over the weekend becomes a ten-minute southwestern steak salad for a few days because I've got lettuce, peppers, frozen corn, avocados, and chipotle dressing around. Salmon cooks quickly, and so salmon in teriyaki sauce plus sautéed broccoli becomes a twenty-minute meal. Eggs and veggies turn into a quick omelet dinner. Stir-fries are lightning fast and healthy; Costco carries frozen vegetable mixes, and thinly sliced chicken, shrimp, or scallops cook in minutes in a hot pan. Add a sauce and dinner is done, leaving enough time to experiment with my quick-prep banana bread, or in-season strawberry shortcake. I love my food. I truly do, and fortunately no one has to spend many hours in the kitchen to make good food happen.

Even if you do prefer dishes that take serious time, you might be able to take making them off your plate. Jennifer Hodgens, an Oklahoma real estate agent and mother of a two-year-old, told me that she hired a student in a local dietitian program to make meals for her family. "She's super ridiculously cheap because she's a student," she says. Indeed, she costs less than what they used to spend going out to eat, "and the meals are wonderful. My husband and daughter don't even know they're healthy." The dietitian student plans to launch her own catering company after graduation, and so

Hodgens set her up with friends who could be clients, and has given her glowing testimonials.

You can make chores fun. If you're going to do chores and errands, you may as well turn them into light moments. Take one kid and score quality time running errands together. Or turn errands into games. One woman turned a Whole Foods trip into a scavenger hunt of sorts, with the parent and child teams charged with finding items on the list as quickly as possible (the children were not tasked with grabbing eggs or other fragile items). Blend in pleasant activities so these undertakings are less annoying. Buy yourself a frozen yogurt while you wait for a prescription to be filled. Bring a friend along to shop for school supplies together and catch up while you're waiting in line.

All these realizations about housework and errands can help make life easier. But the best approach is simply to borrow the theme song from *Frozen* and "Let It Go." Like e-mail, chores will fill any time you give them. No matter how organized you are, there will always be something else you can do. People try to get ahead of the day by packing things up the night before, or setting breakfast dishes on the table, or pulling out outfits. But you can't remove all friction from your mornings. They are often chaotic anyway, with kids wanting different outfits, or the weather forecast being wrong, or the Girl Scout troop leader e-mailing an announcement that everyone must wear something different this week. In this scenario, you've just increased your total getting-ready time by spreading it over the night and morning too. No matter how much we clean and tidy, children just create messes. If we absorb messages of how pristine other people's houses are, we may devote precious minutes to these things when it's ultimately futile, and those minutes could be spent differently.

One lawyer who filled out a log for me was struggling with this trade-off. She worked until close to midnight one night, then came home and washed the dishes that were in the sink. Why? The dishes could have waited until morning and been washed along with the breakfast ones. Or she could have waited until the family members who created the mess got around to cleaning it up. She said she was learning to relax about these things, but letting go is hard. When scripts are committed to memory, it is hard to simply let a dish sit in the sink and not wash it, to see toys on the floor and not pick them up, to see an unmade bed and not pop up to go make it. You may have set aside half an hour to read, but for some people, once you sit down on the living room sofa, a little voice in your head starts saying that those puzzle pieces shouldn't be there, and soon this leisure time is chopped up and scattered to the wind.

I particularly saw this "let it go" mind-set as a process for women with either stay-at-home husbands or ones who did a high percentage of the kid- and home-related work. I don't like generalizations, but in my interviews with these women, some common themes emerged. Men who stay home with their kids often do not view housework as a set of tasks inevitably bundled with the task of child care. That part needs to be negotiated separately. The Pew Research Center published data in 2013 finding that in families with breadwinning fathers and stay-at-home moms, women spend 25.5 hours per week on housework and men spend 7.6 hours. Meanwhile, in families with breadwinning mothers and stay-at-home dads, the father spends 17.9 hours on housework and the mother spends 14.1 hours. The overall amount of housework is similar in these families (33.1 hours versus 32 hours), but the proportion of who does what is entirely different.

Whether they work outside the home or not, men often find housework to be less of a priority than women do. This can lead to tension. Jennifer Owens, editorial director of *Working Mother* magazine, used to take care of her younger brother after school when they were kids, and the deal was that when her parents came home, dinner had to be started and the house picked up. Now, she and her husband each do two nights a week on kid duty while the other works late. "In my mind, when he says he's on the way home, I should go around and pick up the house. It's ingrained in my head that he should come home and the house should be picked up," she says. Her husband never got this memo. So when she comes home late, "He's gotten all the kid stuff done but the house is never picked up. Part of me goes, *seriously?*"

In some families, Dad hasn't even gotten the kid stuff (like their dinner) done. Mom comes home and the kids are having a blast playing with Dad in the mud in the backyard, but she's mad because dinner isn't started and, by the way, *the kids are all muddy.*

Even dads who do run all aspects of the household, including housework, may have different ideas of what tasks need to be done. One law partner whose husband stays home full-time said that "he takes care of all the things that are missing from this log: food shopping, laundry." She appreciated how this worked but acknowledged that part of this arrangement meant "that you need to let go of it being done the way you would do it." Her husband and son would come home from the "weekly" grocery shopping trip and she'd think, "Okay, you've just purchased enough food for fourteen hours. How is this supposed to feed us for seven days?" As she put it, "A kid and a man together is not a recipe for just about any kind of interesting, creative, nutritional food happening." But at least "no one's gotten scurvy yet or anything." It could be a cause for complaint, but this lawyer acknowledged that she had the ability to place recurring orders on FreshDirect for anything she wanted. I mentioned Hodgens's solution of hiring a personal chef, though I quickly couched that with not wanting to step on her husband's toes or imply to him that he was doing a bad job. She laughed. "I don't think he would feel particularly emasculated," she said. Cooking just isn't automatically part of a stay-at-home dad's identity. He wouldn't be insulted. He'd welcome the help.

In life, you can be unhappy, or you can change things. And even if there are things you can't change, you can often change your mind-set and question assumptions that are making life less good than it could be.

The Child Care Dilemma

Housework and errands aren't the only tasks where this philosophy of seeking to make life easier rather than harder had profound effects on people's lives. Women who made peace with their time, rather than battling it, extended this philosophy to child care decisions, too. Since one's parental identity is an intense part of oneself, child care is particularly subject to stories we tell ourselves about what good parents do, and these stories are even more likely to lead us into constrained choices than the ones we tell about cooking and cleaning.

I have seen this in my own life as I've tried to figure out a child care situation that will allow me and my husband the time and mental space to achieve our career goals. It is a process, and the frustrating thing is that it will always be a process, because children's needs change and no child care situation will last forever. The daily trip to day care that worked when you had one two-year-old becomes untenable when you have another baby or you take a job with less predictable hours. Shortly after I finished the first draft of this book, our longtime nanny wearied of her forty-five-minute commute and decided to take a teaching job that was closer to her house. As I figured out what our new child care situation would look like, I recalled a few lessons that came out of the Mosaic logs.

1. THINK ABOUT YOUR DAY-TO-DAY LIFE. Unless your partner is responsible for all things kid related, child care decisions will affect your daily routines and small annoyances can add up. I adore Sam and Ruth's preschool for many reasons, but a key selling point is that it is half a mile from my house. On the days when I am responsible for bringing them, it is a lovely thing to know that the trip takes less than ten minutes, total, including time in the car line, rather than half an hour or more. I have also realized that there are an infinite number of after-school activities I can choose from. Sports and clubs that meet at the children's schools are going to be a lot easier to absorb into a busy family's schedule than those that don't.

For many Mosaic Project participants, this focus on daily quality of life pointed toward choosing child care for their young children that came to them (that is, a nanny), rather than the other way around (day care). A physician married to another physician told me, "Switching from day care to a nanny has made our lives so much more relaxed and pleasant. Instead of rushed mornings, we get to sit with both little ones (ages two and four months) eating a leisurely breakfast. We never have to worry about waking kids up in time to leave. I also no longer have to stress about minor illness (i.e. low-grade fever) necessitating emergency child care arrangements." While it is true that nannies can miss work sometimes too, people who've gone through this more than once tend to prioritize reliability in the hiring process over other things.

Depending on how you structure the arrangement, there may be other benefits to having another adult in the household to help. The physician reports that not only does her family's nanny take amazing care of the children, "she also performs the duties that I would do if I were home: grocery shopping, cleaning (other than the heavy stuff), cooking, and even laundry." There are upsides to day care, too, and "we kept our now two-year-old in day care part-time last year so that she would still have the structured environment/interaction that she was used to," she says. Day care alone can work well for families who live close to a center and have extremely reliable backup care, such as a retired grandma living nearby who can help out with no notice. For this family, though, their setup meant no bottle packing and no loading kids into the car on rushed mornings, which are realities that definitely made daily life easier.

2. DON'T BE CHEAP. From time to time I'm interviewed for articles on saving money on child care. I always try to be careful with the advice I give for such stories, because while you don't want to spend money just to do so, child care isn't an expense in the sense of being money out the door that you'll never see again. It's an investment in your lifelong earning potential. People who go to college or graduate school aren't just considering the tuition per year. They look at the payoff over decades. Likewise, even if child care costs consume a big chunk of after-tax household income, if you stay in the workforce, your income will likely rise over time. Your child care costs will fall as your children grow older, go to school for full days, and take care of themselves after dismissal. Economists would not make this calculation looking at a single point in time. Indeed, economist Sylvia Ann Hewlett has looked at this question, and calculated that women who take three or more years out of the workforce lose 37 percent of their earning power. That's over the remaining decades of their careers, which puts the cost of paying for a full-time nanny for six years into perspective.

You also don't want to skimp on child care in ways that will add to your stress level. You can't concentrate at work if you're worried about your children's safety and happiness. A day care in someone's home with one person watching eight kids might be cheaper than a licensed center with a four-to-one kid-to-staff ratio, but it's hard to believe the children are being carefully watched in the former. I also want to know that my children are being challenged by someone who can help them develop their talents. I like to hire people whose nurturing will complement mine. I have never looked at empty toilet paper tubes and said, "Hey, I bet the kids would have fun making a train out of that!" I'm not crafty, so I like to hire people who are. Nannies with college degrees and other specific skills can command higher salaries than those without, but I've found it's worth it.

Finally, you don't want to skimp in ways that are illegal. Hiring someone to work for you full-time, on the books, with paid vacations and all that, isn't cheap. But neither is prosecution for violating labor laws, and in general, treating the employer-employee relationship as a serious undertaking increases the chances that your caregivers will too.

3. BE REALISTIC ABOUT THE HOURS YOU NEED. Money is a significant consideration in figuring out child care. Because even people with six-figure incomes don't have limitless budgets, it's always tempting to try to pay for as few hours as possible. This impulse is magnified by the constant cultural message that using child care is somehow a sign of parental failure. Once, when I was on a British radio program, the host mentioned my passel of children and asked me how I had found time to write a book. I said I had child care. He said something along the lines of "People are listening to this and saying, 'That's cheating!'" He was a genial sort, and I'd like to think he was kidding, but I don't doubt some listeners thought that. If you hear this message enough, you start to think that using as little child care as you can get away with is a sign of parental success.

I particularly see this play out among women who are self-employed. People who work from home have described to me painstakingly structured child care arrangements that attempt to ensure they won't pay for a second of nap-time coverage. That's fine, except when it isn't. It is inevitably the one day you have an extremely important 1:30 p.m. phone call with your biggest client that your child who naps religiously at 1:00 p.m. elects not to. There are few good ways to deal with the needs of a client and a screaming baby at the same time.

If you work in an office, you don't face this nap-time temptation, but you may encounter another issue: you work longer or more unpredictable hours than a single caregiver can be expected to cover. The solution Mosaic Project participants suggested was to think about stacking multiple kinds of coverage in ways that complemented one another. Indeed, this tendency to stack, and hence devise personalized solutions, is why I couldn't produce a neat number (as I'd originally hoped) for how many families used nannies, or preschools and day care, or family care, and so on.

For those with older children, this stacking sometimes took the form of preschool or school plus an au pair. An au pair is generally a young woman from another country who lives with you for one or two years under a special visa arrangement. International child care placement programs restrict work to forty-five hours per week, and no more than ten hours per day. That's not enough care for a baby if you're away fifty hours a week, but if you have kids who are in school at least part-time, having an au pair can enable longer and less predictable hours than school or day care alone. One woman, whose husband is an army officer deployed to Afghanistan, wrote me that having an au pair was key to making her life work. She was a stay-at-home mom for six years before going back to work in a supervisory position with a government contractor, a job that sometimes results in weekday evening commitments. Their kids are now eight, six, and four, and are in school until 3:15 p.m. "My husband and I struggled with child care, day care/aftercare, etc. when I went back to work," she says. "All of our struggles evaporated when we got an au pair. Three kids makes an au pair really economical, too. A lot of people 'freak out' about the idea of having someone live in their house, but it is not remotely awkward. You have to remember that the au pair is young and they don't have any desire to spend their free time with you. They want to be out with their friends or Skyping with family and friends back home."

Au pairs are not supposed to provide overnight coverage, and because they are generally younger (ages eighteen to twenty-six), not all families want the issues that might come along with having a teenager or not-always-mature twentysomething live with them. In my home, in fall 2014 we took a different approach: stacking a full-time nanny with other coverage. Ruth went to preschool three mornings per week, and we found a nanny who was happy to work from noon to eight p.m. on Tuesdays and Thursdays because she had a morning class at a local university.

I haven't found many families where both parents need to travel unpredictably, though I did have a few single mothers in the Mosaic Project whose jobs involved travel. If you'll have more than a few days' advance notice, having at least one trusted sitter who can stay overnight makes business trips work in these situations. Having family nearby can help on this front too.

Families where both parents need to travel unpredictably, or families with a traveling single parent, often wind up living near family or bringing family to live with them, for precisely this reason. To some degree, if you are flying all over the world, it may not matter where you call home base. If you don't have family who can help, hiring a live-in nanny (a regular employee, not an au pair) is your best option, though you still can't expect this person to work around the clock. Parents who are truly gone frequently and unpredictably will need more than one caregiver to cover the 168 hours of the week, or even the 108 hours between six a.m. Monday and six p.m. Friday. If weekends are in play, you'll definitely need two full-time caregivers. If not, there's this option: a "relief" sitter who comes to your home a few evenings per week to do the postwork shift and put the kids to bed while your regular caregiver has time off. We did this once while I was on the West Coast for three days and my husband was in Europe. Our nanny stayed overnight, but another sitter came from 5:30 to 8:30 p.m. on those nights to give her a break.

For many parents, one of the hardest parts of all this is being honest about how much coverage you need even if one or both parents might wind up being around for some chunk of those hours, but couldn't guarantee it. Recently, our backup sitter came at 5:30 p.m. to take over from our nanny because I was in New York. I thought my husband was flying to Boston that night. I came home at 11:00 p.m. to find my husband's car in the driveway because he'd decided to fly out the next morning. For all I know, he was there at 5:45 p.m., and we didn't actually need a second sitter. But we hadn't been able to guarantee that, so we booked it and paid for a few hours. If you want to keep good caregivers, they deserve to know when they'll get time off.

4. THINK THROUGH TROUBLE SPOTS. Even with the regular child care coverage my family arranged in our new setup—from 9:00 a.m. to 8:00 p.m. two days a week, and 8:00 a.m. to 5:30 p.m. three days a week with an occasional extra evening sitter coming as needed—we still faced logistical challenges. Our nanny can spend the night on the not-too-frequent occasions when we're both traveling, but if her fall semester class was from 8:00 a.m. to 11:00 a.m. on Tuesdays and Thursdays, and preschool started at 9:00 a.m. on those days, this wouldn't work. So I checked with the other sitters in my roster, and found one who had availability from 7:15 a.m. to 9:15 a.m. if we figured out ahead of time that we needed it. This never wound up being an issue, but I wanted to have options. My husband and I also got in the habit of having a weekly or biweekly calendar meeting to confirm our schedules and child care needs.

I will admit that such logistics are not fun to figure out. Over time, this added mental load can wear people down. But if both of you love what you do, it's just part of the game. Just as you manage projects with moving parts at work, you can do it at home too. You staff up a home team as you would at the office. A development officer for a university who kept a log in 2013 described this as creating a sitter "portfolio." She had to cover her travel and her husband's long hours, and because they had young twins, they needed sitters who could handle two toddlers at once. She had a nanny and preschool hours, and made sure to have a few college-age sitters scheduled for regular amounts of time, both to cover leisure and to be trained enough to serve as potential backup for nanny sick days. She'd keep an eye on the mix: "Are there any year-rounders and am I building a pipeline of first- and second-year students?"

•

Of course, the best child care portfolio in the world won't make your life easier if you don't let people help you. One entrepreneur who kept a time log for me employed a nanny to care for her two young children, but still took her older daughter to preschool pretty frequently (twice during her diary week). Because she could do it, she thought she should do it. That would be fine if it were a short jaunt to her daughter's school, like my half-mile journey, but it wasn't. It was a forty-five-minute chunk out of her day.

In a situation like that, the important question to ask is why she was making this decision. What value was she attempting to uphold? Did she want to show her daughter that education is important? Did she want to be involved with the school? Was it important to her that she meet other parents and that she have frequent chats with the teachers? If any of those explanations were deeply held values, then the drive made sense.

But if the value was primarily that she wanted to spend time with her child, then the drive to preschool had some limitations. For starters, the kid wasn't there with her for half the time. As the mother was an entrepreneur and her family's primary breadwinner, that forty-five minutes needed to be made up at some point to keep the business running and the bills paid. She might wind up working later, or on weekends, rather than spending that time with family.

With a situation like this, the best approach is to analyze it from all sides, and then choose a solution that fits with your values without adding hassle to your life. Maybe you do the drive once every other week or so, strategically, on a day when you have time to say hello to people and make playdates. You can volunteer to do something special with the kids like chaperone a field trip, or come in to read to the class three or four times a year. Then you cheerfully let the competent person you hired to care for your children while you work care for your children while you work most of the time.

Because here's the thing: child care is supposed to make your life easier. It is supposed to make life easier so you can work, and it is supposed to make life easier so you can have a life. As I noted in the previous chapter, many Mosaic Project participants expressed surprise at just how many hours they spent with their kids. There is often space to create more me time if we wish. Amy Kellestine had figured out a change in her schedule that would allow her to work about four fewer hours during the week. Since her au pair was already covering this time, these were four found hours. She mentioned that there was a practical thing she could do with them. Children with cystic fibrosis, like hers, are quite susceptible to infections, so she couldn't just pop her two-year-old in the car and run to Target like other parents. Did I think it was a good idea to do errands during those four hours?

My short answer: no. She was already figuring out a way to keep the family fed, clothed, and in possession of toilet paper now. A better approach would be to use those four hours for the personal time she was craving, personal time that caring for a child with special needs can easily obliterate. (She wound up using the time to make personal appointments for pedicures, the dentist, etc., and to volunteer.)

There are no points for martyrdom. This is especially true for people who have far less stressful life situations than Kellestine who still manage to narrate whole playdates or fill entire blog posts with litanies of woes. Ruminating about how hard you have it is, perhaps, a simple pleasure in life, but when we dwell on unhappiness, we get more of it. No one wins in the Misery Olympics.

Instead, people like Lynda Bascelli (whom we met earlier in the chapter) figure out ways to make life work. She chose not to do laundry every morning when she could be writing in a journal instead. She let the kids wear what they wanted to wear, rather than spending time she could be playing the guitar choosing their outfits for each day of the week. She had a child care situation that gave her flexibility (even if there was that scene with the kids on the roof).

Sometimes the answer to "How can I make life easier?" is a big lifestyle decision. An insurance adjuster in Philadelphia included hours of house hunting on her time log. When I followed up with her, I learned that she and her husband were soon closing on a house in the town she grew up in, right outside the city. Her mother had been caring for her baby but with the move could do so more regularly, as could various other relatives and family friends. "We have an army of free and willing child care," she says. Moving out of the city was a tough decision for someone who likes to be part of the urban scene, and it also involved questioning assumptions, like that you can't be cool and live in the burbs and perhaps even drive a minivan (I confess I'm still working on that one, despite purchasing a Toyota Sienna once I learned my fourth kid was on the way). But it did make her life easier. Some other Mosaic women found the opposite. They moved from the suburbs into cities because their commutes ate up too much time. Either way, the point is to look at your daily life and change what you can to make your hours better. We often describe our lives in abstractions, but happiness comes from making our day-to-day lives as good as possible.

That's what Eileen Haley discovered. When she first kept a log for me, this Chicago-area resident had a horrible commute. It wasn't so much the length—it took an hour—as that much of it involved driving on a clogged highway during rush hour with her baby and toddler. She had to find street parking at their day care, which added a huge element of uncertainty to her day. Sometimes, she would find a spot close by, but other days she would have to walk several blocks in the snow with two kids and their gear. She worked through lunch, partly to be sure she could leave on time to repeat the journey in reverse. Her husband had to be at his workplace from 7:45 a.m. to 5:30 p.m., though not because he had the sort of job that could only be done on-site. It was a standard office; "it was just very rigid," says Haley. So he couldn't help. In the midst of such a daily slog, particularly as the long winter made Chicago driving conditions even worse, "you become a negative person," she says. "That negativity was stressing me out."

Fortunately, Haley saw this quite clearly. Fast-forward six months, and her family had moved to a different community. The children transferred to a day care that was four minutes from their house. The trip was a much more tenable part of Haley's day, and she only had to do it half as often, because her husband found a different and more flexible job. That made carting the kids around "a very shared experience now," she told me. After dropping off the kids, she'd hop on the train, and use that time to read or relax. She often took a break at lunch (her log shows shopping and errands and the like, at least getting her away from her desk) because quitting time was no longer so set. "Now I'm not rushing on both ends," she says. "I'm not shortchanging both ends of my day." Indeed, keeping a second time log was her idea; she wanted to show me "proof that my life maybe isn't as grueling as that end-of-winter week made it seem!"

When it comes to housework, child care, and overall life situations, we can choose to make life harder, or choose to make life easier. Sometimes there are good reasons for the former, but sometimes not. The difference between Haley's two logs is so stark it's like two different lives (p. 187 and p. 191).

Log 1

	TUESDAY	WEDNESDAY	THURSDAY	FRIDAY	SATURDAY	SUNDAY	MONDAY
5AM	Sleep	Sleep	Sleep	Sleep	Sleep	Sleep	Sleep
5:30	Sleep	Sleep	Sleep	Sleep	Sleep	Sleep	Sleep
6	Wake up; get ready; wake up boys	Wake up; get ready; wake up boys	Wake up; get ready; wake up boys; nurse T	Wake up; get ready; wake up boys; nurse T	Sleep	Sleep	Wake up; get ready; wake up boys; nurse T
6:30	Nurse T; get boys ready for day; eat breakfast	Nurse T; get boys ready for day; eat breakfast	Play with B; get boys ready for day; eat breakfast	Play with B; get boys ready for day; eat breakfast	Sleep	Sleep	Play with B; get boys ready for day; eat breakfast
7	7-7:10: play with boys; 7:10-7:20: coats, etc to get out door; 7:20: leave for day care	Commute to day care (ugh – another terrible, wintry, snowy, long commute)	7-7:10: play with boys; 7:10-7:20: coats, etc to get out door; 7:20: leave for day care	7-7:10: play with boys; 7:10-7:20: coats, etc to get out door; 7:20: leave for day care	Wake up: read stories with B in bed	Sleep	7-7:10: play with boys; 7:10-7:20: coats, etc to get out door; 7:20: leave for day care
7:30	7:30-7:45: commute to day care; 7:45-8: drop off boys	Commute to day care (ugh – another terrible, wintry, snowy, long commute)	7:30-7:45: commute to day care; 7:45-8: drop off boys	7:30-7:45: commute to day care; 7:45-8: drop off boys	Play with B; T wake up	Play with boys	7:30-7:45: commute to day care; 7:45-8: drop off boys
8	8-8:20: commute to work via EI; 8:20-8:30: settle in at desk	Commute; drop boys off at day care	8-8:20: commute to work via EI; 8:20-8:30: settle in at desk	8-8:20: commute to work via EI; 8:20-8:30: settle in at desk	Nurse T; play with boys	FaceTime with my mom	8-8:20: commute to work via EI; 8:20-8:30: settle in at desk
8:30	Check emails; work at desk	Commute to work via EI	Work at desk	Work at desk	Play with boys	Play with boys	Work at desk
9	Meetings	Work at desk	Meetings	Meetings	Gym	Get ready	Work at desk
9:30	Meetings	Meetings	Meetings	Work at desk	Gym	Play with boys	Work at desk
10	Work at desk	Meetings	Meetings	Meetings	Get ready	Play with boys	Meetings

	TUESDAY	WEDNESDAY	THURSDAY	FRIDAY	SATURDAY	SUNDAY	MONDAY
10:30	Meetings	Meetings	Meetings	Meetings	Drive to Wilmette; stop at little bakery for muffins and coffee	Shedd Aquarium family outing	Meetings
11	Meetings	Work at desk	Meetings	Meetings	House-hunting trip	Shedd Aquarium family outing	Work at desk
11:30	Meetings	Meetings	Meetings	Meetings	House-hunting trip	Shedd Aquarium family outing	Meetings
12PM	Meetings	Pump; grab lunch	12-12:15: meeting; 12:15-12:30: pump		House-hunting trip	Shedd Aquarium family outing	Meetings
12:30	Pump; eat lunch at desk	Work at desk	Walk to grab lunch; eat at desk	Walk to grab lunch; eat at desk	House-hunting trip	Shedd Aquarium family outing	Grab lunch; eat at desk
1	Meetings	Meetings	Meetings	Work at desk	Drive back to city; grocery shop	Shedd Aquarium family outing	Meetings
1:30	Meetings	Work at desk	Work at desk	Work at desk	Grocery shop	Shedd Aquarium family outing	Meetings
2	Work at desk	Meetings	Work at desk	Work at desk	Arrive home; nurse T; color with B	Shedd Aquarium family outing	Meetings
2:30	Work at desk	Meetings	Work at desk	Meetings	Play with boys	Shedd Aquarium family outing	Pump; work at desk
3	Meetings	Meetings	Meetings	Meetings	Play with boys	Shedd Aquarium family outing	Work at desk
3:30	Meetings	Meetings	Meetings	Work at desk	Play with boys	Shedd Aquarium family outing	Meetings
4	Meetings	Meetings	Work at desk	Work at desk	Friends come over to watch bball game with us	Laundry	Meetings
4:30	Work at desk	Meetings	Work at desk	Work at desk	Hang out with friends; play with B	Play with boys	Meetings

	TUESDAY	WEDNESDAY	THURSDAY	FRIDAY	SATURDAY	SUNDAY	MONDAY
5	Commute to get boys	Work at desk	Commute to get boys	Commute to get boys	Hang out with friends; play with B	Play with boys	Commute to get boys
5:30	Pick up boys at day care; commute home	Commute to get boys	Pick up boys at day care; stop for takeout dinner; commute home	Pick up boys at day care; commute home	Hang out with friends; play with B; watch game	Play with boys	Pick up boys at day care; stop for takeout dinner; commute home
6	Arrive home; play with boys	Pick up boys at day care; commute home	Commute home; eat dinner	Play with boys	Hang out with friends; play with B; watch game; play with T	Play with boys	Nurse T; let B watch TV next to us; get dinner ready
6:30	Play with boys; nurse T; eat dinner	Nurse T; let B watch TV next to us; get dinner ready	Eat dinner; play with boys	Eat dinner; play with boys	Hang out with friends; play with B; watch game; play with T	Play with boys	Dinner; play with boys
7	Bath time; play with boys	Dinner; play with boys	Play with boys	Bath time; play with boys	Hang out with friends; play with B; watch game; play with T	Play with boys	Dinner; play with boys
7:30	Put T to bed; laundry; clean up	Play with boys; put T to bed	Put T to bed; play with B	Put T to bed; play with B	Put T to bed	T bedtime	Play with boys; put T to bed
8	8–8:15: check personal emails, updates on baby shower I am hosting later this month; 8:15–8:35: B bedtime	Play with B	Bedtime with B	Bedtime with B	Hang out with friends; play with B; watch game	Laundry	Play with B
8:30	8:35–8:50: clean kitchen; 8:50–9: work emails	Bedtime with B; shower	Surf the web	Put B to bed; surf the web	Put B to bed; friends leave	B bedtime	Bedtime with B; shower
9	Work emails	Work	Work	Watch TV with husband	Surf the web	Talk with realtor	Work

	TUESDAY	WEDNESDAY	THURSDAY	FRIDAY	SATURDAY	SUNDAY	MONDAY
9:30	Work emails	Work	Work	Watch TV with husband	Clean up	Talk with realtor	Work
10	Catch up and relax with husband	Catch up and relax with husband	Work	Watch TV with husband	Watch TV with husband	Talk with realtor	Clean up around house; laundry
10:30	Catch up and relax with husband	Watch Jimmy Fallon with husband	Clean up	Bed	Bed	Read	Catch up and relax with husband
11	Bed; sleep	Bed; sleep	Sleep	Sleep	Sleep	Bed	Bed
11:30	Sleep	Sleep	Sleep	Sleep	Sleep	Sleep	Sleep
12AM	Sleep	Sleep	Sleep	Sleep	Sleep	Sleep	Sleep
12:30	Nurse baby; sleep	Nurse baby; sleep	Sleep	Sleep	Sleep	Sleep	Sleep
1	Sleep	Sleep	Sleep	Sleep	Sleep	Sleep	Sleep
1:30	Sleep	Sleep	Sleep	Sleep	Sleep	Sleep	Sleep
2	Sleep	Sleep	Sleep	Sleep	Daylight savings - lost hour	Sleep	Sleep
2:30	Sleep	Sleep	Sleep	Sleep	Daylight savings - lost hour	Sleep	Sleep
3	Sleep	Sleep	Sleep	Sleep	Sleep	Sleep	Sleep
3:30	Sleep	Sleep	Sleep	Sleep	Sleep	Sleep	Sleep
4	Sleep	Sleep	Sleep	Sleep	Sleep	Sleep	Sleep
4:30	Sleep	Sleep	Sleep	Sleep	Sleep	Sleep	Sleep

Log 2

	TUESDAY	WEDNESDAY	THURSDAY	FRIDAY	SATURDAY	SUNDAY	MONDAY
5AM	Sleep	Sleep	Sleep	Sleep	Sleep	Sleep	Sleep
5:30	Sleep; wake up; get ready	Sleep	Sleep	Sleep	Sleep	Sleep	Sleep
6	Get ready; wake up boys; get boys dressed	Wake up; shower; get ready; wake up boys	Shower; get ready; wake up boys	Wake up and get ready	Sleep	Sleep	Wake up; get ready
6:30	Play with boys; feed boys breakfast	Breakfast for boys; get boys ready; leave for train (6:50)	Wake up boys; breakfast for boys; play with T	Clean the kitchen and do dishes from last night (watch a skunk wander through our backyard while doing dishes!). I prefer to clean up in the morning to the night. Have much more energy in the morning and enjoy the quiet of it while I'm the only one awake rather than doing it at end of the day, exhausted. Leave for train	T wakes up; get up with him, play	Wake up with T; play quietly with him while B sleeps	Boys wake up; get them ready; breakfast
7	7-7:10: get ready; 7:10-7:15: commute to day care (yes - 4 minutes!); 7:15-7:25: day care dropoff; walk to train (2 minutes) get on 7:29 train to loop.	Train to work (read Crains Chicago)	7-7:10: get ready; 7:10-7:15: commute to day care (yes - 4 minutes!); 7:15-7:25: day care dropoff; walk to train (2 minutes) get on 7:29 train to loop.	Train to work; husband working from home today so he is taking boys in at a more leisurely pace	Feed boys breakfast; play with boys	Play with T and put away laundry and organize/sort fall clothes/ summer clothes	Play in playroom with boys; leave for school (7:15); drive to school drop off both boys; walk to train

	TUESDAY	WEDNESDAY	THURSDAY	FRIDAY	SATURDAY	SUNDAY	MONDAY
7:30	Train to work (play aimlessly on iPhone, read through Gmail on phone)	Walk to office; arrive at desk at 7:40, work at desk	Train to work (read a magazine, read through Gmail on phone)	Walk to office; arrive at desk at 7:40, work at desk	Play cars with boys	Play with boys in basement playroom; make coffee	Metra to work (read a book)
8	8-8:10: train to work; 8:15-8:25: walk to office, get coffee	Work	8-8:10: train to work; 8:15-8:25: walk to office, get coffee	Work	Play with boys in basement; get ready	Flip through Sunday paper while watching boys play	Metra; walk to office; arrive at desk
8:30	Check emails; work at desk	Work	Meetings	Meetings	Get boys ready; tidy up	Make blueberry muffins with B	Work at desk
9	Work at desk	Coffee meeting	Meetings	Work at desk	B soccer game; run with T in stroller around park/lake while B at soccer	Get ready; leave for church	Telephone call
9:30	Meetings	Work at desk	Meetings	Conference call	B soccer game	Mass	Telephone call
10	Work at desk	Meetings	Meetings	Meetings	Soccer finishes; head to farmers' market at Wagner Farms	Mass	Meetings
10:30	Meetings	Work at desk	Meetings	Work at desk	Meet up with good friends and their 1-year-old at farm and farmers' market	Arrive home; play in yard with boys	Meetings
11	Meetings	Work at desk	Meetings	Meetings	Farmers' market fun with friends and family	Boys' cousins come over to play; chat with my brother and sister-in-law	Meetings

	TUESDAY	WEDNESDAY	THURSDAY	FRIDAY	SATURDAY	SUNDAY	MONDAY
11:30	Work at desk	Work at desk	Work at desk	Meetings	Farmers' market fun with friends and family	Make lunch for kids; make zucchini pancakes with zucchini from farmers' market	Meetings
12PM	Meetings	Meetings	Meetings	Work at desk	Drop off B to go to cousin's soccer game with his aunt; grocery store with husband and T	Lunch with kids	Meetings
12:30	Meetings	Grab lunch and run into Old Navy to buy a shirt for B for school tomorrow (perks of Loop office is easy access to knocking out errands during lunch break!)	Eat lunch at desk; work	Work at desk	Grocery store	Play in yard with kids	Grab lunch; run into Target
1	Meetings	Meetings	Work at desk	DMV errand to update driver's license, car registration, and voter registration with new address. Good errand to knock out during lunchtime at the express office a block from my office!	Walk home from grocery store with T in stroller; husband drove home with groceries (love our new town and its walkability score!)	Put T down for his nap; clean up kitchen	Work at desk

	TUESDAY	WEDNESDAY	THURSDAY	FRIDAY	SATURDAY	SUNDAY	MONDAY
1:30	Lunch	Meetings	Work at desk	Grab a sandwich, eat at desk while working	Put T down for his nap; eat lunch; set up my home office and do paper work	Relax with newspaper; laundry; check email	Work at desk
2	Work at desk	Work at desk	Meetings	Conference call with remote office	Pay bills, paper work, etc	Play basketball with B; color with chalk	Meetings
2:30	Meetings	Meetings	Meetings	Conference call with remote office	B and my sister (his aunt) arrive back home; chat with my sister	Play basketball with B; color with chalk	Meetings
3	Work at desk	Meetings	Meetings	Meetings	Play in basement with B; chat with my sister	Walk to Library (B on scooter; T in stroller); all got library cards at our new library - including B - so proud of himself!	Meetings
3:30	Meetings	Meetings	Work at desk	Meetings	T wakes up; feed T	Library	Meetings
4	Work at desk	Work at desk	Meetings	Meetings	Play with boys in yard	Library	Work at desk
4:30	Work at desk	Work at desk	Meetings	Work at desk	Make corn muffins; set table for dinner	Walk home from library	Work at desk
5	Work at desk	Walk to train; Metra home on 5:12 to pick up boys	Work happy hour on outside terrace (absolutely beautiful late summer evening)	Work at desk	Play with boys in yard	Dinner out at Irish bar in town as a family	Work at desk

	TUESDAY	WEDNESDAY	THURSDAY	FRIDAY	SATURDAY	SUNDAY	MONDAY
5:30	Walk to train; get on 5:52 Metra (respond to Gmail, read *Crains* magazine)	Train ride (respond to emails via iPhone, chat with husband - rode home together); pick up boys from day care, arrive home at 6	Work happy hour on outside terrace (absolutely beautiful late summer evening)	Walk to train; get on 5:52 Metra home (veg out on train)	Play with boys in yard	Dinner out at Irish bar in town as a family	Walk to train; get on 5:52 Metra (respond to Gmail, draft emails)
6	Arrive in Glenview at 6:18; boys and husband meet me at train w/ stroller and scooter and all walk home (4 minute walk!)	Feed boys dinner, flip through catalogs	Work happy hour on outside terrace (absolutely beautiful late summer evening)	Arrive in Glenview at 6:18, walk home, greet boys and husband	Couple and their dog come over for dinner; take boys and their puppy to park down the street	Dinner out at Irish bar in town as a family	Arrive in Glenview at 6:18, walk home, greet boys and husband
6:30	Play in yard with boys while husband grills dinner	Play outside in the yard (beautiful evening)	Work happy hour on outside terrace (absolutely beautiful late summer evening)	Play inside with boys and husband (rousing game of hide and seek)	Dinner with boys and husband and friends	Dinner out at Irish bar in town as a family	Play in the basement with boys and husband; feed boys a snack
7	Dinner on the back deck	Play outside in the yard (beautiful evening)	Work happy hour on outside terrace (absolutely beautiful late summer evening)	Friday night pizza dinner	Dinner with boys and husband and friends	Bath time for boys	Play in the basement with boys and husband; prep leftovers for dinner; eat dinner
7:30	Playtime; bath time; squeeze in a 20-minute run (!)	Give the boys a snack, play in the basement, T to bed	Work happy hour on outside terrace (absolutely beautiful late summer evening)	Play in the basement playroom	Watch ND football game	Clean up; check/send emails	Bath time for boys; T bedtime
8	Story time; bedtime	Play with B, chat with husband	Work happy hour on outside terrace (absolutely beautiful late summer evening)	Play in the basement playroom	Put T down; watch game	Work in new home office	Respond to emails, hang out with B in basement while he is playing

	TUESDAY	WEDNESDAY	THURSDAY	FRIDAY	SATURDAY	SUNDAY	MONDAY
8:30	Clean kitchen; do laundry, clean up	Put away laundry, eat dinner with husband	Train home	Bedtime for B	Watch ND football game; chat with friends	Read new book from library	Clean up
9	Talk to Mom on phone	Personal computer stuff, write a few letters to mail tomorrow	Walk home from train; B still up so laid with him in bed for 15 mins	Clean up around house	Friends leave; B to bed; watch game with husband	Watch *Downton Abbey* with husband	Work emails
9:30	Work	Work	Chat with husband while he put together new coffee table for our front room	Watch TV with husband	Watch game with husband	Watch *Downton Abbey* with husband	Work
10	Watch TV with husband	Work	Watch TV	Watch TV with husband	Read; get ready for bed; sleep	Get ready for bed; sleep	Watch *Downton Abbey* with husband
10:30	Watch TV with husband; nod off on couch	Watch TV with husband	Fall asleep watching TV	Sleep	Sleep	Sleep	Watch TV with husband; nod off on couch
11	Sleep	Sleep	Sleep	Sleep	Sleep	Sleep	Sleep
11:30	Sleep	Sleep	Sleep	Sleep	Sleep	Sleep	Sleep
12AM	Sleep	Sleep	Sleep	Sleep	Sleep	Sleep	Sleep
12:30	Sleep	Sleep	Sleep	Sleep	Sleep	Sleep	Sleep
1	Sleep	Sleep	Sleep	Sleep	Sleep	Sleep	Sleep
1:30	Sleep	Sleep	Sleep	Sleep	Sleep	Sleep	Sleep
2	Sleep	Sleep	Sleep	Sleep	Sleep	Sleep	Sleep
2:30	Sleep	Sleep	Sleep	Sleep	Sleep	Sleep	Sleep
3	Sleep	Sleep	Sleep	Sleep	Sleep	Sleep	Sleep
3:30	Sleep	Sleep	Sleep	Sleep	Sleep	Sleep	Sleep
4	Sleep	Sleep	Sleep	Sleep	Sleep	Sleep	Sleep
4:30	Sleep	Sleep	Sleep	Sleep	Sleep	Sleep	Sleep

．
．
．
．
．
．
．

SELF

．
．
．
．
．
．
．

.
.
.
.
.
.
.
.

CHAPTER 7

Nurture Yourself

I f you want to make the pieces of life fit together, if you want to build a career, raise a family, and stay sane, it is hard to escape the conclusion that self-care is the secret ingredient. Sleep, exercise, and leisure time are glorious things. Alas, in the popular telling, these are glorious *rare* things, especially for working parents. Twenty-five years ago, sociologist Arlie Hochschild studied employed women with families, and announced that they came home from one job just to start another. What fell away in all of it was any sense of nurturing themselves. As she wrote in *The Second Shift*, "These women talked about sleep the way a hungry person talks about food."

It's an image that stuck, with the modern narrative presuming little leisure and a desperate and obsessive sleeplessness. This impression has been helped along by surveys, most notably the National Sleep Foundation's annual "Sleep in America" poll, which, in 2007, focused primarily on women. Warned the NSF: "Women's lack of sleep affects virtually every aspect of their time-pressed lives, leaving them late for work, stressed out, too tired for sex and little time for their friends." The press release on the study claimed that "Women who are married, with school-aged children and working full-time . . . report being in bed less than 6 hours per night on weeknights."* Media magnate Arianna Huffington has taken on yet another career, as a "sleep evangelist," warning female audiences that they endanger their health by continuing in their dream-deprived lives.

The situation sounds bleak. The assumption that building a career while raising a family means you will have no time to sleep, let alone get the sort of exercise that leads to energy and health, is one reason people believe it's impossible to have it all.

Fortunately, closer examination finds taking care of yourself need not be a casualty of juggling work and life. This is true for sleep and exercise, which this chapter addresses, and for leisure time, which we'll cover in the next chapter.

First, the good news on sleep: women in the Mosaic Project slept a reasonable amount from a quantity perspective. These high-earning women with kids logged about fifty-four hours a week of sleep, on average. That's about seven hours and forty-two minutes per day. Another way to think of it: fifty-four hours is the equivalent of sleeping eight hours five days per week and seven hours the other two.

When I share these numbers, someone will inevitably get wide-eyed and tell me about the horrible night or string of nights she just experienced. So let me be clear: there were bad days. Women got up with babies and sick children. They woke at 3:30 a.m. to catch 6:00 a.m. planes. There was a lower bound to sleeplessness, however. No one in the entire study slept less than forty-two hours (averaging to six hours a day) in her diary week, and most people slept much, much more. Indeed, roughly 90 percent of Mosaic Project participants got *at least* the seven to nine hours per day public health groups have traditionally recommended for adults, averaged over the seven days on the time log. Weekends helped with that, to be sure, but only 191 of the 1,001 days I studied (19 percent) featured fewer than seven hours of sleep. Only 37 of 1,001 days (3.7 percent) featured fewer than six hours.

---

* The study *itself* did not show this; women in the "Briefcases with backpacks" demographic were more likely than other women to claim to be in bed less than six hours, but the difference was 17 percent versus 12 percent overall. The average woman was in bed much longer. Unfortunately, the implication from the press release that six hours was an average was repeated in numerous outlets.

This bears repeating: yes, there are exceptions, but for women who have big jobs and kids, getting adequate sleep is the norm.

Looking at other aspects of self-care, women in the Mosaic Project exercised more than the average American, even though they worked more than the average American too. In 168 hours, there is plenty of space to nurture yourself alongside your career and your relationships. There is no reason to dream of sleep (or a nice solo trail run) the way a starving man thinks of food. This chapter looks at strategies for making those pieces fit into the mosaic in the quantities they deserve.

Sleep

A little confession here—a "confession" because it's not the party line for busy people: most of the time, I get plenty of sleep. I quite enjoy it. I don't just love feeling focused and productive after a good night, though that is nice. I find sleep fascinating and pleasurable for its own sake. I get ideas from dreams, including scenes for my fiction writing and insights into my thoughts. I enjoy seeing what my brain will knit together when I don't consciously force things. My nights can go awry. They go awry more frequently when I'm pregnant, or I've got a kid in the baby stage waking me up before I want. But in general, I aim to be in bed 7.5 to 8 hours before I need to get up, and on the best days, I drift in and out of this most exquisite naturally groggy state in the morning, waking up before my alarm.

I can't claim to have figured out any great secrets to sleeping well. I exercise most days, I limit caffeine, and there's no TV in my bedroom. Then again, I don't always practice good sleep "hygiene," as they call it—those dos and don'ts of preserving the bedroom for sleep and sex and going to bed at the same time every night. I work until fifteen minutes before bedtime some nights, and I still drift off. I'm lucky in that regard, but in terms of getting enough hours of sleep, I'm not as rare as the usual narrative would assume. Indeed, sleep has become a favorite topic of mine, precisely because the assumptions and real-life observations diverge so sharply, at least when you look at sleep quantities. These divergent findings lead to very different accounts of modern life. In one, we are starved for sleep. In another, many of our fellow citizens are indulging in an all-you-can-eat buffet, and even the busiest of us are likely to enjoy regular and reasonable meals.

Here's what's tricky: assumptions of sleeplessness are based on legitimate surveys. If you talk to any group of busy people, they will tell you in great detail how little sleep they think they are getting, on some nights at least, and they will mean it. If you commission a nationally representative poll of one thousand people and you ask them to estimate how much they sleep on a typical day, you will get a number that sounds low. People hear these numbers and they enter our mental models of life. The day before the Bureau of Labor Statistics released one of the best statistical pictures of American life, the American Time Use Survey, in 2014, I polled my Facebook friends about how many hours they thought the survey would show the average American slept per day. Many of my friends guessed in the six-to-seven-hour range.

They were spouting the conventional wisdom, but there are problems in many sleep survey methodologies that don't just come out in the wash. First, *sleep surveys ask about sleep*. This matters. People are primed to think about sleep as they answer the questions, and since negative experiences stand out in the mind more than good ones, the tendency is to call the bad nights to mind first. When primed to think about a certain topic, people are also more inclined to give answers that reflect the common narrative, in which sleep deprivation is a badge of honor. I sat through a conference panel once featuring a woman who introduced herself and all her various accomplishments and then, smirking, announced, "So you can see, I don't sleep." It was an exaggeration, of course. Everyone sleeps, but that she chose this impossibility as her way of conveying her importance isn't random. She knew we would understand what she meant. Getting adequate sleep is a sign that the world doesn't need your attention for seven to nine hours each day. It keeps spinning as usual in its orbit. Who wants to admit that?

Second, surveys sometimes ask how much people sleep "per night," which means that people don't mention unplanned, nonnocturnal sleep. Naps don't register as real sleep, even if the nap starts at eight p.m. in front of the TV and ends when you move to your bed. Sometimes people don't count the snooze time after their official alarms either. Snooze sleep is lousy sleep, but if we're trying to figure out totals, it still counts. (The National Sleep Foundation, incidentally, asks about naps, and finds they happen with some regularity. I found this too, especially on weekends.)

Third, and the biggest problem, is that many sleep surveys ask how much sleep people get on a "typical" or "usual" night, or what time people go to bed and wake up on typical nights and mornings. Asking about a typical night requires, of course, that there be a typical night. The truth is that for many people, typical nights don't exist. I saw this immediately with the Mosaic logs. Monday through Thursday on the first log I looked at featured sleeping times of 7.5 hours, 6.25 hours, 6.75 hours, and 7.5 hours again. That's a gap of 75 minutes between the lowest and highest weekday sleep total. Another early log featured three weekdays in a row with 8.5 hours, 9.5 hours, 7.5 hours. That's a 120-minute difference. Looking at sleep totals for the whole sample on two adjacent weekdays—Tuesday and Wednesday—I found that 22 percent of logs featured gaps of 90 minutes or more.

In a world that views sleep deprivation as a sign of importance, we're often tempted to view the shortest nights as typical, ignoring that much longer nights of sleep occur too, to say nothing of weekends. (Weekends are real days—29 percent of our days, to be precise—even if they never strike us as typical.) One woman told me that it was her goal to be in bed at ten p.m., not eleven p.m. I thought it was a great goal, and according to her time log, she was already doing that three nights per week (Friday, Saturday, Sunday). But she went to bed at eleven p.m. the four other nights (Monday, Tuesday, Wednesday, Thursday). Those nights became "typical," though something that happens four nights per week isn't really much more typical than something that happens three times.

With sleep, a week is a more accurate picture of life than one night. Bad nights can be taken in context, and good nights can be too. By keeping a time log, you record all your sleep, even if it didn't happen at "typical" times, and see whether it fits with your mental picture or not.

Over the days recorded in the Mosaic Project, I got a general sense of what sleep habits look like. Each day is a "diary day"—running from five a.m. to five a.m. So unless you wake up at five a.m., "Monday" includes an hour or two of what most people think of as Sunday night:

MOSAIC PROJECT OVERALL AVERAGE SLEEP/DAY

Mon: 7.4
Tues: 7.5
Wed: 7.3
Thurs: 7.5
Fri: 7.5
Sat: 8.1
Sun: 8.6

While even the lowest day's average—Wednesday's 7.3 hours—is well within the seven-to-nine-hour recommended range, people were more likely to sleep less than recommended amounts on Wednesday than other days. Some 30 percent of Wednesday logs featured fewer than seven hours of sleep, and 6 percent featured fewer than six hours. I'm not sure why Wednesday is so problematic. Perhaps it's midweek stress. Sleep totals and work totals were inversely correlated, and people did work longer hours on Wednesdays than other days. In any case, because sleep is a biological function, not a testament to how important you are, most people's bodies then force them to make up this time.* Thursday was much better than Wednesday. Only 17 percent of logs featured fewer than seven hours, and 1.4 percent featured fewer than six. This alternating pattern somewhat repeated itself through the week. Friday was another low total day. Nearly a quarter of logs featured fewer than seven hours, and about 5 percent featured fewer than six. Saturday improved, with only 13 percent featuring fewer than seven hours, and 3.5 percent featuring fewer than six.

It was interesting to see exactly how people caught up on sleep, day to day. One woman fell asleep in her toddler son's room four times in the course of one week. I'm not sure if that habit would be reflected in her vision of a typical night (even if it happened more often than it didn't), but on the days that didn't happen, she slept seven to eight hours. On the days it did, she slept

---

* This is not the case with chronic insomniacs, whose bodies may lack the catch-up impulse. But chronic insomnia is a serious medical condition that doesn't fit neatly into narratives of people being too busy to care for themselves.

eight to nine. People would make up time in the morning, too. They'd turn off alarms. A five a.m. workout might happen Wednesday, but not Thursday.

The good news, though, is that 54 hours of sleep per week is not bad. To be sure, that sleep total is less than that of the average American. According to the American Time Use Survey's 2014 report on its 2013 data, the average American sleeps 8.74 hours per day. That's 8.48 hours on weekdays and 9.34 on weekends. A blog reader dug up the previous year's numbers for me on the ATUS sleep range and found that the 25th percentile was 450 minutes, the 50th was 524, and the 75th was 600 minutes.

At roughly 462 minutes a day, women in the Mosaic sample are just a bit above the 25th percentile. Working parents in general are a little higher. The ATUS finds that employed parents with kids under age six sleep 8.26 hours per day (about 495 minutes), and employed parents with kids ages six to seventeen sleep 8.38 hours (about 504 minutes; mothers average a bit more sleep than fathers). These are also a little under average for all Americans, but keep in mind that the 75th percentile, 600 minutes, comes out to *10 hours a day*. That's what I mean about the all-you-can-eat buffet line. It is not that working parents are sleeping so little. It's more that some Americans—whoever they are—sleep so much. To continue the eating metaphor, 7 or 8 hours a day does not suggest a starving man talking about food. Rather, it suggests that feeling you get about 80 percent of the way through a decent meal. You could eat more . . . but you don't need to.

Of course, quantity and quality are not the same. Someone could sleep lightly for 8 hours or get 9 interrupted hours and still feel lousy the next day. Averages also mean nothing about individuals. Mosaic Project participants were a varied group. A few women got 63 hours of sleep *or more* over the week, the equivalent of 9-plus hours a day.

Natasha Dwyer, an Australian academic who was parenting solo while waiting for her partner's visa to be finalized, told me she was "obsessed with being horizontal by ten p.m." At night, "I keep an eye on the time and start winding everyone up around nine p.m. We usually watch an episode of Agatha Christie's *Poirot* and I skip the gory bits." Then she and her two-year-old son would co-sleep. "The advice we are given here is to have the kid in the same room overnight for the first year. I'd put my kid in a cot beside me, he'd wake up in the night and ask to come in with me. To improve everyone's sleep, I just put him in with me from about eleven months old." While some people don't co-sleep well, it worked for her. She and her son would both sleep from ten p.m. to a little after seven a.m. (he would nap during the day, often on the later side, which made the ten p.m. bedtime work). "I've made an effort to make sure I get enough sleep because I feel so rotten if I don't," Dwyer says. While going to bed early precluded late-night me time, "I don't feel like I'm missing out as I get to have meaningful conversations at work."

Some people got much less sleep. No one slept less than forty-two hours a week (averaging to six hours a day) in my sample, though I counted fifteen logs in my sample, or just over 10 percent, with sleep totals under forty-nine hours for the week (seven hours a day).

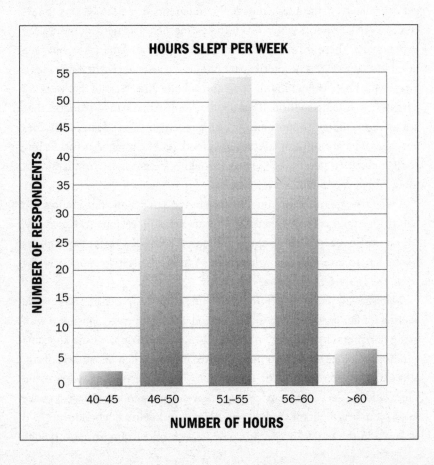

	MONDAY	TUESDAY	WEDNESDAY	THURSDAY	FRIDAY	SATURDAY	SUNDAY
5AM							
5:30							
6							
6:30							
7				Breakfast, get kid ready			
7:30	Breakfast, get kid ready	Wake up, breakfast, get kid ready			Breakfast, get kid ready	Breakfast, get kid ready	Breakfast, get kid ready
8		Check emails	Wake up, breakfast, get kid ready		Check emails	Trip to park	Trip to park
8:30	Travel to work	Travel to work	Check emails		Housework		
9	All-day planning meeting		Shower		Travel to work		
9:30		Meetings with students	Housework	E-learning training course		Food shopping	Housework
10			Reading for journal article				
10:30		Prepare groundwork for next				Put kid down for a nap	Put kid down for a nap
11		research project	Travel to work	Student enrollments		Put kid down for a nap	Put kid down for a nap
11:30						Academic reading	Academic reading
12PM							
12:30		Prepare curriculum for		Meetings with colleagues		Edit article	

	MONDAY	TUESDAY	WEDNESDAY	THURSDAY	FRIDAY	SATURDAY	SUNDAY
1		coming semester	Print course outlines				
1:30							
2							
2:30						Housework	Housework
3		Travel home			Travel home		Meet up with friend
3:30		Put kid down for a nap			Put kid down for a nap		(take kid)
4				Travel home			Housework
4:30				Play with kid			
5	Travel home	Prepare article for publication	Travel home	Put kid down for a nap		Trip to another park	
5:30	Play with kid outside		Food shopping				Food shopping
6	Bath/housework		Put kid down for a nap				
6:30	Television			Catch up on emails		Food preparation for next	Emails
7	Emails		Catch up on emails		Housework		
7:30	Walk	Walk		Walk	Walk	few days	Walk
8				Housework			
8:30				Walk	Housework		
9	Housework	Housework	Housework	Television	Television	Television	Television
9:30	Television	Television	Play				
10	Bed for everyone	Bed for everyone	Bed for everyone	Bed for everyone	Bed for everyone	Bed for everyone	Bed for everyone

	MONDAY	TUESDAY	WEDNESDAY	THURSDAY	FRIDAY	SATURDAY	SUNDAY
10:30							
11							
11:30							
12AM							
12:30							
1							
1:30							
2							
2:30							
3							
3:30							
4							
4:30							

While these women were not the norm, I was curious about their lives, so I took a closer look at their logs and talked to them to see what was happening. I found a statistically significant inverse correlation between work hour totals and sleep hour totals, something larger time use surveys have found too, though I'm not sure what is cause or effect. Some people may be sleep deprived because they work too much, but some people have more hours available to fiddle with their inboxes at night or in the early morning hours because they need less sleep.

Indeed, some people may legitimately need less sleep than others. Eight hours a night sounds good, but this isn't a universal rule. Some large-scale sleep studies have suggested that getting closer to seven hours of sleep per day (and perhaps a bit under that) might actually be associated with lower morbidity and mortality than sleeping eight hours, though plenty in the medical community dispute that finding. One sign of needing less sleep would be getting six to seven hours of sleep on weekdays, and then roughly this same amount on weekends too.

Helen Fox, whose "Inbox Zero" tale is told in chapter 4, may be an example of this. She woke up at 6:45 a.m. on Saturday without an alarm and without a small child waking her up. She didn't show signs of sleep deprivation, like falling asleep in her children's rooms when she put them in bed, or passing out in front of the TV, which are all things the human body does when it's tired and trying to catch up. She told me that she thinks seven hours a day is her set point, and she got 47.75 hours of sleep during her diary week, which averages out to about ten minutes under that. "I feel like I'm mostly functional," she says. "Other people have commented that I have more energy than average." Likewise, Em Hillier, who had the lowest sleep total at 42.25 hours for her diary week, never crashed while working on her businesses at night, or during the afternoon while she was caring for her youngest child. I know that if I were getting six hours of sleep night after night, my kids would be watching a lot of *Mickey Mouse Clubhouse* while I was lying somewhere in a heap. Hillier can honestly claim that she needs less sleep than I and many other people do.

A few women with low totals, though, did show evidence of sleep deprivation, taking multiple naps on the weekends or falling asleep during movies.

Some added up their own totals and knew that clocking under forty-nine hours didn't work for their lives.

Why were these women falling behind? Some had life situations that precluded orderly sleep. One woman, who was eight and a half months' pregnant when she logged her time, woke up every few hours to go to the bathroom. She wound up with just 46.5 hours for the week. She joked that it was nature's way of preparing her to plunge back into the newborn stage. One woman traveled internationally during the week she logged, and sleeping on planes, and while jet-lagged, is tough. She clocked 46.75 hours for the week. Others had children who woke during the night. While having young kids (under age two) did not correlate with getting less sleep overall, for some that was the issue. One single mom I spoke with had three young children who didn't sleep well. On her log, she was waking up two or three times per night, and hit just 44 hours for the week (p. 212).

This was a tough situation. The children's father wasn't available to help much on this front, and she didn't have many family members around. Strategizing together, we talked about her trying to go to sleep earlier, and prioritizing her own sleep above just about everything else. With a big job and three young kids, she was craving me time, as many others in this situation would too, and she would stay up late surfing the Web. The problem was that, for her, this strategy extracted a much steeper cost than most people's late-night Internet wandering. It would be better to get to bed early and try to get at least another hour of sleep before the interruptions started. She was building in some me time during the day, which was a good idea, and she was also hoping for relief in another year or so, as her children grew up (her oldest child woke up a lot less frequently than the younger ones).

Frustrating as this situation was for her, though, it is not evidence of some larger narrative of stressed-out womankind having no time for sleep. Some parents win the kid sleep lottery and some lose it; some kids take well to sleep training and others don't. This mother had tried what she could, and even worked with baby sleep specialists, but eventually kids are who they are. There is a three-hour-per-day difference between Dwyer's log and this one. If you lose the kid sleep lottery as a single mom, life is going to be hard.

I was more intrigued by cases where women had low sleep totals, at least

	MONDAY	TUESDAY	WEDNESDAY	THURSDAY
9:30 PM	Leisure - TV/Internet	Leisure - TV/Internet	Leisure - TV/Internet	Chores - housecleaning and food prep
10	Leisure - TV/Internet	Leisure - TV/Internet	Leisure - TV/Internet	Leisure - TV/Internet
10:30	Leisure - TV/Internet	Sleep	Sleep	Sleep
11	Sleep	Sleep	Sleep	Sleep
11:30	Sleep	Sleep	Sleep	Sleep
12AM	Sleep	Sleep	Sleep	Sleep interrupted/up with R
12:30	Sleep	Sleep interrupted/up with R	Sleep interrupted/up with T	Sleep
1	Sleep interrupted/up with R	Sleep interrupted/up with M	Sleep	Sleep
1:30	Sleep	Sleep	Sleep	Sleep
2	Sleep interrupted/up with M	Sleep	Sleep interrupted/up with M	Sleep
2:30	Sleep interrupted/up with M	Sleep	Sleep	Sleep
3	Sleep	Sleep	Sleep	Sleep
3:30	Sleep	Sleep	Sleep	Sleep
4	Sleep	Sleep	Sleep interrupted/up with R	Sleep interrupted/up with M
4:30	Sleep interrupted/up with M	Sleep	Sleep	Sleep

during the week, and fewer obvious life circumstances that kept them from sleeping. Their children weren't that young. They didn't work extreme hours. What was going on in their lives?

Various cultural narratives, like the ones I talked about in chapter 6, may play a part here. One woman, who got up early to do chores, compared herself with friends who didn't work outside the home. If she believed their homes were spotless, then trading sleep for housework could be a way to achieve what she viewed as the norm. Nearly half of women worked a "split shift," meaning they went back to work after their kids went to bed at some point during the workweek, as a way to log lots of family time and heavy work hours too. Sometimes this leads to sleep deprivation if people stay on their computers too long in the misguided hope that they'll ever be truly finished. Women who handled this well generally gave themselves a bedtime. They'd stop work at least half an hour before lights out, and then read or relax. A bedtime alarm can help with this, providing an external signal that it's time to wind down. In some cases, women did this split shift in the early morning, before their kids woke up. This can work too, if you go to bed on time the night before. This is easier said than done. "I am apparently trying to have all my fun on top of regular work hours, and it is not a good system," a woman with a below-average sleep total (47.75 hours a week) told me. "I don't find myself nodding off, but I have noticed that it gets harder to focus and I get more emotional, particularly as the week goes on. I'm generally not tired right at bedtime. I should probably start the routine earlier." She'd read for a while at night, but then wake up before five a.m. to get quiet social media time in too before she did some work.

As I looked at this burn-the-candle-at-both-ends log, I was reminded that sleep doesn't exist independently of everything else in life. Sometimes sleep deprivation is about how content you are with the rest of your hours. People want a certain amount of joy, or at least autonomous time, in their lives. When you are not getting enough of this during work hours, and if you have a lot on your plate at home, you want to create hours around these obligations for activities you choose. If you work long enough hours, that means you have to choose to sleep less. This woman told me that she was spending "too much energy forcing myself to do something I don't really want to do." So I wasn't surprised to learn, when I circled back a year later, that she had taken the opportunity presented by new family developments (moving for her husband's job, having a new baby) to take some time away from work.

Even people who like their jobs, though, can want more me time, and can adopt questionable habits as a result. Paula Beck is a public sector lawyer with two kids, ages ten and six. She slept fifty hours over the week she logged, which is more than seven hours a day, but only because she managed to get nine hours on Saturday. Some chunk of those fifty hours also came as snooze button sleep. "The log pointed out more clearly what I already knew—I have been trading sleep for TV and computer time at night," she says. "I have had the snooze habit for as long as I can remember." She would set two alarm clocks. "I am afraid if I only set one alarm, I can't count on myself. I might sleep through it or be late." She called the second alarm "my security blanket." Unfortunately, she set her alarms quite a bit apart, and so had the worst of all worlds: interrupted sleep, without the extra time to read, or exercise, or do something else that would come from getting up.

Studying Beck's log, I saw that her morning issues started the night before (p. 215). After her husband went to bed, she'd stay up for what could be hours. Some nights she read (see the one late night devouring Harry Potter), but other nights she'd play sudoku, watch TV, or fold laundry, activities that she described as not particularly meaningful to her. She wouldn't go to bed until after midnight some nights, and then she'd set her two alarms, with the first one ringing long before she intended to wake.

Habits are hard to give up. A better approach is to work with the habits you have. I suggested to Beck that rather than setting her two alarms far apart, she set them close together, and closer to the time she actually intended to get out of bed. Snooze sleep is lousy sleep, so better to have it consume five minutes, rather than twenty. That way, she'd be able to enjoy her sleep until close to wake-up time. Because she also called her late-night computer game playing "the most mindless and the least fulfilling" of all the things she did, I suggested she start doing more enjoyable leisure activities earlier in the evening.

We all want me time, and the key to getting enough sleep is making sure that you do things you want to do at times that don't require you to burn the midnight oil. Beck loved to knit, and did that with a group during Tuesday lunches. She could start on a project as soon as the kids went to bed, and get

	MONDAY	TUESDAY	WEDNESDAY	THURSDAY	FRIDAY	SATURDAY	SUNDAY
5AM							
5:30							
6		6:20 alarm: snooze til 6:40	6:30 alarm: snooze til 6:45				
6:30		Laundry, get ready					
7	7:10 alarm: snooze		Get ready, get son ready, breakfast, drive to school	7:10 alarm: snooze	7:10 alarm: snooze	7:00 alarm: snooze	
7:30						Up 7:20, breakfast	
8	Get ready, get kids ready, eat	Doctor's appointment	Sit in on piano lesson, knit, drive to work	Up at 7:40, get ready, get kids ready, eat	Up 7:35, load dishwasher, get ready, kids ready, breakfast		
8:30		Commute, breakfast	Sit in on piano lesson, knit, drive to work			Work out, get coffee	
9	Commute		Get coffee	Drop kids off at school, drive to work, get coffee	Get coffee, take cats to vet, drive to work		
9:30							Up at 9:30, family time (breakfast, Easter egg hunt, games, lunch)
10	Work	Work	Work	Work	Work	At horse barn with family for riding lessons	
10:30							
11							
11:30							

	MONDAY	TUESDAY	WEDNESDAY	THURSDAY	FRIDAY	SATURDAY	SUNDAY
12PM	Work			Work	Work		Up at 9:30, family time (breakfast, Easter egg hunt, games, lunch)
12:30	Get lunch, eat at desk, surf web	Get lunch, eat and knit	Get lunch, eat at desk, surf web	Get lunch, eat at desk, surf web	Work		
1							
1:30						At horse barn with family for riding lessons	Yard work
2					Get lunch, eat at desk, surf, calls re dr. appts.		
2:30	Work	Work	Work	Work			
3					Work		Family bike ride
3:30							
4							
4:30							
5						Have dinner with family and my brother, hang out	Get kids dinner
5:30	Drive to YMCA, work out		Get groceries, drive to church				
6							
6:30		Commute					
7				Attend son's school play, out for ice cream, drive home	Errands on way home		Dinner and a movie with husband
7:30	Run errands on way home	Dinner	Wait during kids' choir practices		Eat dinner	Web surfing, email	
8	Supervise piano practice, kids' bath and bedtime	Supervise piano practice, kids' bedtime	Drive home		Kids' bath and bedtime	Kids' bedtime	
8:30			Kids' bedtime	Kids' bedtime			

	MONDAY	TUESDAY	WEDNESDAY	THURSDAY	FRIDAY	SATURDAY	SUNDAY
9	Supervise piano practice, kids' bath and bedtime	Supervise piano practice, kids' bedtime	Kids' bedtime	Kids' bedtime	Kids' bath and bedtime	Kids' bedtime	Dinner and a movie with husband
9:30	Computer games, surfing	Computer games, surfing, shopping	Computer games, surfing	Computer games, surfing	Laundry	Hard boil eggs	Computer games, surf
10	Laundry, take care of cats					Watch TV	
10:30							
11	Watch TV	Laundry, sort kids' clothes	Read	Make self dinner, eat and watch TV	Computer games, surfing	Computer games, surf	Watch TV
11:30						Read	
12AM	12:00–6:40: sleep	12:00–6:45: sleep		Take care of cats, read	Read	12:00–9:30: sleep	Read
12:30			12:40–7:40: sleep	12:20–7:35: sleep	12:30–7:20: sleep		12:30–7:30: sleep
1							
1:30							
2							
2:30							
3							
3:30							
4							
4:30							

hours of creative time if she wanted, and still get to bed on time. If she got to bed by midnight, and didn't set her alarm until close to 7:30 a.m., she'd be getting plenty of sleep.

Beck agreed with this. However, wisely, she decided to focus on fixing one habit at a time, starting with getting to bed at a reasonable hour. By aiming to wind down by 11:30 p.m., she could make it into bed by midnight almost every night. She had a harder time giving up her staggered wake-up. She did move the two alarms later, though, and found that compressing her morning routine didn't actually make her late to work. Sometimes she ate breakfast on the go, but that was a trade-off she was willing to make in order to get more sleep. In the grand scheme of things, that is what matters. Indeed, getting more sleep makes big steps possible. When I checked back in six months later, Beck's alarm clock had broken, so she took the opportunity to start setting just one alarm on her phone, sans snooze. Even long-standing habits can be changed in time.

Exercise

While I normally sleep well, on the night of April 24–25, 2010, I did not. I woke at three a.m. Sunday morning in my rental house in Carmel, California. I headed to a bus in the center of the seaside town, bound for the Big Sur International Marathon starting line. I remember my nerves as we rolled twenty-six miles along the Pacific Coast Highway. In the next few hours I would have to run every single one of those miles back.

I had wanted to run a marathon since I'd started running a few years prior, but I was more interested to see if I *could* run a marathon. Could I fit the training in with my life? It was a quintessential mosaic question. My training required that I run for about seven hours a week. If I worked forty-five hours and slept fifty-six, the time should be there among the remaining sixty-seven hours. As it happened, I did make the time, with long runs early Thursday mornings and trips to the track for speed work on weekends. I managed to cross the finish line grinning and in reasonably good shape. I have not felt compelled to train for any other marathons since. I now know, though, that that's not because I don't have time. I have time. *I just don't want to.*

When it comes to exercise, there is no way around this matter of choice. The majority of people don't exercise enough. Only one in five adults meets the CDC's guidelines for adequate aerobic and strength-building exercise (just shy of half meet the aerobic guidelines alone). It's not because people don't have time, which is a fundamental flaw of articles trying to convince people that intense workouts can do the job in fifteen minutes, or gadgets that pledge all-over fitness in four minutes a day. We have plenty of time. Averaged over the entire American population, people watch almost as much television as they work. If people don't exercise, it's because *they don't want to exercise*. Time becomes the scapegoat. Time becomes the scapegoat for all sorts of things, which explains the phrase "If you want something done, ask a busy person." I was researching volunteering statistics a few years ago when I came across the phrase "the more, the more." I'd presumed that people with jobs, and people with children, would be less inclined to volunteer. The reality is that people with these claims on their hours are more likely to volunteer than similar people without such claims. The more you have going on, the more you do.

This theme emerged as I studied exercise totals. Not all Mosaic logs showed exercise, though of the 135 logs that were detailed enough to measure exercise, 123 (91 percent) showed some physical activity. The average for the 135 was 3.3 hours of exercise per week, which is more than the 2.5 hours per week many public health experts tell us we should get. I counted 33 logs featuring 5 hours of exercise a week or more. Interestingly, unlike sleep hours, exercise was *not* inversely correlated with work hours to any degree of statistical significance. Indeed, if you want evidence that exercise is a choice, not a function of free time, I found that exercise and total number of children were *positively* correlated. People with larger families exercised more than those with smaller families.

I'm not sure other samples would replicate that. Statistics are slippery, and this may be the one-in-twenty chance of being a fluke, but it does suggest that if you want to exercise, you can make it work. There are good reasons to make it work. One woman summed up her dedication to exercise like this: "I noticed that my best self was most likely to emerge on the days I run."

Another woman, an IT director at a health care research company, started working out at lunch most days to see what would happen. The report:

"Immediately, I started sleeping better. I had been an insomniac before, and couldn't shut my brain down at night. Even though I took time away from work, I had much greater mental clarity in the afternoons after I exercised, and was able to accomplish more in less time. My ability to handle work stress increased exponentially. I stopped caring whether I was clocking in enough. I've been doing this for a year now, and I had a terrific year at work."

Fitting in exercise requires some careful placing of tiles, but it is not an inevitable casualty of a full life. Indeed, given the benefits of energy and focus, sometimes it's what makes a full life possible.

Making Time

How did people make time to exercise? Many of the women with the highest exercise totals engaged in what I'd call functional fitness. There was a reason beyond exercise that they did what they did. They biked to work, or walked to and from the train station; because commutes have to happen, this exercise didn't feel as contrived as going to the gym. A Danish woman in my survey biked behind her youngest son for the ride to school, then biked to work from there. She did once get caught in a downpour, but she easily got an hour of activity each day. However, while I counted her biking as exercise, she didn't. It wasn't particularly strenuous, she said. An easy, flat ride in which you are trying not to get your work clothes sweaty may not have much in common with taking your mountain bike out on some serious hills.

In a case like that, I was perhaps overcounting exercise. In others, I undercounted, as there is little aerobic difference between going for an hourlong walk that is specifically labeled as such, and doing normal family activities such as walking around the zoo on a Sunday. The zoo trip could easily translate into two or three miles. My tallying system would count a time log entry that said "walk" as exercise, but not "zoo," so I am not capturing all aerobic activity. I also overcounted other entries. Three half-hour blocks labeled "gym" would get counted as ninety minutes of exercise, even if someone spent a big chunk of that in the locker room or examining her muscles in the weight room mirror.

That said, I was fascinated to see the ways people built movement of all sorts—both functional exercise and deliberate exercise—into their lives. One of the best examples came from an engineering professor at a major California university who had a toddler son ("S"). She took advantage of the California climate and biked everywhere: to the pediatrician on Monday, to work most days, to pay S's preschool tuition on Thursday. In the evenings, she'd load S in the stroller and go for a run (her husband stayed home with the boy during the day, so this served the dual function of exercise and giving S's dad a postwork break). Despite working 54.5 hours, including an all-day business trip on Friday, she managed to go on five stroller runs (p. 222).

If functional fitness wasn't a possibility, the next most consistent exercisers tended to get their workouts in early in the day. Lisa Camooso Miller, profiled in chapter 4, got up every morning at five a.m. to do CrossFit with a handful of girlfriends.

Marissa Levin, the CEO of a company called Successful Culture, has two teenagers, and tells me that many mornings she's up at 4:50 and at the gym by 5:15. She trains for a little over an hour before coming home to make breakfast for her kids, and possibly meditating or walking the dog. "My husband sleeps through most of this," she tells me, but "I crave my alone time to take care of my mind, my body, and spirit in the morning. It is my gift to myself. I have been weight training/running/spinning, etc., consistently for thirty-two years, since I was fifteen. I used to be a certified trainer, in high school and college. I have never not worked out. I can't imagine my life without it. I say that I train for two reasons—please attribute this to me—for 'sanity and vanity.'"

Morning is a great time for exercise because we tend to have the most willpower then (think about it: diets aren't broken with a spoon going straight into the Häagen-Dazs at seven a.m.). Also, you're less likely to be interrupted. Few people schedule emergency meetings at six a.m., whereas a planned six p.m. workout can be derailed by a five p.m. call from a needy client. Then there's the matter of hygiene: you only need to shower once if you work out in the morning. While driving to a gym can add time to the morning routine, it may not add much, especially if you live nearby. A biology professor who kept a time log for me lived five minutes away from the Bikram yoga studio she frequented most mornings. Those with home exercise equipment (like Lynda Bascelli from chapter 6) had an even shorter commute, and hence didn't need to wake up much earlier, or find child care if the other parent was

	MONDAY	TUESDAY	WEDNESDAY	THURSDAY	FRIDAY	SATURDAY	SUNDAY
5AM	Sleep	Sleep	Sleep	Sleep	Transport to airport	Sleep	Sleep
5:30	Sleep	Sleep	Sleep	Sleep	Arrive at airport/ check in/ security	Sleep	Sleep
6	Sleep	Sleep	Sleep	Sleep	Work on grad student paper in boarding area	Sleep	Sleep
6:30	Sleep	Sleep	Sleep	Dressed S/brushed his teeth, etc	Pump breast milk/get coffee/ comment on paper	Sleep	Sleep
7	Woke up and took care of S	Sleep	Dressed S/brushed his teeth, etc	Dressed S/ brushed his teeth, etc	Comment on student paper/ board plane	Sleep	Give S a bath
7:30	including: feeding, clothing	Woke up, took care of S, made breakfast	Walked to Starbucks w/ S	Fixed S breakfast and ate with him	Work on student paper on plane	Wake up/dress S	Play w/ S/dress him
8	Housework, cleaned up after S, ready for work, emails		Made S breakfast, prepped backpack	Got ready for work/ light housework	Work on student paper on plane	Play w/ S	Go to get Starbucks and bagels
8:30	Worked on post doc paper	Biked to work, bought coffee	Got dressed, walked S to nursery school	Rode to pay S's tuition/bike to Starbucks, to work	Talk to neighbor on plane about research	Walk to Starbucks/ eat breakfast w/ S	Go to farmers' market
9	Call with another post doc	Advising meeting with new student	Drop off at nursery school, rode bike to work	Call	Travel from airport to meeting spot	Play w/ S outside	Go on walk with S
9:30	Worked on post doc paper	Advising meeting with new student	Conference call on project	Lecture prep/notes review/pay bills	Meeting	Play w/ S outside	Go to park with S

	MONDAY	TUESDAY	WEDNESDAY	THURSDAY	FRIDAY	SATURDAY	SUNDAY
10	Worked on post doc paper	Email/met with grad student/ submit manuscript	Conference call on project	Emails/work on talk/bike to dentist	Meeting	Make raw key lime vegan pie with friend	Come home, give S a snack
10:30	Call w/ grad student	Meet with grad student about research	Meet with grad student	Dentist	Meeting	Play with S	Relax with S
11	Bike to pediatrician office/ buy lunch		Meet with grad student about research	Dentist	Meeting	Play with S	Relax with S
11:30	Pediatrician appointment	Email	Meet w/ grad student/ admissions/meet w/ colleague	Bike to work from dentist/buy lunch	Pump breast milk/ meeting	Play w/ S and friend	Go running with S
12PM	Bike to office	Pump breast milk/ email/finish submitting paper	Pump breast milk/ make lunch/emails	Pump breast milk/ eat lunch/email	Go to lunch with colleagues	Eat lunch from Chipotle with friend	Go running with S
12:30	Pump breast milk/ read emails/eat lunch/class prep	Admissions/eat lunch	Review lecture notes/ admissions	Discuss admissions w/ colleague	Meeting	Take nap with S	Emails/light work and housework
1	Teach class	Meeting on project	Teach class	Meet with MS student	Meeting	Take nap with S	Give S lunch
1:30	Teach class	Meeting on project	Teach class	Meet with PhD student	Meeting	Take nap with S	Play with S
2	Teach class	Admissions/email	Teach class	Try to deal with budget problems - stressful	Meeting	Take nap with S	Give S a bath
2:30	Teach class	Admissions	Teach class	Research group meeting	Meeting	Take nap with S	Try to get S to nap
3	Teach class/walk to office hours	Admissions/ review lecture notes	Teach class/walk to office hours	Research group meeting	Meeting	Take nap with S	Take nap with S

	MONDAY	TUESDAY	WEDNESDAY	THURSDAY	FRIDAY	SATURDAY	SUNDAY
3:30	Office hours	Finalize lecture notes for Wed.	Office hours	Meet with students discuss budget; problem solved	Meeting	Feed S a snack	Take nap with S
4	Office hours, help students w/ homework	Pack up/drop off admission folders/ bike home	Office hours	Emails/flight check in/bike home	Meeting	Play w/ S/take S on a run	Take nap with S
4:30	Office hours, meet with colleague	Review grant proposal email	Office hours	Have snack/talk with friend staying with me	Meeting	Take S on a run	Take nap with S
5	Bike home/light housework	Play with S, cook him dinner	Bike home/light housework	Play with S/go on a short run with S in stroller	Meeting	Play w/ S	Read emails/get ready for dinner
5:30	Spend time with S; cook him dinner, play, take on walk	Play with S, cook him dinner	Make S dinner	Run with S in stroller	Transport to airport	Make S dinner/ feed S	Travel to restaurant
6	Spend time with S; cook him dinner, play, take on walk	Take S on a 4 mile run	Play with S	Fix S dinner/feed S	Eat dinner at airport with post doc	S is playing alone/ chores/talk to friend	Take research group to dinner
6:30	Spend time with S; cook him dinner, play, take on walk	Take S on a 4 mile run	Go running with S to watch trains	Light housework	Prep lecture notes	Give S a bath	Take research group to dinner
7	Give S bath	Give S bath	Give S snacks	Bathe S/prepare for bed	Prep lecture notes/board airplane	Put S to bed	Take research group to dinner
7:30	Put S to bed	Put S to bed	Give S bath/put to bed	Put S to bed/have Indian food dinner with friends	Prep lecture notes	Put S to bed	Take research group to dinner

	MONDAY	TUESDAY	WEDNESDAY	THURSDAY	FRIDAY	SATURDAY	SUNDAY
8	Light housework	Light housework	Work on presentation for next week's meeting	Dinner with friends	Prep lecture notes/work on presentation	Eat dinner with friends	Transport from restaurant to home
8:30	Answer emails	Answer emails	Lecture prep	Dinner with friends	Work on presentation	Eat dinner with friends	Give S bath and put to bed
9	Lecture notes prep	Buy mom and sister bday presents	Lecture prep	Dinner with friends	Land at airport, transport home	Work on presentation for Monday	Call with collaborator/ answer email
9:30	Lecture notes prep	Read book for lecture prep	Emails	Prepare house for cleaners to come tomorrow	Transport home	Go buy ice cream	Work on presentation for tomorrow
10	Read work paper	Read textbook for lecture prep	Emails	Prepare for trip tomorrow/enroll in fitness class	Say hi to S/eat a snack	Go buy ice cream	Work on presentation for tomorrow
10:30	Read work paper	Read textbook for lecture prep	Watch Netflix	Watch Netflix	Eat snack/talk to husband and friend staying with me	Work on lecture notes / email	Work on presentation for tomorrow
11	Emails	Watch Netflix	Sleep	Sleep	Watch Netflix/ sleep	Work on lecture notes/read workbook	Get ready for bed/ watch Netflix
11:30	Watch Netflix	Watch Netflix	Sleep	Sleep	Sleep	Read workbook/ watch Netflix	Watch Netflix
12AM	Watch Netflix	Watch Netflix	Sleep	Sleep	Sleep	Sleep	Sleep
12:30	Sleep	Sleep	Sleep	Sleep	Sleep	Sleep	Sleep
1	Sleep	Sleep	Sleep	Sleep	Sleep	Sleep	Sleep
1:30	Sleep	Sleep	Sleep	Sleep	Sleep	Sleep	Sleep
2	Sleep	Sleep	Sleep	Sleep	Sleep	Sleep	Sleep
2:30	Sleep	Sleep	Sleep	Sleep	Sleep	Sleep	Sleep

	MONDAY	TUESDAY	WEDNESDAY	THURSDAY	FRIDAY	SATURDAY	SUNDAY
3	Sleep	Sleep	Sleep	Sleep	Sleep	Sleep	Sleep
3:30	Sleep	Sleep	Sleep	Sleep	Sleep	Sleep	Sleep
4	Sleep	Sleep	Sleep	Sleep	Sleep	Sleep	Sleep
4:30	Sleep	Sleep	Sleep	Wake up and prepare to leave house	Sleep	Sleep	Sleep

traveling or had to leave for work. Waking up a mere twenty to twenty-five minutes before the usual alarm time can be enough to squeeze in a two-mile run. Put the morning shows on in front of you and you can do a workout in what could be kitchen puttering time.

As with the engineering professor, some women found ways to exercise with their children. A one-mile run with a jog stroller to the playground can be a fun excursion for everyone. You get a two-mile round-trip run, and maybe even some strength work if you attempt the monkey bars, and the kid gets to play. Paula Beck took horseback riding lessons with her kids on Saturday, and her family did a bike ride together on Sunday. Kimberli Jeter, the PYXERA executive who's profiled in chapter 5, scheduled her children's sports practices for the same night at the YMCA and then exercised while they were with their teams. We joined our Y for this reason as well. If my husband and I have to trade off running outside on weekends, each of us aiming to do just forty-five minutes can somehow eat up a whole afternoon. Our Y has child care, so we put the kids in the playroom, simultaneously dash off a 5K on our treadmills, and then we can all go for a family swim at the indoor pool together. There's even a water slide, and there is something particularly wonderful about being able to go down a water slide in January as you see snow falling outside.

A few women worked out at lunch, particularly those who had scheduled evening conference calls. I didn't see too many workouts during what single childless people think of as prime gym time, five to eight p.m. People might take one evening class per week (Beck's log shows a YMCA trip on Monday night). One hospital development executive ran on her home treadmill at six p.m. predinner, and others sometimes exercised in the space of time before day care pickup or before a sitter needed to go home. Someone who worked eight a.m. to five p.m. most days might work eight a.m. to four p.m. two days, and go to the gym before heading home.

Late-night exercise doesn't work for many people, either because it keeps you from sleeping, or because you're already sipping a beer by the time it would be an option. If that doesn't describe you, though, it's a possibility. If your kids go down around 8:00 p.m., you can hop on a home treadmill or elliptical for thirty minutes as soon as you've said good night. If you don't go to bed until 10:30, you'll still have two hours after exercising to wind down.

If you've got a partner who's willing to stay home with the sleeping kids, you could go for a walk if it's light out or even if it's not (reflective clothing is pretty advanced these days). In a pinch, you could even run laps around the backyard.

Plenty of busy people do exercise. Other busy people, though, do not, or don't that much. Many want to, at least in theory, and in interviews with Mosaic Project participants, I heard the various reasons why exercise wasn't happening. Most of these explanations fell into the same 24-Hour Trap that limits the way people think about work. I'd suggest a time to exercise and people would tell me why that time wouldn't work *every single day.* I'd love to exercise, but *I'm not the kind of person who can just leave for an hour at lunch every day.* I'd love to exercise, but *I can't because I want to see my children in the evening.* Or, I'd love to exercise but *my husband stays home with the kids and I feel bad asking him to cover even longer hours.* People recognized that mornings might be a good time to fit exercise into their schedules, but couldn't stomach setting the alarm for five a.m. daily.

So here's an idea: don't set the alarm for five a.m. daily. Yes, daily rituals are nice, but they're not the only strategy for building a productive life. Stop looking for a time to exercise that is perfect *every single day.* Instead, look at the whole 168 hours that make up a week. Maybe just one day a week you can get up half an hour early, go for a half-hour run, and compress your morning routine by a few minutes to make up the time. Maybe on a different day, you can take a brisk walk at lunch. Then you run around the soccer field for thirty minutes on Saturday during your kid's ninety-minute practice. You exercise on Sunday at some point while the rest of the family is passed out on the couch in front of the TV, not requiring your presence. None of this has happened at the same time every day. But it's still occurred four times per week, which is not bad at all.

When it comes to time, the perfect is a disarmingly subversive enemy of the good. Sometimes it is easier to hold on to the story that "parents with big jobs like myself just can't exercise" than to recognize that you might be able to walk with a friend at lunch for thirty minutes twice a week, or walk your dog while on an internal conference call when you're working at home. I've recognized that even on days I can't run as much as I'd like, I can slip into my exercise clothes during a five-minute break somewhere, then slip out for a run during a half-hour break somewhere else. A twenty-five-minute run isn't going to have me winning races, but it is twenty-five minutes better than nothing, which is the default in our sedentary society. Even if you worked seventy hours a week and slept fifty-six, that would leave forty-two hours for other things, which is the equivalent of six hours per day. Anyone can fit in thirty minutes here and there around the margins of their lives. And to be honest, exercise doesn't just have to fit in around the margins. Unlike work, the sheer nature of exercise means that even if you do a lot of it, it's not going to consume much time because it can't. One woman who works at a tech company kept a log for me three weeks before she ran the Boston Marathon. That's right at the peak of training before the taper, when you're doing a twenty-mile-long run. For a Boston-caliber runner, a twenty-mile training run takes around three hours. The other runs that week clocked in closer to an hour. All told, she devoted just a bit over ten hours to physical activity. The average American watches ten hours of TV in about three days.

The happiest people know that in the mosaics of our lives, there is space for both work and family, and sleep and our own interests. If these interests improve our health, all the better. I even saw a handful of sports leagues on time logs. Playing softball or soccer is an excellent way to combine exercise with friends and score a great deal of fun. One single (Canadian) mother played in a ladies' curling league on Monday nights, and curled in a mixed league, which alternated on Friday evenings and Sunday afternoons. "I normally take the kids to the curling club with me when I curl, as long as it is an early game," she told me. She watches her nine-year-old's games and he watches hers. She called hers a "curling crazy family," but I don't think it's crazy. She worked more than fifty hours and slept fifty-seven, but there was still plenty of space for fun, too. She wasn't talking about sleep, or her sports passions, the way a starving man might talk about food.

Instead, she'd arranged her life to get her fill.

.
.
.
.
.
.

CHAPTER 8

Savor Space

I don't know what it is about Wednesdays. There is something to the "hump day" image that you're struggling up the steepest part of the summit; on the Mosaic logs, that's the day people worked the most and slept the least. Alicia Meulensteen certainly had a busy Wednesday during the February week she logged (p. 232). As her husband, baby, and three-year-old slept, she woke around 5:00 a.m. to pump milk and get her gym clothes on. By 5:45 a.m., she was out the door to go to spin class a few blocks from her New York City home. She came back by 7:00 a.m. to get the baby and her three-year-old ready. By 8:40 the family was in transit, with her husband bringing the kids to day care and Meulensteen, an executive at a major nonprofit, hopping on the subway to head to her midtown office. She was booked in meetings for much of the day. She left a bit before 5:00 to head home for the evening routine: playtime, dinner, bath, books, bed. She was in charge of the baby; her husband took the three-year-old. She got the baby down before 8:00 p.m. but, like most nights, the three-year-old took a bit longer. She heard her husband still wrangling him through his bedtime routine.

So, what should she do with the uncertain quantity of time until he finished? Clean the house? Sort the mail? "I'd be just kind of waiting around," Meulensteen tells me. "So I thought maybe I should use that time." On that particular Wednesday night, as she does once a week or so, she headed out the door to the little nail salon around the corner in their TriBeCa neighborhood. "They're open until nine thirty or ten," she says. "I'll get my nails done, I'll bring a book, something to read and kind of hang out for an hour, then walk home." Since it's two minutes away, "I come home and I haven't really lost any time." She and her husband can then watch TV on the couch together before going to bed. On that busy Wednesday, counting her exercise class, manicure trip, and TV time, she scored at least 2.5 hours of grown-up-oriented personal time, doing things she wanted to do. This time didn't come in bits and pieces. It came in reasonable chunks. "I'm a big introvert and need alone time to recharge," she explains. "I make a point of being up before the family so I can unapologetically do my own thing in or out of the house." The weekly manicure means she can "just zone out without anyone needing a thing from me." It's a conscious choice, and "I'm kind of loving this," she says.

●

Meulensteen, busy as she is, has space in her life. Yet it is an article of faith for many of us that busy people have no leisure time. Between the demands of work and family, free time must come only in bits of "time confetti," to use *Washington Post* reporter Brigid Schulte's memorable image. In 2010, when Schulte publicized John Robinson's claim that mothers had around thirty hours of leisure time per week, Dr. Phil had the sociology professor on his show to defend this statistic to viewers. Judging by the audience members' reactions, it was clear that most didn't just think Robinson was wrong. They were offended at the suggestion that they had any free time at all.

This struck me as strange. Watching the *Dr. Phil* show is pretty much the definition of a leisure time activity. Yet the audience members no doubt believed they were beleaguered. They were busy. They were starved for time.

I've been trying to figure out why we cling to this narrative, and often react so negatively—sometimes complaining on Facebook, another quintessential leisure time pursuit—to any insinuation that life is not a death march from dawn to midnight. While many Mosaic Project participants were matter-of-fact about their leisure time, noting manicures and get-togethers with friends, others had bought into this worldview. We have stories we like to tell

	MONDAY	TUESDAY	WEDNESDAY	THURSDAY	FRIDAY	SATURDAY	SUNDAY
5AM	Sleep	5:25 awake and out of bed. Put on gym clothes. Feed cat, get coffee. Pump milk for baby. Check personal email, Facebook	5:05 awake and out of bed. Put on gym clothes. Feed cat, get coffee. Pump milk for baby. Check personal email, Facebook, read dining section of NYT	5:15 awake and out of bed. Put on gym clothes, feed cat, coffee, pump milk	Sleep	Sleep	Sleep
5:30	Up, put on gym clothes, coffee, feed cat			Feed baby	Sleep	Sleep	Sleep
6	Get ready to leave—baby is up. Go feed baby	Trainer	Spin class!	Trainer at gym	Sleep	Sleep	Sleep
6:30	At the gym	At the gym	Still spinning	At the gym	Wake up, feed baby	Sleep	Wake up, feed baby, get baby dressed
7	7:15 home. Feed baby again	7:10 home. Feed baby. Get baby dressed	Home. Chat with son and husband. Shower, dress, makeup. Start breakfast	Home. Feed baby. Shower, dress, makeup	Get baby dressed. Hand baby off to Mom. Shower, dress, makeup	Wake up, feed baby	
7:30	7:45 shower, dressed, get breakfast ready	7:35 shower, dressed, get breakfast ready	Breakfast with son and husband. Wake up baby at 7:45. Feed baby	7:45 cook breakfast	Older child is up. Get him dressed. Breakfast for him 7:50	Kids up, breakfast	Older child is up. Get him dressed. Breakfast for him at 8
8	8:15 eat breakfast at the counter, quickly	Breakfast for everyone	Dress baby, pack day care bags, brush teeth. Feed baby one more time	Breakfast for everyone. Feed baby again. Finish dressing, brush teeth, pack lunch bags	Eat own breakfast in between feeding of baby, diaper changes, packing lunch bags	8:15 leave for spin class	

	MONDAY	TUESDAY	WEDNESDAY	THURSDAY	FRIDAY	SATURDAY	SUNDAY
8:30	8:40 everyone out the door. In office 8:50. Unpack lunch, change shoes	Out the door with baby to day care (I do drop off today; son goes swimming). Leave day care 8:50	8:40 everyone out the door. 8:45-8:55 commute on subway	8:40 everyone out the door. 8:45-8:55 subway time. Listen to podcast	Everyone out the door 8:30. subway 8:35-8:45. At office 8:50	Spin class!	
9	Check calendar for the day, emails, call hotel to cancel reservation for conference	8:55 in subway. At office 9:05. Unpack bags, check emails, calendar for day	At office. Check email. 9:15 sign invoices, check voicemail	At office. Make copy of meeting attendee list for boss, review emails and meeting calendar for the day	9:20-9:45 review data for upcoming appeal	Still spinning	Shower, dress, play with kids
9:30	9:45 pump milk for baby, start staff review	9:30-9:45 call	Pump milk, check personal email and social media. 9:50 review year-to-date mail costs	Database call	9:45-10 chat with direct reports	9:45 shower, get ready	
10	Work on review	Emails	Status meeting	Pump milk, check personal email	Pump milk for baby, checked LinkedIn invites and messages	Play with kids	Lay out kids' clothes for the week, pack sheets and blankets for day care
10:30	Phone call	Pump milk for baby. 10:45 sign invoices		Benchmarking meeting	Phone call with audit. 10:40 ordered lunch online, 10:45 review January numbers and write notes for boss		Take older child to community center
11	11 eat lunch at desk and read deck for meeting. 11:30 meeting with colleague	11-11:15 meeting with boss	Discussion, 11:15 staff check-in call			Playground and farmers' market	

	MONDAY	TUESDAY	WEDNESDAY	THURSDAY	FRIDAY	SATURDAY	SUNDAY
11:30		11:15-11:30 call with direct report					
12PM		Lunch at desk, read white papers	12:15 lunch, read HBR articles			Lunch for everyone	12:30 lunch
12:30	12:45 pump milk for baby. Eat some pineapple and check social media		12:30 stop in at meeting, catch up with industry peers. 12:45 pump milk. Emails	12:45 pump milk	Pump milk for baby	Playing with kids	
1	Meeting 1-3	Pump milk for baby, read corporate culture docs	Strategic plan work	January revenue review	Mental break		
1:30		Meeting with boss	Call to Mom	Vendor call, meeting scheduling	Work on team-building plans		
2		Development leadership meeting	Staff check in	Benchmarking			
2:30			2:45 memo to HR		Office cat visit		Pack lunch for son for tomorrow
3	Meeting with consultant: staff changes 3-4	Corporate partner chat/office cat visit. 3:45 pump milk for baby. Call husband to discuss day care pickup and dinner plans	Meeting		2:45 database plan review		Mom leaves, husband comes home
3:30				Staff chat	3:30 pump milk		
4	Chat with colleague 4-4:10; check email 4:15		Call/pump milk	Pump milk			

	MONDAY	TUESDAY	WEDNESDAY	THURSDAY	FRIDAY	SATURDAY	SUNDAY
4:30	Pump milk for baby, wrap up emails. Leave office at 4:50		4:50 head out	4:45 leave office	Next week project planning/4:45 leave		
5	Home, change, play with kids and cook dinner, bathe kids, books, bed	Leave at 5	Home, change, play with kids and cook dinner, bathe kids, books, bed	Drop off bags, go to day care to pick up kids. Home, cook dinner, get kids ready for bed	Home, change, play with kids, cook dinner, bathe kids, books, bed	Cook dinner, play with kids, dinner, bathe kids, books, bed	
5:30		Home, change, play with kids and cook dinner, bathe kids, books, bed					5:45 cook dinner
6							6:15 dinner for everyone
6:30							
7							7:15 start bath time and bedtime drill for baby
7:30							
8	8:15 kids asleep, make son's lunch for tomorrow	8 baby asleep. Make son's lunch for tomorrow. Intervene in some bedtime drama	Baby asleep/8:15 head out to get manicure and read				8:15 baby asleep
8:30	Send meeting invites to team for upcoming review; check work email	8:25 head out and read a business book I've been neglecting		Kids asleep. pack lunches for tomorrow	Kids asleep. chat with Mother, visiting	Kids asleep. Clean up kitchen, go through mail	
9	Watch Olympics 9–9:45		Home. Pack lunches for tomorrow, get out gym clothes	Chat with Mother, visiting	Sleep	Watch Olympics	Catch up with husband, home from travel

	MONDAY	TUESDAY	WEDNESDAY	THURSDAY	FRIDAY	SATURDAY	SUNDAY
9:30	9:45 bath, read magazines	Home. Olympics on TV	Watch some TV with husband, chat	Bedtime for me	Bedtime		Take much needed bath, get ready for bed
10						Get ready for bed	
10:30	Sleep	Sleep	Sleep	Sleep	Sleep	Bed	Bed
11	Sleep	Sleep	Sleep	Sleep	Sleep	Sleep	Sleep
11:30	Sleep	Sleep	Sleep	Sleep	Sleep	Sleep	Sleep
12AM	Sleep	Sleep	Sleep	Sleep	Sleep	Sleep	Sleep
12:30	Sleep	Sleep	Sleep	Sleep	Sleep	Sleep	Sleep
1	Sleep	Sleep	Sleep	Sleep	Sleep	Sleep	Sleep
1:30	Feed baby	Feed baby			Feed baby	Feed baby	Feed baby
2	Sleep	Sleep	Sleep	Sleep	Sleep	Sleep	Sleep
2:30	Sleep	Sleep	Sleep	Sleep	Sleep	Sleep	Sleep
3	Baby awake/feed baby; son wakes up give him water and tuck in; baby wants food again	Sleep	Sleep	Sleep	Sleep	Sleep	Older child up, nightmare
3:30	Sleep	Sleep	Sleep	Sleep	Sleep	Sleep	Sleep
4	Try to go back to sleep	Feed baby	Sleep	Sleep	Sleep	Baby awake and upset, 4-4:45	Feed baby
4:30	Sleep	Sleep	Sleep	Feed baby	Feed baby	Sleep	Sleep

ourselves, stories that may have arisen out of something that was true at one point, or at least closer to true, and so we choose which data points to see. If our time logs show leisure, and yet our story is that we lack leisure, we might claim various instances are just exceptions, or something we had to do because life is so crazy, and we're stealing it and it's rare. People would write, "This never happens" on their logs next to some leisurely pursuit and yet, obviously, it did.

Everyone in the Mosaic Project had leisure time. Most people watched at least some TV. Most people read. People had time for friends and neighborhood barbecues. Even the women working north of sixty hours per week had leisure time: shoe shopping, parties, watching movies.

Did these things happen as much as people hoped? Probably not. Nor was everyone mentally present during her downtime. Humans invent all sorts of ways to make themselves miserable. You can be lying on a massage table and thinking about your grocery list. But that is a different story from having no leisure time at all. Leisure time is a choice, and celebrating life's fullness means not only making leisure a priority, but acknowledging that it is happening, and relishing one's own sweet time in the nail salon when it does. This chapter looks at how to recognize and savor space—that ultimate source of contentment and sustainability in full lives.

.

I know, from tracking my hours, that I have leisure time. Sometimes it comes in big, obvious dollops, like an adults-only trip to Sonoma, California, that featured tours of vineyard after beautiful vineyard and wine flights at noon. But more commonly it looks like a half hour spent reading a magazine on the porch while the kids are playing inside. It can mean meeting a friend for a run or watching *The Daily Show* with my husband. As the kids get older, I can do things that feel like real leisure while I'm with them: watching a speedy, three-actor version of *Macbeth* at a Maryland festival over Memorial Day weekend, or taking in the fireworks on the Fourth of July.

I am far from the only one with space in my life. When the first logs came in, as I was trying to figure out if a project like this would work, *The Bachelor* had just finished a dramatic season. It became a running joke for me when I'd see yet another time log featuring this program. Sometime later, I recounted this to a friend who has three young kids and a rather intense job herself. She laughed, then later confessed that she had watched *The Bachelorette*.

That said, women in the Mosaic Project did not watch a lot of TV. On the logs where I could calculate it, TV time averaged 4.4 hours per week.* By contrast, according to the American Time Use Survey, employed mothers with kids under age six watch about 11 hours per week of TV as a primary activity, and those with kids ages six to seventeen watch 13 hours. An ATUS project that looked at married mothers who worked full-time found that they watched 9.7 to 10.6 hours of TV per week, depending on the age of their youngest child. Since these "average" women worked around 35 hours a week, versus 44 for the Mosaic Project, the lower TV totals mean you can account for a big chunk of the difference in hours available to work right there. The 4.4 hours I calculated may actually overstate the normal state of affairs. I collected the bulk of my logs during February and March 2014, months that featured the Winter Olympics and the annual NCAA basketball tournament. These events draw in people who are not necessarily regular TV watchers, to say nothing of the Super Bowl and the Oscars.

This approach of minimizing TV has a lot going for it if you want to build a full life that leaves enough space for meaningful leisure. TV is fun, but it's not that fun. Scales of human enjoyment place it somewhere in the middle. It's better than commuting or getting your car repaired, but it's less fun than socializing or sex. So if you're sitting on the couch with your spouse at the end of the day, and wind up watching TV until you're too tired for anything else, a rational person could calculate that there's a better way to optimize happiness: turn the TV off half an hour earlier, and do something more enjoyable with that time instead.

Reading scores better than TV on scales of human enjoyment too, although, as with TV, it scores lower than sex. The Mosaic logs showed 3.9 hours of reading per week, or about 33 minutes per day. The ATUS finds that the average American reads, as a leisure activity, for about 19 minutes on weekdays and 20 minutes on weekends, though this averages in a lot of zeros. Parents

---

* Of the first 143 complete logs, 137 were detailed enough to figure out TV and other specific leisure pursuits. A few people simply labeled evenings as "family time" or "leisure time" and didn't specify their specific leisure activities.

read for a few minutes with kids as well, though also averaging in a lot of zeros. An ATUS report from a few years back found that only 21.3 percent of married, stay-at-home moms with kids under age six read to or with their children on their diary day.

On the whole, reading and TV showed little correlation, inverse or otherwise, though the fifteen logs showing more than 1 hour a day of reading (7 hours a week) showed 3.4 hours of TV a week, slightly less than the overall average. For many of these women, reading occupied what could be TV time before bed, or on weekend afternoons. A few jacked up their totals by listening to audiobooks on their commutes. One woman read for 17 hours during her diary week, thanks in part to her hour-long commute and the 8 hours of audiobooks she devoured during that time. That said, even minus the commute time, she clocked in at more than twice the average. People who like to read like to read. Wendy Rose, a consultant who lives in New Jersey, read for 15 hours during her diary week. She explains it this way: "I am a voracious reader and have been since I was a kid, with my nose stuck in a book on every car ride, during every vacation, in every spare minute." She vastly prefers books to TV. When her son, now a teen, was diagnosed with a rare genetic condition early in life, her reading took a hit as she dealt with his medical care. He's doing well now, and she is "so happy to once again have been able to read for pleasure, and no doubt am trying to make up for lost time." She's in an adventurous book club (they became beta readers for my novel) and they trade recommendations and books. In a good month, "I probably read three or four novels, depending on their length and my energy level. I would say that at least four nights out of seven, I fall asleep reading and wake up when my husband is trying to get my glasses off my face without waking me up."

Reading and TV were far from the only leisure time activities. There was the highbrow: an opera, a play. There was the surprisingly agrarian: "Pick oranges to make drinks." Several women managed to visit the spa. Among the domestic pursuits I found: quilting, knitting (often while watching TV), gardening. One woman went to a Friday night neighborhood party; others invited friends over to watch a game. People did devotionals, sometimes as part of a morning routine.

As I interviewed women about their time choices, I found that making leisure happen involved managing two sides of the equation. I refer to these as "demand" and "supply." You need demand for turning time into leisure, meaning there is something you want to be doing with that time that is compelling enough that you will ignore your inbox and the laundry. Then you need a "supply" of hours (or at least minutes) available to do it in.

You'd think the demand side—having a good idea of what you want to do with your leisure time—would be easy. And yet precisely because we presume we don't have time, we don't think this matter through. Leisure time appears and we are not prepared to seize it. We fritter it away with activities like, as one woman wrote on her log, "Hanging out around the house (family gone), ate Girl Scout cookies, read FB, Twitter, let dog in and out 5 times . . ."

I'm guessing you don't work from the assumption that you have thirty hours of leisure time per week. But let's suppose that you did. If you had thirty hours to spend on personally pleasurable pursuits, what would you do with that time?

I've been pondering this question recently. For years, I sang in a choir that I made time for weekly, including for four years after I had kids, and I enjoyed it immensely. Singing, and perhaps playing the piano too, could both be on my thirty-hour list. I might get together with friends for drinks. I'd have more dinner parties. I'd go to more choral concerts and dance performances and professional basketball games. Years ago, as a girl, I built a dollhouse out of a kit I got for Christmas. I filled it with furniture that I carefully saved up for. I'd likely enjoy that now too. I like to bake. I love to read mindless magazines, particularly when they feature stories about weight loss. For whatever reason, I love sitting down with a glass of wine and some dark chocolate, and reading a story about how someone else lost fifty pounds, probably not by drinking wine and eating desserts. I like reading poetry. I like writing poetry. I'd like to try a longer bike ride one of these days. I live close enough to several art museums that I really should visit more often.

Whatever your favorite activities are, knowing what they are, and keeping them at the top of your mind, helps you take advantage of the pockets of time we all have in our lives. Time is elastic. It stretches to accommodate what we need or want to do with it.

I saw that best on a time log from a financial planner who came home one night to find her water heater had exploded all over her basement. If you've ever experienced this, or know someone who has, you know that it is a giant sopping mess. This woman spent some hours that night dealing with the disaster. The next day, she had to deal with getting plumbers out to the house as she worked from home between their visits. The next day she called in a professional cleaning crew and got them started on this project. All of this was being recorded on her time log and consumed about seven hours of her week.

This is a reasonable chunk of time. Finding seven hours a week requires finding an extra hour a day, a claim deemed so lofty that magazines put that line on the cover. I suspect if I'd asked this busy woman at the start of the week if she could find seven hours to read *Mrs. Dalloway* or train for a triathlon, she probably would have said what most of us would have said: no. And yet, when there was something she urgently needed to do, she found those hours.

Perhaps you have noticed this too. If you're deeply absorbed in a book, you make magical amounts of time appear as you binge-read to see what happens. While most Americans don't read that much as a matter of habit, millions of grown-ups found time to read the seven Harry Potter books. Some 27.7 million copies of *The Hunger Games* books sold in 2012, and not all of them to teenagers or retirees with time on their hands. When you have something you want to read, you get up on Saturday morning and read while the kids watch cartoons. You read late at night. You decide not to go grocery shopping and read during that time instead. A page-turner, or a TV series like *House of Cards* that inspires binge watching, answers the demand side of the equation. Indeed, if you think you have no leisure time, you might try starting a binge-worthy series, and see where that hidden time may be.

People who make time for leisure become adept at boosting the demand side of the equation. If you want to read more, you can make sure there are always piles of books around that you want to read. When you've got lots of enticing books you want to read, you're marginally more inclined to pick up a book during what could be leisure time but could not be, too. You can take the same approach for other hobbies as well. I recently hauled my keyboard out of storage, bought a stand and a bench, and stuck it in my office. Seeing it boosts demand to sit down and play through my old sheet music. You can take this too far, of course. Houses are cluttered with the detritus of hobbies that people thought they would pursue and then did not. I'd recommend not shelling out a lot of cash until you're sure the habit will stick. But sometimes the difference between making time to scrapbook and not making time to scrapbook is having a table you pass by regularly with your scrapbooking material there. It is waiting for you, beguiling you to not turn on the TV or your laptop tonight.

The second side of the equation—the supply side—is more straightforward. To make leisure part of your life, you need to make space for it. In terms of sheer volume, the time is there. I'm inclined to believe something around the thirty-hours figure for the average parent, though it's likely lower for the Mosaic women just because they work more than most people. While studying the numbers, the researcher I hired to do some calculations pointed out where the lack-of-leisure narrative may stem from: those hard early years when we're adjusting to parenthood. Women in the Mosaic Project with kids under age two didn't work less or sleep significantly less than other women, but they spent about a third less time on exercise, a third less time reading, and 40 percent less time watching TV than women with older children. They didn't spend zero time on these activities, but they didn't spend a lot of time on them either, probably because much time that could be spent on leisure was spent on the active physical care of their kids.

The good news is that children grow up. They may need more emotional tending later on, but they need less physical tending. Time available for reading, TV, and exercise increases when the children can be sent to a basement playroom on a Saturday afternoon and trusted to entertain themselves.

The problem is that we form our understanding of parenthood when the kids are little. This makes sense; the baby and toddler years are a searing season. When things are seared deep, narratives become hard to change, especially if they become part of our identities. That would be fine, except failing to recognize where leisure time might be means we use it mindlessly. Instead of going outside to savor a wintry sunset, we take random online polls that attempt to quantify how little time we have for ourselves. Our tendency is not to say, "Hey, I have some leisure time, even if it's not as much as I want." Our tendency is to subtract our leisure time from others' and focus on the difference. If you are watching about three hours of TV a week in a world in which the average person watches north of twenty hours, you can feel as if, by comparison, you have no leisure time at all.

So where does leisure time occur? Some does happen in short spurts of time but that doesn't mean you can't use it. Anne Bogel, the blogger known online as Modern Mrs. Darcy, devours books at the rate of twelve per month. She told me, "I read in the pockets of time that other people use to check their phones and their e-mail, again." She'll read while waiting for food to heat up in the microwave. Even if that's just five minutes a day, that buys you thirty-five minutes of extra reading time per week. She'll listen to audiobooks while running, and finishes another two books per month that way. There's more about using bits of time in the next chapter, but it might help to specifically brainstorm leisure activities that you can dip in and out of quickly. Cross-word puzzles might fit in this category. Crocheting might too, more so than creative pursuits that require more setup, like painting.

Other leisure time comes in big chunks. Even the busiest people have these potential chunks, but making the most of them requires making a conscious choice to use them and not to spoil the opportunity with random e-mail checks and social media puttering, or errands. With Mosaic housework and errand totals ranging from two hours a week to more than twenty-five hours a week, there's a lot of room to play around with here.

Here's how you can make the time:

Look at your workday. My favorite approach to enjoying blocks of leisure is to build some of them in during traditional work hours. If you have young kids, you have child care during this time, so that makes these hours a reasonable option. More important, people *already* engage in vast quantities of leisure activities at work. That's why *BuzzFeed* and *The Huffington Post* are the phenomena they are. The reason we choose these leisure activities is that they're fun, and yet we can fool ourselves and our colleagues into believing that we're still working. After all, if you're looking at a computer or smartphone, it's work, right?

As a blogger myself, I don't mind people reading my musings at work, but let's be honest about it. Better to acknowledge that this is leisure time, and ask yourself if Pinterest is really where you'd like to be spending it. Women in the Mosaic Project had quite a bit of control of their time, which should at least partially counter the need to be seen at a computer (to say nothing of those who worked from home regularly). If you normally surf the Web for half an hour after lunch, you can meet a friend once a week for a longer lunch instead. You can go for a walk when you'd normally take a social media break in the afternoon. One physician wrote on her log that she "played hooky" during a slow time between appointments by heading over to Starbucks and relaxing. A few women observed that lovely British tradition of teatime. If you work from home, you can go on a bike ride during breaks. This just requires making a conscious choice not to clean the kitchen during breaks instead.

A number of employers at least claim to support volunteering, and so if you'd like to volunteer more, you could look into during-the-day options. (Volunteering may not be actual "leisure" per se, but because most people find it meaningful, it can certainly qualify as enjoyable time.) One engineer took time during the day to go judge a math contest. An accountant took a few hours to help a nonprofit with its books during the day. Roping in team members might turn this into a group bonding experience, and one that would be more fun than a contrived ropes course.

Take a day off. Another option for blocking in leisure is to strategically take a personal day, or at least a personal half day. In Sheryl Sandberg's *Lean In*, she recounts an observation from Larry Kanarek, who managed the Washington, D.C., office of McKinsey while Sandberg was there. He talked to everyone who was quitting and, over time, realized that "people quit for one reason only: they were burnt out, tired of working long hours and traveling. Larry said he could understand the complaint, but what he could not understand was that all the people who quit—every single one—had unused vacation time. Up until the day they left, they did everything McKinsey asked of them before deciding that it was too much. Larry implored us to exert more control over our careers. He said McKinsey would never stop making demands on our time, so it was up to us to decide what we were willing to do. It was our responsibility to draw the line."

If you're entitled to time off, take it. You don't win points in the game of life for working through vacation and personal days if you wind up burned out as a result. The single mother from the previous chapter who had a rough week of kid wake-ups took two hours to sit in Panera by herself on a Friday morning just to recharge. A woman whose travel consumed part of her weekend took Monday off as a trade. A biotech project manager occasionally took a half day to go to the mall when she needed to decompress. She wasn't going to be getting much done at work, so it was better to realize that and go relax in the mall food court than sit at her desk.

Extend your child care a bit. Tacking on an additional hour or two once or twice a week can create space for personal pursuits. If your sitter stays until 6:30, you can leave work at 4:30 and meet friends for a drink. Another option, if you're normally the person doing pickup, is to have someone else, perhaps your partner or a sitter, do pickup once a week and use that time for relaxing or socializing.

If you're the extroverted sort, hanging out with friends one night a week can help you feel like you still have an individual identity beyond employee and parent. One woman in the Mosaic Project had a regular sitter on both Friday and Saturday evenings after her young kids went to bed. She could go out with friends one night and her husband the other. In the grand scheme of already paying for full-time child care, those six to eight hours weren't that much of an additional expense, but it meant she had almost the same sort of social life she would have had in her younger, child-free days.

Embrace your nights. I turned on the TV around ten o'clock the other night. The channel was set to Nick Jr., which my kids watch. All of a sudden, a strange thing happened. The TV told young viewers to go to bed, and then switched over to new programming called "NickMom," featuring stand-up comedy, sitcoms, etc. As Nickelodeon says of this programming, "Since being a mom is a 24/7/365 job, we're gonna give you the break you deserve. Get your daily dose of funny photos, funny videos, funny stories and funny shows created just for you. Really, where else are you going to laugh at last-minute diorama projects, sleep deprivation and what to say at the goldfish's funeral all in one place? (You're welcome.)"

Nickelodeon has obviously spent quite a bit of time analyzing the moms of young children who are its primary customers, and realized that late-night hours are often prime mommy "me time." While running three to four hours of programming each night aimed at people who claim to have no leisure time is somewhat humorous, the programming does take advantage of an important insight: young kids generally go to bed before adults. If your kids go down at 8:00 p.m., and you go to bed at 10:30 p.m., you could work for an hour, do something fun for an hour, then spend half an hour winding down. TV is one option for this time, but you could also read a book, call a friend, carve out time for crafting, or, like Meulensteen, slip out for a little personal time if your partner is there. If he's happy enough to watch TV—if probably not NickMom—then it really doesn't matter what you do.

Get smart about kid activities. Modern parenting seems to require shuttling kids around to endless events. Fortunately, some creative parents have figured out how to use the time during kids' sports and activities for their own pursuits. Partly this is about reframing the situation, turning what could be a dull activity into a positive one. One mother, whose son had an intense soccer schedule, noted, "I'm inside all day, I love just being outside, and getting the fresh air." She also made friends with a group of other soccer moms and reported that "three of us moms, we'll get sushi, and grab it to go and get a bottle of wine and sit in the car." Even if you do want to watch every second of every game, there is often time before games or during breaks that doesn't require your presence. "It depends on our mood and how much each of us has to do," she reports, but when these parties happen, "those are great nights."

Sign up for your own activities. Adults, just like kids, can benefit from extracurricular enrichment. Lynda Bascelli (from chapter 6) took guitar lessons and played for 2.5 hours during the course of the week. Wendy Rose took a mosaic making class. "I have been wanting to learn to make them for years and years," she told me. She sent me an e-mail with evidence of her work. "What I am finding is that it is a wonderful escape and 'gets me out of my head.' The 3 hour class flies by in a blink and I am also now finding some time to work on a mosaic project at home and have lots of ideas about others." This state of "flow"—when you are so absorbed in a project that time seems to stand still—is associated with peak happiness. Anytime you can seek it out, it's good to do so. Rose reports that making mosaics is "making me more creative at work. Maybe most of all, I can tell it is making me happier."

Turn travel time into me time. Business travel can be wearying and lonely, but the dirty little secret is that it's also a great time to catch up on sleep, order from room service, visit the hotel spa, call friends, and watch TV that you don't have to justify to anyone else. On a business trip to New York, one woman managed to go out with friends and get her hair done in addition to doing the work she was being paid to do. While at a conference, another woman went for a hike. With careful planning, you might be able to hit a gallery between your last meeting and dinner, or start your first meeting late enough that there's time for a run by some famous landmark before you start working. Or you might be jet-lagged enough that you're up by 4:30 a.m., leaving plenty of space for me time, if not the space you might find ideal. There's more on maximizing travel time in the next chapter.

Think through your weekends. Even with using all these techniques, there's only so much leisure time available during the workweek. That makes weekends critical to enjoying a full life. There are sixty hours between six p.m. Friday and six a.m. Monday; you're probably awake for around thirty-six of them. While planning leisure time sounds like a contradiction, we have a tendency to do things that we plan, especially if they involve commitments to other people. If you and a friend have plans to go to a museum together at ten a.m. on Saturday, you're more likely to do it than if it's just you thinking that maybe you'd like to visit sometime. Overcoming that initial resistance to planning can massively increase the amount of fun in your life.

Rama Karve, a software engineer, told me that she wanted to spend her weekend time better. "Usually we just spend it aimlessly, doing chores/going to the neighborhood park, etc.," she says. The weekend she logged, however, was fantastic. It was the week of the Hindu New Year, and she, her husband, and their two-and-a-half-year-old son spent lots of time with friends—going out for lunch twice, cooking special dishes, and attending a potluck party on Saturday night. What made that weekend successful was "having something that I actually know is going to happen, that I didn't have to think about it and it was already planned," she says. With a few anchor events on the calendar, "the rest of the time I could completely do nothing and I'd be okay. I'd feel accomplished for that weekend."

Not all weekends can be major holidays, but there is a big space between planning a lot and planning nothing. Like many of us, "during the week I'm all focused on the week," says Karve. "Then I come to Friday and I'm like, whoops! I didn't plan for the weekend." Her husband would plan major family vacations, she told me, but wasn't much into weekend strategizing. On the other hand, "he never says he doesn't want to do stuff," so this was less of an obstacle than if he refused to leave the house.

One option? Karve's log showed that common leisure woe—"the nightly time sink," as she put it—after her son went to bed. "Unless I have work stuff lined up or am in the middle of a book, that time goes into the Internet black hole." She could build a pipeline of books on her Kindle. But one night a week, perhaps Wednesday, she could spend fifteen minutes thinking about what she wanted to do that weekend, and making any necessary arrangements, such as purchasing tickets and making reservations. Then she could relax, and anticipate her fun to come. She tried the strategy, and after a few months was regularly making time on Wednesday evenings to plan her weekends. "An unexpected aspect of this is that although I put an entry in my calendar for nine p.m., I get the reminder on Wednesday morning," she told me. "I find that the reminder makes me subconsciously think about the weekend during the day, so by the time nine p.m. rolls around I usually have a good idea of what I want to plan. My weekends have been way more productive as a result."

I tend to find that planning three to five fun activities—and I mean fun for grown-ups—per weekend is the right balance between a weekend that feels wasted and a weekend that feels draining. That could mean one activity Friday night, one Saturday during the day, one Saturday night, and one Sunday. These plans need not be elaborate; it could mean renting a movie you want to see on Friday, going for a short family bike ride Saturday morning, getting together with friends on Saturday evening, and going to church on Sunday. That's just a few hours of your thirty-six waking ones, leaving many more hours for downtime. For a few minutes of planning, you set yourself up to make memories over the weekend, and you don't lose the whole weekend to chores and puttering. Getting that right mix is what makes a weekend feel rejuvenating, so you hit Monday ready to go.

Think different. One strategy for getting the most out of your 168 hours is to choose to recast time you're already spending on an activity as leisure time. One woman with young toddlers put this entry on her log: "Floor play with my twins. This is part leisure when I have a drink."

To me, one of the biggest dividends of my children growing older (before I plunged myself back into the baby stage) is being able to relax at my house when they are there with me. Ruth can go up and down stairs by herself, and can be trusted not to eat the Legos. She doesn't need constant supervision. One Saturday morning recently, I let all the kids watch cartoons while I sat and read a few articles in back issues of *The New Yorker.* I didn't particularly care about innovations in business class plane seats, or the architect overseeing the renovations on the National Aquarium. It was more for the sheer thrill of being able to do something without anyone tugging on my leg.

On too many logs, I saw this potential benefit of kids getting older turned into more chore and errand time. A four-year-old does want to play with you, so you do. A fourteen-year-old doesn't want to play with you, so you spend Saturday at Target or organizing the basement. The problem, as we saw in chapter 6, is that the chores will always be there. A woman who spent five hours on her 2013 time log organizing her basement told me, when I caught back up with her in 2014, that this chore was back on the list. The basement will always be a disaster.

The best way to find time for leisure is simply to claim it—to let the dishes sit in the sink while you read the paper on the porch, to take time for that art project or photo book despite whatever might be lurking in your inbox. Some people do this, and some don't, and looking at the variance in time logs, I cannot subscribe to the belief that there is something about modern life that makes us harried and maxed out. If we are, then it's time to examine our own choices and the scripts that are running through our heads. You don't become a better parent or employee by not enjoying your life. There are likely lots of options available to you that would make life more fun. Don't assume anyone is judging you, or actually cares, if you choose some of them.

In my interviews, I found that single mothers often handled this better than their partnered counterparts. If you have a partner, you may assume that you will trade off kid time and chores, or that your partner will know that you need two hours to yourself on a weekend. Then he doesn't recognize that, because he can't read your mind, and you feel unhappy and use that potential uncontaminated leisure time checking Facebook instead of browsing in a bookstore, which is what you really wanted to do. Single parents know they cannot make this assumption and so must plan for anything they need to do that can't involve the kids.

Mothers who are their children's sole means of financial support were quite straightforward about this with work. One woman was going up for tenure shortly after the two daughters she adopted on her own came home, and she recognized that it was in her new family's best interest that she get it. "We have to eat," she said. Rather than agonize over part-time schedules and flexible options, she put the girls in full-time day care as soon as her leave was up. It paid off; she received tenure shortly thereafter, and then had a lot more flexibility with her schedule. She could confine her work largely to school hours. Single moms learn to take this same no-nonsense approach for personal time too. A single parent of young kids knows that unless she plans for care, she will never be able to get her hair cut.

This is just life, and there is no point feeling guilty about it. One single mother had a four-year-old son with significant special needs. Upon moving to Canada, she learned that her community had programs for "respite care" for caregivers. The financial upsides of subsidized care were nice, she noted, "but the psychological impact is even greater." It's a validation that "you're under somewhat extraordinary pressure, and you need to take time for yourself to be a better parent. It really changed my approach." She got together with friends for a spa night during the week she logged. She told me that her son's nanny came for a few hours on Sunday so she could have coffee with her sister. Getting a three-hour break made a huge difference, and because she knew it was coming, and knew it was precious time, she planned for it and used it well.

You don't need to be a single parent to take this same approach to leisure. You just need to be mindful about it. You can block in the time, think about what you'd like to do with it, and then savor the time as it's happening.

Of course, this savoring brings up the issue of muddled mental states. People sometimes look at time logs that show obvious leisure (surfing the Web and looking at Facebook) and say, "Maybe, but I didn't really enjoy it." It was passing the time or coping with stress. The person was watching TV, but her mind was on that difficult conversation happening the next morning.

Indeed, such ruminations are one reason I suspect people estimate longer workweeks than their time logs show them working. One woman told me, "I'm thinking about work constantly. Even if I'm cooking dinner or at the gym, I'm thinking through an approach to solving a problem or a way in which I need to be prepared to work on something when I'm actually at my desk. In this way, I 'work' much more than forty hours a week, though I am not physically present in front of a computer for all of it."

I will admit that I'm somewhat skeptical of this reasoning. If your mind wanders to an argument you had with your partner during a conference call, you don't mentally subtract this from your work total. That said, I know people do think about work outside of work a lot. I also don't think that thinking about work outside of work is a bad thing. Inspiration can strike at any time. Many people get their best ideas while driving or in the shower. But if ruminating about work interferes with being able to relax, and with savoring space in your life, it can be a problem, and unfortunately telling yourself to stop thinking about work is about as effective as telling yourself to stop thinking about a kangaroo. (You know what just came to mind.)

Instead, there are a few approaches that can calm this pattern. The first is to create transition rituals between "work" and "home." This transition time is one of the few upsides of a commute, although even if you work out of a home office you can give yourself space. Go for a walk around the block. Read the newspaper for ten minutes. Even if you'll be signing back on to check e-mail later in the evening, enforcing a few hours of device-free time can give your brain a break.

Second, and somewhat counterintuitively, you might try *not* downloading your day on your spouse. When I interviewed Peter Shallard, a business psychology expert who works with entrepreneurs, for a *Fast Company* post, he mentioned that talking about your problem can trigger the same cascade of thoughts you just spent your commute distancing yourself from. Instead, ask your spouse about his day, and see if you can be helpful to your kids as they figure out how to solve their problems. Being a good listener gets you out of your own head.

Third, get a hobby. The human brain is amazing, but it can only focus on a few things at once. If you're busy helping your daughter build a ship in a bottle, you won't have much mental energy left for rehashing a meeting.

Fourth, give yourself a designated worry time. Shallard told me that long-term clients will often e-mail him to "remind me to talk about *X* on Friday." That simple action then gives the conscious part of their brains permission to procrastinate thinking about the issue. That, in turn, kicks the subconscious mind into gear, triggering the sorts of solutions that come to you while you're driving. When Shallard broaches Problem X on Friday, the person has often figured it out. You can meet with a coach, or an accountability partner, or a mastermind group—whatever will give you a time to consider your problem.

And finally, if you have trouble making time to relax in general, whether it's because of work, or housework, or parenting concerns, it might help to set rules for yourself. You can even create a budget for leisure, a concept that sounds insane at first, but has its merits. Perhaps you own a hammock and would like to enjoy it but never do because lolling in the hammock feels too decadent for a busy person such as yourself. When a spot of time opens up, you go pick up your kids' toys, even though they'll be back out on the floor the next morning, if not inside thirty minutes. Though I will argue with people that this urge to fill time with unpleasant but "productive" tasks is irrational, I also know that such beliefs stem from scripts that are hard to change.

Instead of beating yourself up over it, work with the personality you have. You can assign yourself two twenty-minute sessions in the hammock each week. You put it on the to-do list for Wednesday evening when another parent is on carpool duty and again on Saturday afternoon. You check "hammock time" off the list when done, and then can resume pointless playroom cleaning. Or not. Ideally, the hammock will feel so nice you'll want to stay out there. Either way, carving out time for leisure eventually becomes a habit.

You can also listen to a higher power and carve out a whole day for leisure, or at least for more leisure than you'd have otherwise. Several women in the Mosaic Project kept the Sabbath for religious reasons. Paid work is out, and in many cases so are driving and using electricity. Chores are more of a muddled message. You have to eat, which means someone has to do at least light food preparation. But I like the concept of major chores being pushed to the other weekend day, rather than being on the docket both days. That way, you have a full day to relax, or relax as much as you can. If you've got young kids, this day of rest isn't going to look all that restful. But there is always downtime, and if you can't watch TV, then you may nap, or stare at the clouds. Either way, there is space, and white spaces make for striking mosaics.

Perhaps the most radical idea is to turn a leisure activity you love into paid work. For some people, this ruins the fun. For others, paid work has privileges in our hierarchy of time that hobbies never will. If you're getting paid, the upstanding citizen part of your brain gives you permission to devote time and energy to it. In our free agent age, starting a creative business need not be an either/or proposition. If your day job doesn't forbid it, you can do a "normal" job sometimes, and run your artisanal business at others.

That's what Anandi Raman Creath does. By day she works from her home in Seattle on a contract for a major software company. Then, many nights after her young girls go to bed, she works on her own elegant scrapbooks and "ghost scrapbooks" for other people through her business, the Papercraft Lab. She's thought about making her various creative projects into a full-time endeavor, but she eventually decided that this hybrid model creates the best of both worlds. She earns a good income from the tech work, so she doesn't have to hustle for her side business. She can take on only the scrapbooking work she wants to take on. On the other hand, when it comes to scrapbooking, "I like having a hobby that pays for itself," she says. "It makes me feel a little less guilty." Because she's making money from it, she can invest in classes and purchase fancy papers and ribbons and other things she might think twice about if they were just for her own enjoyment.

With a toddler, a four-year-old, and a job, it would be easy for Creath to decide that she has no time for making art. Instead, she tells herself this story about pursuing passions post-children: "You'll still find a way to do the things you really want to do." Sure, things she didn't care about "sort of disappeared." But "always, even when both girls were really little, I've been doing crafty stuff. I was still doing it for myself. If it's important enough, you'll find a way to make it work." In her case, she simply chooses to use the hours of 7:30 to 10:30 p.m. for crafting, rather than catching up on episodes of *Dr. Phil.* The night before we talked, Creath told me she and her husband had watched TV for the first time in ages. Surveying the multiple hours spent that way—"All we did was watch TV, then it was time for bed!"—she decided "this is not something I want to start doing again. It's more satisfying when you actually have something you made at the end of it."

•
•
•
•
•
•

CHAPTER 9

Master the Tiles

I n my years of writing about time management, I have found this: when I talk about how to use hours well, inevitably someone will tut that life is not well lived by filling every minute. Take this quote from an early 2015 article in the *Financial Times*: "Though Ms Vanderkam's obsessive approach to time management will no doubt help some people become more productive, its controlling rigidity could leave others feeling suffocated." Sometimes people will wax poetic about lingering in a café over coffee, or with friends on an October evening, talking around a backyard fire pit and drinking wine. They will recount these pleasures as if they are somehow in opposition to my worldview, either not recognizing or ignoring that they are choices. They are choices to use time to create the good life, rather than letting time disappear into puttering with the mail pile, or watching TV you didn't mean to watch.

I don't believe in "using" every minute of every day. I *don't* use every minute in the sense of doing some sort of Protestant work ethic–approved task with it. Many a summer night after the kids have gone to bed, I like to sit on my back porch and do nothing but listen to the breeze in the pines. I don't believe in brutalizing my time into some joyless dirge of work and chore charts. I do believe, though, that since life is lived in hours, the proper stewardship of time is the key to making any sort of pleasure happen. When you start being aware of where time is, and where it goes, you can master the tiles to create a mosaic containing more joy than most people think is possible.

This chapter looks at some of my favorite time management strategies. They don't fit neatly into categories of work, home, or self. At first, they seem to affect just small clusters of minutes, but these are powerful tactics nonetheless. Taken together they can transform life into something even more brilliant and fun.

Strategy 1: Learn to Estimate

Knowing how long things take seems like a simple skill, and yet people live in chaos because they cannot figure this out. They miscalculate what they can take on, and then have to chuck things that are meaningful to them, or would positively impact their careers. When I interviewed Mark Langley, president and CEO of the Project Management Institute, he told me that organizations lose or waste almost 11 percent of their project dollars due to poor estimates and bad planning. If that were true for individual efficiency as well, that implies that we could find an extra 18.5 hours per week if we had a better sense of how long things take.

I doubt that statistic actually transfers from organizations to people, but it is true that estimating time is hard. It's hard for me, and I write about time management for a living. When Ruth graduated to having the same bedtime as Jasper and Sam, I realized I was chronically underestimating how long it took to get all three in bed. I wanted them in their bedrooms and quiet at 8:30 p.m., but something would go awry and I'd be dealing with final requests at 9:15. We didn't have as much time for stories as we wanted and I would get increasingly frustrated as time ticked away.

I eventually realized that if door-shut time was 8:30, bath time needed to start by 7:30 on the nights that happened. If it was not a bath night (parenting tip: small children do not need to be bathed daily), we needed to head upstairs by 7:45 if we wanted to read for twenty minutes and not be rushed. This has led to calmer bedtimes. I am forty-five minutes less tired at 8:30 than I am at 9:15. More realistic estimations mean I don't have to choose between story time and whatever I intend to do after the kids go to sleep. I get both.

If you want to get better at estimating time, the first step—always the first step—is to keep track of it. A time log can show you that your "one hour" ten a.m. Monday morning meeting has never taken less than seventy-five minutes, which explains why you are always late and apologizing when you schedule anything for eleven a.m.

Once you have a true sense of how your days fit together, you need to embrace your inner pessimist. Some people overestimate the time tasks require; I do this when I'm writing rough drafts of articles, though I try to convince myself that I'm building in slack rather than being risk averse. But the more common curse is unbridled optimism. People think they will do everything right on the first try, that tonight is the night no child will be missing a requisite stuffed animal, that no one will suddenly remember he is hungry or that he forgot to put his homework in his backpack. Good estimators know that this time must be accounted for.

Good estimators also learn to think like a chef. If someone is coming to dinner at eight p.m., you need to figure out what steps will allow you to put dinner on the table at that time. You count back from eight p.m. to figure out when you should start various dishes, and which steps can run concurrently. One complication with getting the kids to bed is that the boys are in a separate room from my daughter. She requires rocking and singing, which can be done concurrently with the boys' brushing their teeth, but cannot be done concurrently with reading them a story in *their* beds. All this must be built into the model.

Then you must make sure the model is complete. Project managers call this the "100 percent rule." People fail to account for all the steps of a project. Getting groceries doesn't just involve driving to the store, choosing and paying for groceries, and driving home. It requires taking the groceries out of your trunk and putting them away, too, and if you don't account for this, you will be late for whatever you think you'll start next. Stuff is inside the frame and outside the frame, but often there's more inside the frame than you think. The kids' bedtime ritual always involves at least one child calling me back upstairs for something. Frustrating, perhaps, but if you build it into the model, at least it's expected.

If you hone your estimation skills, you can plan your life in a more rational fashion. Here are some things that could fit in twenty-four hours: eight hours of sleep, one hour of getting ready and eating meals, nine hours of work (plus a thirty-minute commute both ways), a thirty-minute walk, ninety minutes of family time, and two hours of TV, with the extra hour likely disappearing into transitions. Here are some things that cannot fit into those same twenty-four hours: getting drinks with a friend, paying bills, spreading mulch in the yard, and attending your nephew's baseball game.

With time, we have an absolute limit on what is available to us. When a resource is scarce, we should make decisions that optimize this scarce resource. If something has to give, you want to make sure it's the right thing.

Strategy 2: Use Travel Time (Part 1)

Commuting time can be hard to estimate, even though people do it every day. We become used to most things that are uniformly good or bad in life, but the variability of traffic means that every day entails new suffering. That explains why scales of human happiness have put the morning commute at the absolute bottom of the list, with the evening commute not far behind. Commute time is generally wasted time, and unfortunately, the first idea people come up with to use it better—talking on the phone—is a terrible one. The National Safety Council estimated that in 2012, 26 percent of motor vehicle crashes involved cell phone use or texting. People who drive and talk on the phone frequently don't get any better at their ability to multitask, and people who think they're good at multitasking generally turn out to be worse at it than those who acknowledge their limits. Here are other ideas for improving your commute that still allow you to focus on the road when you need to.

Find a friend. Whether gas prices rise or fall, few people choose to carpool because most of us like having a sense of control over our time. We like to choose when we come and go. But what if you recast this? You don't have to carpool every day. A bit of inconvenience can be worth it if you share the drive on occasion with a mentor or mentee, or a coworker you need to meet with and now don't need to shoehorn into your nine-to-five schedule. Calee Lee (from chapter 2) drove to two events with an employee during her logged week, which meant they could hash out business during the ride. You can carpool with a friend who works nearby and have a girls' night out even if there won't be drinks involved. Or you can commute with your spouse and turn wasted time into a date. If you do this just once a week, that's another hour or so of your 168 hours spent together. Do it daily and you'll spend more quality time together than newlyweds. Of course, you don't actually have to like your fellow carpoolers. You can decide not to talk, and let the nondriving person read or sleep while you use the HOV lane.

Try public transit. People discount buses and trains for the same reasons carpooling isn't that popular. We like the sense of autonomy. But while it might be annoying to have to leave work at a certain point to catch the bus, being able to work for thirty uninterrupted minutes on the bus can win you back all of the time you'd "save" by driving.

Start carschooling. Morning shock jocks are funny for about two seconds. Instead, try something more edifying than listening to bad prank calls: think of your car as a one-room schoolhouse where you can get an education on whatever subjects you choose. Get in the habit of packing your listening material as you pack your bag for work. Check out audio versions of classics from your library. If you've got a long commute, you could make it through *The Odyssey* in a few weeks. Use iTunes for modern audiobooks or informative podcasts. You could try listening to lecture offerings from the Great Courses, which feature big-name professors teaching physics, history, and art, among other things. Commute time is also good for learning a language. If you're in the car by yourself, you can repeat phrases without people staring at you. If traffic gets intense, you can always hit pause.

Practice. Even though I've given my time management speech dozens of times, I still practice it before each gig. Doing this the night before the speech in front of the mirror is one option, but so is rehearsing a talk behind the wheel. You can rehearse tricky conversations such as a salary negotiation or feedback for an employee, and hear how the words sound out loud, so you won't flinch when you say them. If you've got a hobby that involves performing, commute time might work for this too. You can practice singing scales, or delivering your lines for that community theater version of *Hamlet*.

Move. The women with the highest exercise totals often incorporated exercise into their commutes. They speed-walked to the train. They biked to work, which, on a nice day, can make you feel incredibly alive as the wind whips against you. As someone once told me, "Biking is my caffeine." To be sure, a rainy, frigid day can be miserable, somewhat like having cold coffee thrown in your face, but you don't have to choose any of these active commuting options *every day*. The point is to sprinkle them in as a way to move more. Even parking in a spot far away from your office building one day a week and taking a few minutes to walk outside can help you start the day with more energy.

Think and revel. Done well, commuting time can be me time. Perhaps you take the scenic route to work. A woman once described her long California commute to me in a way that made it seem like a visual adventure. She drove along the Pacific Coast Highway as the sun rose. The waves foamed, surfers unloaded their cars, she once saw a whale. Her subsequent train ride ended in downtown San Francisco, where she walked across a bustling marketplace just waking up, with the flowers and ice and fresh produce all producing a riot of color. Morning by morning, the world was shiny and new. It brimmed with possibilities. She could feel blessed that she was awake to see it.

A commute can be an aural experience, too. I recently listened to the Bach B-Minor Mass twice on the way to and from a speech outside Washington, D.C. I rarely just sit and listen to beautiful music, but the piercing strains of the alto *Agnus Dei* solo created a meditative sphere inside my car despite the gridlocked traffic on the Beltway. Some people listen to ball games or comedic podcasts. If you consciously use your car time as personal time, then you might not need as much Facebook surfing time during the day to decompress. You can use this time to work, and then hopefully get in your car early enough to beat traffic on the way home.

Skip it—sometimes. A number of women in the Mosaic Project worked from home at some point during core work hours. If you need to speak to someone face-to-face, you can video chat. Incidentally, you can video chat with friends and family too. Many Mosaic logs featured weekend chats with grandparents in far-flung locales. You do want to visit people, but skipping the long drive with little ones in a car has its upsides too. It's worth throwing Skype into the mix.

Strategy 3: Use Travel Time (Part 2)

If commute time is easy to squander, airport time is even easier to waste. Brandy Hebert, the consumer products company manager from chapter 4 who worked remotely three out of every four weeks, likes being able to live where she wants. But the transaction costs are notable. There is no direct flight between her home in Maine and the office in Cincinnati, meaning she's always connecting through Detroit, LaGuardia, or Dulles, airports not known for their stellar on-time records. She recently spent eight hours stuck in Detroit. Though she used the time to read a technical book she hadn't had a chance to wade through, long delays are never an ideal situation.

"What I do when I do it well is that I have a library card in Cincinnati and a library card in Maine. I check out books for the month and read books on the plane," she says. She also keeps a list with "a lot of nonurgent reading-type material—a lot of things around personal development plans." Because she manages others, she'll look at their development plans too, "and then I start to run out of stuff." This is why I'm a big fan of airport bookstores (especially when they're selling my books!). I hate to board without at least a few magazines to page through should I get through the work I've assigned myself for the flight. If you get stuck without enough to do, or plenty to do but no energy to do it with, feel free to watch a movie and revel in this me time at thirty thousand feet. I'm not a huge TV watcher, but if I'm traveling for work, I'll let myself watch idiotic stuff I'd never watch on the ground. It's the same with running on the treadmill, really. The larger context covers a host of sins.

Frequent fliers generally weather ground delays in their airline lounges, and even if you're not a "Platinum" or "Priority" level traveler, it might be worth buying a day pass for access. For short delays, though, those aren't the only options. You can make friends at the airport bar. No one is there with their usual posse and no one will judge you for drinking before noon. Order a beer and practice the fine art of small talk in a situation with lower stakes than an industry networking event. Simply lead with something travel or weather related, or about the sporting event playing on the bar TV. Wait for your partner to volunteer something about himself, and then ask questions designed to find common ground. You can also take in something visually fascinating. Lots of airports have art on display. The Philadelphia airport recently featured an exhibit of historic communications technology including old typewriters and rotary phones, and another exhibit of pencil sharpeners shaped like every object known to man. You can walk around the airport, and maybe get a few miles in. Or you can just zone out. Many airports have chapels, and few people use them. If the blaring televisions elsewhere are making you tense, go in and relax. You don't have to participate in any formal religious practices while you're in there.

Strategy 4: Multitask Better

As mentioned in the commuting section, multitasking is the bête noire of productivity literature. It is inefficient, and yet when you're not in danger of driving your car off the road, the inefficiency may be worth what you gain in happiness. Few people like to fold laundry. Few people like to iron. But many people do like to talk with their loved ones. So one accountant noted that she called her sister while folding laundry, and a manager at a tech company called her sister while ironing. If the laundry takes a little longer, so be it. At least you'll enjoy yourself during the process.

The best categories for multitasking are things that use different parts of your brain. A few studies have found that doodling actually helps you pay attention and retain more information in meetings, as it absorbs that slight bit of extra capacity that can lead your mind to wander. Knitting likely does the same thing. While making a scarf during a staff meeting isn't going to fly in most offices, if you run the place, why not?

Strategy 5: Use Unexpected Moments

How do you use time you didn't expect to be there?

I think the answer to this question separates the time management masters from everyone else. Anyone can plan something fun or meaningful for an open block on the calendar. The best stewards of hours, on the other hand, can pivot in the moment. To these mosaic makers, a broken tile is an opportunity, and not a source of angst.

Jennifer Hodgens, the Oklahoma real estate agent mentioned in chapter 6, uses unexpected time to indulge in one of her favorite activities: a massage. Whenever a client cancels, she tries to fit one in. "Half the fun of getting the massage for me is being able to sneak away. You just kind of feel like you're escaping from the world for a little bit, and everyone else thinks you're in an appointment with a client," she says. To be sure, some spas operate on long lead times for appointments, which is why she compromises and patronizes a particular place in town. "It's not necessarily the 'best' massage, but if I e-mail or text they can get me in within thirty minutes," she says. She's happy enough to have a place where "they know me by name and can squeeze me in. It's good to have that on hand."

It's always good to have ideas on hand for time that might appear, like when a meeting ends early, or a trip gets canceled. You can go for a walk. You can text friends to see if they can meet you for dinner. But keeping the mindset that *any* unexpected time is "found time" can make even unorthodox hours more fun.

Most of us hope to sleep at normal times—say, 11:00 p.m. to 6:30 a.m.—and in general, Mosaic Project participants got adequate sleep. But that doesn't always happen. Whether I travel east or west, if I cross more than one time zone, I wake up ridiculously early. Flying to Phoenix from Philadelphia recently, I was up at 5:00 a.m. Mountain time. Then, flying to Europe two days later, I woke up at 4:00 a.m. during my first night there. I've learned to embrace it. The world is quiet in these early morning hours, and you can get a lot done, even in the hotel bathroom if you're traveling with someone who's managed to stay asleep. The woman who kept a log for me when she was eight and a half months pregnant decided to play video games when she got up in the middle of the night and her baby was too busy practicing kicks against her rib cage to let her go back to sleep. Another woman finished a book proposal from 3:00 a.m. to 6:00 a.m. when she couldn't turn back in.

I think my favorite example of using overnight time came from Jenny Powers. When she kept her log (p. 263), she planned events for the National Multiple Sclerosis Society as her full-time gig (she later left to lead a professional women's networking group she'd founded called Running With Heels). She volunteered overnight at a homeless shelter, serving the clients a meal. During her shift, she spent some time watching shows and relaxing,

	MONDAY	TUESDAY	WEDNESDAY	THURSDAY	FRIDAY	SATURDAY	SUNDAY
5AM	Sleep	Sleep	Sleep		Wake up, wash up, brush teeth		Arrive at work
5:30	Sleep	Sleep	Sleep		Set up breakfast for shelter		Work event
6	Sleep	Sleep	Sleep		Wake up shelter guests		Work event
6:30	Sleep	Sleep	Sleep		Serve breakfast; make to-go lunches		Work event
7	Sleep	Sleep	Sleep		Sign out guests; load bus		Work event
7:30	7:45 wake up, make breakfast and pack lunch for M	7:45 wake up, make breakfast, pack lunch for M	7:50 wake up, make breakfast, pack lunch for M		Clean up; leave		Work event
8	Wake M, get her dressed	Shower, wake M, both get dressed	8:15 wake up M get her dressed	Wake up, shower, get dressed	Home, make M's lunch		Work event
8:30	Shower, get dressed, give M breakfast	Give M breakfast	Shower, get dressed	Wake up M for school, make her breakfast, pack lunch	Set up M's breakfast		Work event
9	Leave house; drop M at school	Leave house, drop M at school	8:45 leave for work, commute	Drop M off at school; head to office	Wake M; get her dressed and fed		Work event
9:30	9:15 commute to work	Commute, arrive at work	9:20 arrive at work, check emails	Commute	Drop M off at school		Work event
10	9:45 work	All staff meeting	9:30 senior staff meeting	Arrive at office 9:45	9:15 meet class parent for breakfast		Work event
10:30	Work	All staff meeting	Senior staff meeting	Work	Breakfast with class parent	Wake up, wash up	Work event

	MONDAY	TUESDAY	WEDNESDAY	THURSDAY	FRIDAY	SATURDAY	SUNDAY
11	Breakfast at desk	Check emails, voicemails	Senior staff meeting	Work	Breakfast with class parent	Family breakfast	Work event
11:30	11:45 leave for meeting	Leave office, commute to meeting	11-11:30 breakfast at desk, respond to emails	Work	Go home, check emails	Family breakfast	Finish work; leave
12PM	Commute; read	12:15 meeting	Work on script for event	Check personal emails/Facebook	Respond to emails, work	Hang out with M	Walk to lunch
12:30	Arrive at meeting	Meeting	Work on script for event	Lunch with new colleague at restaurant	Sleep	Hang out with M	Lunch with friend
1	Meeting	Commute back to office, pick up lunch	Work on script for event	Lunch with new colleague at restaurant	Sleep	Hang out with M	Lunch with friend
1:30	Lunch	Eat lunch, go online	Work on script for event	Lunch with new colleague at restaurant	Sleep	Get dressed, dress M	Commute home; read
2	Meeting concludes; commute to work; read	Conference call	Work on script for event	Work	Sleep	Get dressed, dress M	Locked out :(Starbucks/read
2:30	Check personal email	Conference call	Production meeting	Work	Sleep	Clean up apt.	Read
3	Work	Call completed; work on project	Production meeting	Work meeting	Wake up, wash up	Clean up apt.	Get home; nap
3:30	Work	Work on project	Eat lunch at desk	Work meeting	Pick up M from school	Car ride	Sleep
4	Work	Conference call	Work on script for event	Check personal emails	Come home, have snack with M	Car ride	Sleep
4:30	Work	Call ends; another call 4:45	Work on script for event	Work	Play with M	Arrive at Legoland	Sleep

	MONDAY	TUESDAY	WEDNESDAY	THURSDAY	FRIDAY	SATURDAY	SUNDAY
5	Personal emails	Call ends; work on project	Work on script for event	Review calendar for next 3 days	Play with M	Legoland	Sleep
5:30	Online reading	Calls	Work on script for event	Leave office; commute; begin new book on subway	Shower, get dressed	Legoland	Sleep
6	Finish up at work	Leave office, taxi to event	Complete script	Arrive home; get and sort mail; pack for overnight	Commute, read book	Legoland	Sleep
6:30	6:45 mani, pedi, eyebrow wax	Arrive at sushi and sake tasting event	Check voicemails	Eat dinner with daughter	Date night with husband	Legoland	Sleep
7	Mani, pedi, eyebrow wax	Sushi and sake tasting	Leave office, commute	Arrive to volunteer overnight at homeless shelter	Date night with husband	Legoland	Wake up
7:30	Mani, pedi, eyebrow wax	Sushi and sake tasting	Meet husband and 2 friends for dinner	Organize dinner and pantry for shelter guests	Date night with husband	Leave Legoland; walk around	Run dishwasher
8	Mani, pedi, eyebrow wax	7:45 event ends, walk to train	Dinner	Organize cots and bedding for guests	Date night with husband	Walk around	Watch movie with M
8:30	Head home; commute; read	Commute home	Go to NY Nets game	Serve dinner for guests	Date night with husband	Car ride to grocery store	Watch movie with M
9	9:20 get home	Arrive home	Nets game	Sit for dinner; talk to Mom, Dad on phone	Date night with husband	Grocery shop	Watch movie with M
9:30	Go through mail	Have dinner with husband	Nets game	Clean dinner dishes; put leftovers away	Commute, read book	Grocery shop	Watch movie with M
10	Eat dinner	Check emails, pick out M's clothes	Leave game, go to garage, pick up car, drive home	Go online, respond to emails, go on Facebook	Get in bed, check emails	Stop for quick dinner	Eat
10:30	Go online	Leave notes for housekeeper/ leave pay	Get home, relieve babysitter	Online	Online	Car ride home	Internet

	MONDAY	TUESDAY	WEDNESDAY	THURSDAY	FRIDAY	SATURDAY	SUNDAY
11	Go online, pick out M's clothes	Pay bills online, return work emails	Check personal emails	Call husband and M and say goodnight	Go to sleep	Put M to sleep	Internet
11:30	Go to sleep	Go to sleep	Sleep	Fill out time log	Sleep	Shower	Sleep
12AM	Sleep	Sleep	Sleep	Watch *Orange is the New Black*	Sleep	Sleep	Sleep
12:30	Sleep	Sleep	Sleep	Watch *Orange is the New Black*	Sleep	Sleep	Sleep
1	Sleep	Sleep	Sleep	Watch *Orange is the New Black*	Sleep	Sleep	Sleep
1:30	Sleep	Sleep	Sleep	Read book	Sleep	Sleep	Sleep
2	Sleep	Sleep	Sleep	Sleep	Sleep	Sleep	Sleep
2:30	Sleep	Sleep	Sleep	Sleep	Sleep	Sleep	Sleep
3	Sleep	Sleep	Sleep	Sleep	Sleep	Sleep	Sleep
3:30	Sleep	Sleep	Sleep	Sleep	Sleep	Wake up 3:45 am	Sleep
4	Sleep	Sleep	Sleep	Sleep	Sleep	Wash up; get dressed	Sleep
4:30	Sleep	Sleep	Sleep	Sleep	Sleep	Leave house; commute to work	Sleep

with a bit of sleep thrown in. She took a nap the next day, but enjoyed being able to indulge in me time while doing good.

Strategy 6: Use Bits of Time

Of course, when most of us find time, we know exactly what we'll do with it: check e-mail. The ubiquity of smartphones means we never lack for the opportunity to do this. If the elevator takes a mere thirty seconds to arrive, your phone is out, and you're deleting ads and updates from groups you don't remember joining.

Cleaning out the inbox feels productive, but it isn't accomplishing much. Here are better ways to use bits of time to bring joy into your life:

- Seize quality time. The five minutes before you need to hop in the car is enough time to read through many children's books. If you've got a few minutes before the bus comes, you can play hopscotch on the driveway or chat through the day's challenges.
- Work on your List of 100 Dreams. What's on it now? What could you add? What could you cross off in the next year? Go visit BucketList .org for thousands of ideas that other people have thought up.
- Pull out your headphones and listen to a favorite song.
- Text your partner or your children. Tell them you love them and you're thinking about them. Suggest something fun for the evening. Text a friend to ask her about her life.
- Read. Keep a list of articles or blog posts to read later, and open one up anytime you've got a few minutes.
- Write a letter. Keep note cards in your desk or purse and write a note to a relative, friend, or colleague who did something intriguing. It can be short. Three or four lines will suffice to make someone's day.
- Write in a journal. Check out Gretchen Rubin's *The Happiness Project One-Sentence Journal* for a low-key way to make this part of your life.
- Write a novel (or at least a draft). This sounds like the sort of activity that would require long stretches of time, but that's not necessarily the case. Every November, thousands of people participate

in National Novel Writing Month, a challenge that requires writing a 50,000-word novel in thirty days. Quality isn't the goal; finishing is. I tried it in November 2014, and found that when I turned off the inner critic, I could crank out 100 to 200 words in five minutes flat. Sneak in a few of these creative bursts during the day and it's not hard to hit 1,667 words daily.

- Go on social media with a purpose. Look through your LinkedIn contacts or Twitter followers until you see an update that makes you smile. Respond (perhaps via e-mail or a phone call) and renew a connection. Look at Facebook's birthday reminders, and send these friends a real note.
- Stretch. You can also lie on top of a tennis ball or use a foam roller to release tension.
- Get stronger. If you're in an office with a door or a home office, you can knock out some push-ups or sit-ups. Jump rope for five minutes, or do some lunges or squats.
- Get strategic with your calendar. Study your commitments. What can you get rid of? In a few minutes, you may be able to buy yourself several hours by chucking things that don't deserve a place in your life. In five minutes, you can also reach out and schedule a meeting that you know should happen but hasn't.
- Memorize an inspirational quote or a verse in a sacred text.
- Think through your leisure time. People are generally good about setting work goals, but we're not as good about personal ones. In five minutes, you could decide that next week you'll make dinner plans with friends, watch a favorite movie with your family, and make your famous apple pie over the weekend. Planning a few fun events gives you something to look forward to. One trick? Structure your to-do lists this way, with three side-by-side categories: work, family, self. Such a setup reminds you that there should be at least something on all three sublists.
- Peruse DonorsChoose.org, and pick a classroom project to sponsor. Two minutes and ten dollars can bring someone's field trip closer to fruition. GlobalGiving.org offers international projects, and

ModestNeeds.org lets you help people who are down on their luck and are dealing with onetime financial emergencies.

- Learn something. Watch a Khan Academy video on some random topic like the quadratic equation. Watch a TED talk or read Wikipedia's featured article of the day.
- Walk the halls for five minutes. If you can get outside, do. The fresh air will wake you up. If you're working from home, seize five minutes to change into your workout clothes, so you'll be ready to race out the door for a run when you've got thirty minutes between phone calls.
- Look through photos on your phone. They can conjure up happy memories of that ski vacation, or the way your toddler sang "Happy Birthday."
- Get artistic. If you've stashed crayons in your purse to distract your kids, try using them yourself. A few pictures from magazines can become the start of a vision board.
- Peruse your idea file. Start a collection of miscellaneous tidbits, images, and articles. Take a few minutes weekly to ponder them, play with them, or purge them when you no longer find them intriguing.
- Nap. Some people do this accidentally, but you can also be strategic and do it between calls. If you wake up refreshed, you'll be able to focus on the topic at hand.

Strategy 7: Look at the Whole Mosaic

Sometimes the most important time management strategy is to take any bit of time in context. Any moment is fleeting. Things will look different in minutes, days, or years.

I remind myself of this during busy times. I try to work hard when I work, but I like to take frequent vacations too, something that keeps life manageable over time, even if a particular stretch of time looks bad.

April 2014 was an uncommonly crowded month, with multiple speeches and conferences, yet I wrote this on a lazy afternoon at a farmhouse called

Vinca Minor outside Uddel in the Netherlands, where I'd come with my family for spring break. It had been a mosaic sort of day. I did some work, but I also went for an hour-long run past horses and sheep into the village, where all the "Van" names and people who looked like me created quite a rush of feeling for this country my grandfather left ninety years before. I had an hour communing with my agrarian roots as I washed our clothes by hand and draped them outside to dry. There were hugs, too—snuggles over breakfast, and Sam, in his earnestness, calling me over from the kitchen table to tell me a secret: *"Mommy, I love you."* There had been trying moments during the week, of kids misbehaving in museums and melting down as international travel disrupted their schedules. But there were also sweet moments, and dandelions, sprinkled all over this fertile land and picked by my little four-year-old, who wanted me to put them in my hair.

A mosaic can contain all these things. When you look at all the tiles, it often does.

This ability to look at all the tiles is something I saw in Emma Johnson's log, and in her life. I've been quite intrigued by her story, partly because of how different her existence looks now from how she thought it would look seven years ago. When I first got to know her, she was freelancing just a few hours a week and primarily caring for her new daughter. She was happy with this life, to be mostly home while her husband built his career.

Then, one night several years ago, she was supposed to meet me and some friends for dinner. She never showed. She didn't show the next morning for a conference session she was supposed to help lead on freelancing, which was a completely uncharacteristic move for a reliable woman. She sent a note later that day explaining that her husband had sustained a severe head injury while on a business trip to Greece. She had flown with her daughter to Athens the night before. He survived, and soon after, she got pregnant with their second child. These were happy developments, but accidents change people and change situations. Their marriage couldn't take the changes. Johnson's husband moved out shortly before their son was born. They got divorced. She received child support from her ex-husband for a bit, but not for long.

I wouldn't blame her for fixating on the horror of the dark tiles from that year. Instead, she's chosen to look at life more broadly. *Remember the berry season is short.* When she realized she would need to support herself and her

children, she threw herself into rebuilding her career, which has also fascinated me, since we do similar work yet she earns more while working fewer
hours. "I've just been doing what I've been doing for so long I've got it down
to a little machine," she tells me. "I've learned to ask questions in a very efficient way to evoke the answers I want." She gets people on and off the phone
in twenty minutes, and schedules meetings back-to-back to compress them
into the least possible time. Packing well-paying work in tightly is key to the
rest of her life: building a brand as "The Wealthy Single Mommy"—an expert
on the huge and growing demographic of women parenting solo. She hosts a
radio show, comments on pop culture (like Tyler Perry's *The Single Moms
Club* movie), blogs, and spends time with her son and daughter, of whom she
has primary custody. "I don't just want to spend time with the kids. I want to
really hang out with and enjoy them," she says, which means she does such
crazy stuff as take a five-year-old and three-year-old on a ten-day solo road
trip ("It was terrible. Terribly awesome!"). She also wants to have a lively social and dating life, taking advantage of the heaping options New York City
and OkCupid have to offer.

Sometimes life is hectic. Her log (p. 272) showed a birthday, family visits,
a client emergency, even this quintessential mom moment: a quick run to the
bodega for craft supplies to make a whale for her daughter's school project.
But ask her how she does it and she will tell you this: she chooses to be grateful for the calm moments, and to take the others in stride. She walks her
daughter to the bus stop in the morning. She hangs out with her three-year-
old until it's time to bring him to school. "As the kids are getting older, they
don't need that much from me. The kids just want to be near me sometimes,"
she says. She'll sit with her laptop and her son will sit with her, lingering over
breakfast. She practiced yoga and wrangled five little girls at a nail salon for
a party. She did a radio show and went on a second date. It was a full week,
and a good week. "I'm honoring all of those things," she says of the tiles in
her life. "If anything is out of whack, I'm just not productive." But when you
arrange the tiles to create a compelling mosaic, one with work, family, and
your own sweet time too, life can be pretty good.

	MONDAY	TUESDAY	WEDNESDAY	THURSDAY	FRIDAY	SATURDAY	SUNDAY
5AM							
5:30							
6	Woke up, made breakfast, packed lunches, dressed kids, daughter to bus by 7:25		Wake, make bfast, kids lunches, kids dressed, run through emails, off to bus stop	Wake, make bfast, lunches, kids dressed, emails, finish whale, color H's hair with marker gels, bus	Cooked bfast, made lunches, got kids dressed, off to school for H		
6:30						Clean house, prep for 6-y-o bday party	
7							
7:30	Social media for blog post (written night before), email, hung out with L				Finished story and filed		
8		Misc work - emails, created blog post, social media	Mess of writing, filing three stories, email social media, and client 911	Try to occupy L with videos while work before picking up Mom at airport			
8:30					Dropped L at school, yoga		
9	Yoga class						Roll out of bed, breakfast with my mom at home
9:30							
10				Pick up Mom from airport, return home	Emailed w/ editor, prepped for radio show		Jog

	MONDAY	TUESDAY	WEDNESDAY	THURSDAY	FRIDAY	SATURDAY	SUNDAY
10:30	Walked to Modell's to shop for H's bday (her dad ALSO got her a skateboard!), take sked call w/ potential speaking client		Mess of writing, filing three stories, email social media, and client 911	Finish/file 2 stories, eat lunch, settle Mom in	Radio show!		
11	Interviewed sources, client meetings, wolfed lunch (during week I almost always make self a salad)					Wrangle 5 little girls at nail salon for party, pick up pizza on block, walk to my apt.	Shower, lunch, lounge
11:30					Lunch w/ Mom		
12PM					Shower, hair, makeup, coffee		Start cooking dinner and catch up on phone with friend
12:30		Went out for Mexican take out mainly to get fresh air/quick phone chat w/ my mom			Story edits, write story, follow up emails, flirt with furniture maker on OkCupid	Pizza and cake at my house	Run errands re kids' bday and dinner
1	Shower, coffee, dressed	411 friendly colleague meeting w/ fellow blogger/ entrepreneur	Mess of writing, filing three stories, email social media, and client 911				
1:30	More emailing, following up, wasting time on social media	Misc writing/emails and set up account with HomeExchange.com for summer home swap!				Chill with Mom, bro, SIL, and kids	

	MONDAY	TUESDAY	WEDNESDAY	THURSDAY	FRIDAY	SATURDAY	SUNDAY
2				Weekly media training w/ my agency			
2:30	Moved car, ran errands for H's bday (flowers, card)					Drive kids across Queens for ANOTHER bday party	
3	Picked kids up at school and walked to H's dance class, L and I went to bank and had a mommy date at café	Source interview	Pick up kids from school and hang out with them		Pick up kids from bus/day care, run errands, home	Drop kids at party, head to café, realize I'm near the comedian	
3:30		Writing story, FB time wasting, BOOK WRITING!		Cook special dinner, hang out with kids and Mom		I've been chatting w/ on OkCupid, text him	
4			UNUSUAL: send kids to neighbors' while I work. I never do this!			He meets me for impromptu coffee date	Pick up kids from their dad's, hang out at my place w/ Mom and cook dinner
4:30					Kids goof off with my mom, I cook chicken pot pies from scratch		
5		Yoga					
5:30	Cooked/ate dinner, fielded birthday calls from relatives for H					Pick up tired, grumpy kids at party, drive to drop them at their dad's house for night	Family birthday dinner and party. My house looks like Christmas tree minus tree

	MONDAY	TUESDAY	WEDNESDAY	THURSDAY	FRIDAY	SATURDAY	SUNDAY
6			Run to bodega for supplies for H's school project and make whale; neighbor comes for dinner		Weekly movie night (Shirley Temple) while eating dinner - kids to bed		
6:30		Writing		Bath, jammies, I read Little House book while H beaded and L threw epic fit. Bed!			
7	Cake/presents/ neighbors and SIL stopped by					Restaurant dinner with Mom, bro and SIL	
7:30		Kids home from dad's, snuggle and bed	Kids' bath and bed	Kids' bath and bed			
8	Kids in bed w/o bath and only 1 brushed teeth as both were stoned on sugar	Interview and single mom blogger meeting	Attempt to work but too exhausted. Read and tiny bit of yoga then BED		Emails, listened to Marc Maron WTF while baking birthday cake for H		
8:30	Cleaned kitchen, caught up on emails, prepped for bed and read news a bit						
9				Little work, little reading, early bed		Second date with the comedian! Café in my hood	
9:30		Web and bed					BED!! SO TIRED!

	MONDAY	TUESDAY	WEDNESDAY	THURSDAY	FRIDAY	SATURDAY	SUNDAY
10							
10:30					Bed!		
11							
11:30						Bed, exhausted!	
12AM							
12:30							
1							
1:30							
2							
2:30							
3							
3:30							
4							
4:30							

Afterword

On January 14, 2015, shortly after a noon drive to pick up my mom at the airport, I turned in the close-to-final edits of this book. I remember it was around 4 p.m., and I was happy to get the project off my desk: I was scheduled to be induced to deliver my fourth child early in the morning on the 15th. But later that evening, around 11:30 p.m., I woke up with sudden contractions. After figuring out that this was the real thing a few hours early, my husband and I zoomed toward the hospital. The GPS in the car put our arrival time in the parking lot at 1:13 a.m. Alex entered the world at 1:32 a.m. My friends joked that I am efficient even at childbirth.

It was the start of what was quite a year. *I Know How She Does It* was published a few months later, and I spent the rest of the year discussing it with audiences ranging from MBA students to attendees of Chicago Ideas Week.

In the usual "recitation of dark moments" narrative that dominates the literature about women, work, and life, this combination of frequent travel and raising four small children might have been hectic. Indeed, there were low moments, like using my breast pump in train car bathrooms, or being up multiple times during the night with the baby when I had to be on a plane early in the morning.

Yet there were so many high moments, too. The most profound involved hearing from readers who saw their lives reflected in this book. As one put it, "Finally, a book that's optimistic versus doom and gloom and guilt." In particular, I was touched to hear from young women who said that *I Know How She Does It* made them feel that a full, rewarding life was possible. They could start their families while building their careers, secure in the knowledge that women had blazed that trail before them. In the rush to proclaim that "women can't have it all," we just don't hear these stories.

I'd be happy to make my life busier in the service of sharing those stories, but to be honest, I'm still not *that* busy. I know that my life features swaths of open space, leisure time, downtime. In April, inspired by the time logs in *I Know How She Does It*, I decided to start tracking my time continuously. I'm still going, as of this writing, nine months later. In page after page of 168-hour logs, I can see rhythms. I can see that I have time to read. If I elect to read *People* magazine rather than *War and Peace*, well, "I don't have time" really means "it's not a priority." The logs show that I got together with friends, which keeps me from telling myself the story that I am so busy with work and family obligations that friendships are forced to take a back seat. I can see that even during the craziest weeks, like one from the time log printed here featuring trips to New York and London and a half-marathon, I also fit in a tea party with my daughter, baked banana bread, and watched a lot of bad TV on the plane.

This is not the description of a life that lacks for space. Sometimes enjoying these open blocks of time requires creativity, but as I study my logs and those that people continue to send me, I see that these open spaces exist just as busy times exist. Life is a mosaic. Success requires some stressful moments, but not all of life will be harried or crazed. Neither busyness nor openness is necessarily emblematic of life. All of it must be taken in context.

As I navigate my busy times and slower times, I have been trying to use lessons learned while writing *I Know How She Does It*. I make the most of family breakfasts; my Monday morning in this log shows me making waffles for the crew. I try to invest in the soft side of work, like meeting a friend who was launching a new media business while I was in New York on Monday afternoon. I adopted the "do it anyway" motto about getting to church on Sunday. I was tired—the baby was up early with the clocks falling back overnight, and I'd just traveled internationally and run a half-marathon. And we were running late. There were reasons not to go, but I also know that I'm tired from time to time, and I draw energy from meaningful things. Once there, I was so glad we'd gone. The choir sang the Durufle Requiem, which is one of my favorite choral works.

I also tried to make the most of unexpected time. On Monday, I'd packed my bags to go straight to the Philadelphia airport after arriving at Philadelphia's

30th Street Station. But the stars aligned, and I made an earlier train from NYC. I had enough time to drive home, and though I was there for just an hour, I was able to change clothes, nurse the baby (which meant one less airport pumping session), and my husband made me pad thai. It was a nice moment of calm in an otherwise intense day. I have come to appreciate these rhythms: calm moments in intense days, a few intense days surrounded by calmer ones. When you look at life in terms of the 168 hours in a week, or even the 8,760 hours in a year, you realize that much that seems contradictory is just part of a good, full existence. Work and life are not in opposition. When you view time from a perspective of abundance, there is space for career, relationships, and self, too.

A year into life with four little ones, I know this: building a career while building a family is not always easy. But it is doable. I also believe it is worth doing. We have the power to design lives that work for us, whether that's within the traditional pattern of a nine-to-six job or something more wild like mine. We can embrace these patterns and see them for what they are. Knowing where the time really goes has assured me that I am making space for what matters to me. Many of my readers have told me this as well: a clear look at life in all its messy glory helps them avoid the false narratives that encourage women to feel guilt that is not justified. Some moments must be endured, but in the broader view of time, there are many moments to be enjoyed, too.

Life is stressful and life is wonderful. There is no contradiction here. In this new chapter of my life, I see that more and more.

	MONDAY	TUESDAY	WEDNESDAY	THURSDAY	FRIDAY	SATURDAY	SUNDAY
5AM	To sleep; 5:15, sleep	Land, through customs	Shower, email	Sleep		5:20 up, ready	Up, feed
5:30	M wakes me up 5:45, sleep	Heathrow Express	Email			Ready, drive	Play while in office
6	Drift until 6:20, shower	At Paddington, walk	Pump, hair			Drive to 30th, sit in car	Feed A cereal
6:30	Ready, check in for flight	Walk through Hyde Park	Dress, check out, walk			Wait in (warm) station	Go outside
7	Up w/A, R, their breakfasts	To hotel, pump	Walk (window shop on Bond)		7:15 up, nurse	Walk to start	Play inside
7:30	Making waffles, others up	Sleep	Walk (window shop, F&M)	Wake, shower, bfasts	Shower, bfast	Find L, wait	Make banana bread
8	Work, getting ready	Sleep	Walk to Villandry St. James	My breakfast, clean up	Bfast, kids ready	Wait, start run 8:20ish	A down, shower
8:30	Bus, drive R, nurse A	Sleep	Event at VSJ	Bus, start work	Bus, play w/R	Rock n Roll half	Work (NaNoWriMo)
9	A down, work	Sleep	Event at VSJ	Work (revise Fortune)	Try to get A down	Rock n Roll half	Hangout w/M
9:30	Work, ready, drive	Sleep	Event at VSJ	Work (revise Fortune)	Work (teacher call)	Rock n Roll half	Ready for church, car
10	Still driving, arrive 10:25	Up, email	Event at VSJ + change	Work email triage	To parade	Rock n Roll half	Church (Requiem)
10:30	Wait, on train, work	Email	Tube to Paddington, train	Work	Halloween parade	Rock n Roll half	Church (Requiem)
11	Work (my blog)	Shower	Train to Heathrow	Work, ready	Home, play	Finish, walk to car	Church, home
11:30	Work (my blog)	Ready, walk in London	Check in, security	Drive downtown	Play w/A, S, diaper	Get coffee, drive	A, S lunch

	MONDAY	TUESDAY	WEDNESDAY	THURSDAY	FRIDAY	SATURDAY	SUNDAY
12PM	To midtown (subway)	Walk around Green Park	To gate	Pick up race bib	Get R, lunches	Drive, home, shower	S lacrosse, kids, clean
12:30	Give talk/lunch	Walk, to hotel	Read at gate	Drive back, snack	My lunch, drive to Y	Feed A, make lunch	Clean, A play, down
1	Give talk/lunch	Email, blog, ready	Board, on plane, read	Work	YMCA (kids in, work)	A down, nap	Make chicken, S home
1:30	Sign books, to Harvard Club	Work	Read on plane	To boys' school	YMCA (work), get R	Nap, tea party R, S, J	Kids go with dad
2	Meet w/C re her new biz	30% Club reception/talk	Watch BBC TV— sharks	Halloween parade/party	Drive home, work	Read mag, drink beer	Work (NaNoWriMo)
2:30	To 3% Conference	30% Club reception/talk	Watch BBC TV— sharks	Home, work	Work	Read The Economist	Work (NaNoWriMo)
3	Green room, take stage	30% Club reception/talk	Eat, watch BBC TV—Japan	Work (Fast Co interview)	A up, nurse, watch TV	Read, hang out w/M	Work (NaNoWriMo)
3:30	3% Conference talk	30% Club reception/talk	Watch BBC TV—Japan	Write Fast Co	Watch TV w/kids, get J	Hangout w/M + kids	Work (blog)
4	Sign books, to Penn Station	30% Club reception/talk	Work	Work (blog)	Home, outside S, A	Kids outside, read, A up	Work (admin)
4:30	Eat, board train, work	30% Club reception/talk	Work	Work (blog, newsletter)	Walk outside w/A	Feed A, start dinner	Work, do puzzle
5	Work on train (slow internet)	Back to room	Work	Work (Fast Co)	Play downstairs A, R, S	Kids' dinner	Kids, feed A cereal
5:30	Work on train	Read, work	Work	Work, make kid dinner	Play downstairs, mail	Ready to trick or treat	Make, eat dinner
6	Read, train in, get car	Work	Work	Play w/A, R	Make dinner, feed A	Trick or treating	Hang out, clean
6:30	Drive, home 6:50, change	Work, internet time	Work	Play w/A, R	Finish eating, A plays	Trick or treating, home	Kids' baths, jammies

	MONDAY	TUESDAY	WEDNESDAY	THURSDAY	FRIDAY	SATURDAY	SUNDAY
7	Nurse A, eat dinner w/M	Sleep	Read on plane	A bath, nurse, down	Nurse A, to bed, dishes	Make guac, watch A&M	Get A down for night
7:30	Pack up, say goodbyes	Sleep	Read on plane	Call for teacher event	Dishes, outfit tomorrow	A down	Kid desserts, email
8	Drive to airport, park	Sleep	Read on plane	Dinner (M made)	Plan week	Watch A&M game	Kids in bed, talk M
8:30	Security, to gate, email	Sleep	Read, land	Desserts, showers	A up, others ready	Watch A&M game	Read in bed
9	Read at gate	Sleep	Customs, to car	Find costumes, work	A not down, kids bed	Watch A&M game, ready	Read in bed, get ready
9:30	Board, read on plane	Sleep	Drive home	Work	Read in bed	To bed by 9:45	Down by 9:45
10	Read on plane, take off	Sleep	Pump, talk to kids	Talk to M, ready for bed	Read, A down		
10:30	Read, eat, ready for bed	Sleep	Hang out w/M	Asleep 10:45	Sleep		
11	Read	Sleep	Sleep				
11:30	Sleep	Sleep					
12AM	Sleep	Sleep					
12:30	Sleep	Sleep			Up w/A, feed		
1	Sleep	Sleep					
1:30	Sleep	Sleep			Up w/A, feed		
2	Sleep	Sleep					
2:30	Sleep	Sleep, up briefly					
3	Sleep	Sleep			Up w/A, give to M	(+ 1 hour sleep)	

	MONDAY	TUESDAY	WEDNESDAY	THURSDAY	FRIDAY	SATURDAY	SUNDAY
3:30	Wake up, breakfast	Sleep		Up w/A, feed bottle	Sleep		
4	Read	Up 4:15/8:15 London	Up w/A, feed	Try to sleep			
4:30	Read	Lie in bed, think	Up, back to sleep by 5	Fall asleep		Up 4:45 w/A	

Acknowledgments

I am deeply grateful to everyone who helped make this book possible.

I've kept many time logs over the years, and while it's an enlightening process, it would be easier *not* to record the minutes of my life on a spreadsheet. So I feel incredibly lucky that so many women took time out of their busy lives to give me a glimpse of how they spent their hours. I am grateful for their time logs, for the time people spent on the phone and in person with me, and for the strategies and struggles they shared. I learned a lot from everyone who participated. Thanks to Emily Snell for helping me sort through the data, and for figuring out what was significant and what was not.

I'm also grateful that my editors at FastCompany.com gave me a platform to try out some of this material. *Fast Company*'s readers are an engaged and enthusiastic bunch. When certain topics, such as working "split shifts" or thinking of leisure in terms of supply and demand, garnered thousands of Facebook and Twitter shares, I knew these topics had to be discussed here. Thanks especially to Erin Schulte, Maccabee Montandon, and Kathleen Davis for their guidance. I'm also grateful to the readers of my personal blog (LauraVanderkam.com) who provided feedback on my ideas and helped me recruit many participants in the Mosaic Project. Nancy Sheed of Sheed Communications likewise helped me test out these ideas on social media and in my "Just a Minute" newsletter, whose readership has grown spectacularly under her watch.

This is my fourth book with the team at Portfolio (part of Penguin Random House), and I continue to be thrilled at how fruitful this partnership has turned out to be. Thanks to Brooke Carey for her initial interest in the topic, and then to Natalie Horbachevsky for acquiring, editing, and shaping the manuscript. Thanks to Will Weisser and Adrian Zackheim, to Stefanie Rosenblum, and the merry crew of copy editors, designers, and salespeople. Thanks to Emilie Stewart for negotiating the contract particulars.

On the home front, I am blessed to have the sort of support that makes a full life not just possible, but enjoyable. Thanks to Lauren, Promise, and Pam for their help with the kids and the household. Thanks to my mother-in-law, Diane Conway, and my parents, Jim and Mary Vanderkam, for their help and involvement with family life.

My husband, Michael Conway, continues to make life quite an adventure. As for my kids, they always remind me why the metaphor of "balance" isn't quite right. Work and life aren't pitted against each other on opposite sides of the scale. When one grows, the other doesn't lose. It is because I want to figure out how best to enjoy life with these little ones that I write about time in the first place. Likewise, writing about how amazing women make life work assured me that all would be okay as we continued to see our family grow. I have loved watching Jasper, Sam, and Ruth welcome their baby brother into their tribe since they first learned of his existence. The berry season is short. Someday I won't be asking editors to set deadlines around my due dates. But in the meantime, I'm looking forward to this new chapter in the story of our increasingly boisterous home.

Notes

Chapter 1: The Mosaic

5 **Ever since *The Atlantic* put Anne-Marie Slaughter's manifesto on this topic on the cover:** Anne-Marie Slaughter, "Why Women Still Can't Have It All," *The Atlantic*, July/August 2012, available at www.theatlantic.com/magazine/archive/2012/07/why-women-still-cant-have-it-all/309020/.

6 **In 2012, the legal world posted reams of comments in response to a widely circulated departure memo:** For one take, see Elie Mystal, "Departure Memo of the Day: Parenting Gets the Best of One Biglaw Associate," November 8, 2012, available at http://abovethelaw.com/2012/11/departure-memo-of-the-day-parenting-gets-the-best-of-one-biglaw-associate/.

7 **logged more time reading to her kids than, according to the Bureau of Labor Statistics' American Time Use Survey:** From the Married Parents' Use of Time analysis, "Time spent in primary activities (1) and the percent of married mothers and fathers who did the activities on an average day by employment status and age of youngest own household child, average for the combined years 2003–06," available at www.bls.gov/news.release/atus2.t01.htm (married, stay-at-home mothers of kids under age 6 average 0.12/hours day reading to or with children). This is 7.2 minutes.

9 **Influential economist Robert Shiller explained the phenomenon best in a different context:** David Wessel, "Nobel Knowledge," WSJ.Money, March 26, 2014, available at http://online.wsj.com/news/articles/SB10001424052702304256404579451513719842826.

10 **A commenter on the *Modern Mrs. Darcy* blog summarized this worldview:** Anne Bogel, "Bad for the Game: Women, Work, and Hockey," May 8, 2013, available at http://modernmrsdarcy.com/2013/05/bad-for-the-game-women-work-and-hockey/. In the comments section, this observation came from commenter Rebecca.

12 **One study of medical researchers who won K08 or K23 grants:** Shruti Jolly, M.D., et al., "Gender Differences in Time Spent on Parenting and Domestic Responsibilities by High-Achieving Young Physician Researchers," *Annals of Internal Medicine* 160 (2014): 344–53.

13 **one recent poll done by Citi and LinkedIn found that women:** Press release on Business Wire, "New Survey from Citi and LinkedIn Explores the Factors That Shape Men's and

Women's Professional Paths—and Their Varied Definitions of Success," October 30, 2012, available at www.marketwatch.com/story/new-survey-from-citi-and-linkedin-explores-the-factors-that-shape-mens-and-womens-professional-paths-and-their-varied-definitions-of-success-2013-10-30.

13 **A few minutes spent perusing the Bureau of Labor Statistics' Occupational Employment and Wage Estimates:** These figures are for 2011. The figures for lawyers are available at www.bls.gov/oes/2011/may/oes231011.htm. For writers and authors, see www.bls.gov/oes/2011/may/oes273043.htm.

13 **Very few women (in the United States, less than 4 percent of employed women overall):** One analysis found that 2.4 million working women in the United States earned more than $100,000; see Carol Morello and Dan Keating, "More U.S. Women Pull Down Big Bucks," *Washington Post*, October 7, 2010, available at www.washingtonpost.com/wp-dyn/content/article/2010/10/06/AR2010100607229.html?sid=ST2010101100168. According to the U.S. Department of Labor, there are 72.7 million women in the labor force. About 6 percent are unemployed in recent times, giving us about 68 million employed women. If 2.4 million of these earn more than $100,000, that puts the figure at about 3.5 percent.

15 **One of the most poignant scenes in Brigid Schulte's 2014 book:** Brigid Schulte, *Overwhelmed: Work, Love, and Play When No One Has the Time* (New York: Sarah Crichton Books/Farrar, Straus and Giroux, 2014), 13.

18 **We know from surveys of moment-by-moment contentment:** Daniel Kahneman and Alan Krueger, "Developments in the Measure of Subjective Well-being," *Journal of Economic Perspectives* 20 (2006): 3–24, available at www.princeton.edu/~kahneman/docs/Publications/Development_DK_ABK_2006.pdf (p. 13).

18 **Hour-by-hour happiness doesn't rise with household incomes past $75,000 a year:** Daniel Kahneman and Angus Deaton, "High Income Improves Evaluation of Life But Not Emotional Well-being," *Proceedings of the National Academy of Sciences*, August 4, 2010, available at www.pnas.org/content/107/38/16489.full.

18 **the vast majority of people in high-income ($100,000-plus) households called themselves "very happy":** Betsey Stevenson and Justin Wolfers, "Subjective Well-Being and Income: Is There Any Evidence of Satiation?" available at www.brookings.edu/~/media/research/files/papers/2013/04/subjective%20well%20being%20income/subjective%20well%20being%20income.pdf (p. 13).

18 **women find every activity more tiring than men do:** Wendy Wang, "Parents' Time with Kids More Rewarding Than Paid Work—And More Exhausting," October 8, 2013, available at www.pewsocialtrends.org/2013/10/08/parents-time-with-kids-more-rewarding-than-paid-work-and-more-exhausting/.

19 **In two-income households with kids, fathers have about 4.5 more hours of leisure per week than mothers:** Kim Parker and Wendy Wang, *Modern Parenthood*, Pew Research Center, March 14, 2013, chapter 6, "Time in Work and Leisure, Patterns by Gender and Family Structure," chart of "Work and Leisure for Dual-Income and Single-Income Couples," available at www.pewsocialtrends.org/2013/03/14/chapter-6-time-in-work-and-leisure-patterns-by-gender-and-family-structure/.

19 **"My friends are buying second homes and I'm falling behind"**: www.wealthysingle
mommy.com/fwf-im-worried-friends-make-money-grateful-need/.

19 **"My cleaning woman was slow with the laundry which made me late for my vacay"**:
www.wealthysinglemommy.com/cleaning-woman-slow-laundry-made-late-vacay-first
worldfridays-fwf/.

Chapter 2: Seek True Balance

31 **According to historical charts from the St. Louis Fed:** "Average Hours of Work per
Week, Total, Household Survey for United States," available at http://research.stlouis
fed.org/fred2/series/M08354USM310NNBR.

31 **In August 2014, the Bureau of Labor Statistics reported that the average private,
nonfarm workweek:** Bureau of Labor Statistics, "Average Weekly Hours and Overtime
of All Employees on Private Nonfarm Payrolls by Industry Sector, Seasonally Ad-
justed," available at www.bls.gov/news.release/empsit.t18.htm.

32 **On the other side, men with college degrees:** Mark Aguiar and Erik Hurst, "The Increase in Leisure Inequality, 1960–2005," American Enterprise Institute, available at
www.aei.org/files/2014/03/27/-increase-in-leisure-inequality_095714451042.pdf.

32 **the average employed mother with a child under age six:** American Time Use Survey,
"Time Spent in Primary Activities for the Civilian Population 18 Years and Over by
Employment Status, Presence and Age of Youngest Household Child, and Sex, 2013
Annual Averages," available at www.bls.gov/news.release/atus.t08.htm.

32 **when the ATUS produced a report looking at married parents' time between 2003
and 2006:** American Time Use Survey, "Time Spent in Primary Activities and the
Percent of Married Mothers and Fathers Who Did the Activities on an Average Day by
Employment Status and Age of Youngest Own Household Child, Average for the
Combined Years 2003–06," available at www.bls.gov/news.release/atus2.t01.htm.

32 **I wrote a column for** *USA Today* **called "White-collar Sweatshops Batter Young Workers":**
Laura Vanderkam, "White-collar Sweatshops Batter Young Workers," *USA Today*, November 25, 2002, available at http://usatoday30.usatoday.com/news/opinion/editorials/
2002-11-25-vanderkam_x.htm.

34 **In his and Geoffrey Godbey's 1997 book,** *Time for Life*: John P. Robinson and Geoffrey Godbey, *Time for Life: The Surprising Ways Americans Use Their Time* (University
Park: The Pennsylvania State University Press, 1997), 88–93, and Appendix E, 331.

34 **In an article for the June 2011** *Monthly Labor Review*: John P. Robinson et al., "The
Overestimated Workweek, Revisited," *Monthly Labor Review*, June 2011, available at
www.bls.gov/opub/mlr/2011/06/art3full.pdf.

34 **The Executive Time Use Project, run out of the London School of Economics and
Political Science:** Oriana Bandiera, Andrea Prat, and Raffaella Sadun, "Managing the
Family Firm: Evidence from CEOs at Work," November 25, 2014, available at http://
sticerd.lse.ac.uk/dps/eopp/eopp49.pdf.

35 **who earns about $37,000 a year working full-time:** Bureau of Labor Statistics, "Median Usual Weekly Earnings of Full-time Wage and Salary Workers by Sex, Quarterly Averages, Seasonally Adjusted," available at www.bls.gov/news.release/wkyeng.t01 .htm. The average woman with a full-time job earned $715/week in the second quarter of 2014.

39 **The average commute time in the United States is about twenty-five minutes:** "Commuting in the United States: 2009," American Community Survey Reports, published by the Census Bureau, September 2011, available at www.census.gov/prod/2011pubs/acs-15.pdf.

44 **there are plenty of strategies for knocking time off your workweeks:** See Laura Vanderkam, "7 Ways to Knock an Hour Off Your Work Day," FastCompany.com, April 28, 2014, available at www.fastcompany.com/3029712/7-ways-to-knock-an-hour-off-your-work-day.

44 **One study done by researchers associated with Johnson & Johnson:** Janet Nikolovski and Jack Groppel, "The Power of an Energy Microburst," Wellness & Prevention, Inc., 2013, available at www.jnj.com/sites/default/files/pdf/WHITEPAPER_Microburst.pdf.

47 **A few years later, she wrote a guest post for my blog about her decision to embrace these new ambitions:** Calee M. Lee, "Want to Write a Book? Don't Do Laundry," October 11, 2011, available at http://lauravanderkam.com/2011/10/want-to-write-a-book-dont-do-laundry/.

Chapter 3: Take Charge of Your Time

53 **accurately pointed out in a post for *Harvard Business Review*:** Joan C. Williams, "Why Men Work So Many Hours," *Harvard Business Review* (HBR.com), May 29, 2013, available at http://blogs.hbr.org/2013/05/why-men-work-so-many-hours/.

54 **Indeed, about a third of full-time workers already work "remotely":** "It's 10 a.m. Do You Know Where and How Your Employees Are Working?" Flex + Strategy Group/Work + Life Fit, Inc., 2014 report, available at www.worklifefit.com/sites/default/files/pdfs/WorkLifeFitReportFINALUPDATED—with%20Updated%20Hyperlink.pdf.

55 **A 2014 survey from Cali Yost's Flex + Strategy Group:** "Ambivalence Is Not a Strategy: Employees Sense Waning Commitment to Work Life Flexibility," Flex + Strategy Group/Work + Life Fit, Inc., 2014 report, available at www.worklifefit.com/sites/default/files/pdfs/WaningCommittmentReportFINAL.pdf.

56 **In 2013, the American Time Use Survey found that 36 percent of Americans with college degrees:** "American Time Use Survey—2013 Results" (news release), June 18, 2014, available at www.bls.gov/news.release/atus.nr0.htm.

68 **As her head of human resources put it in a memo:** For a copy of the memo, see http://allthingsd.com/20130222/physically-together-heres-the-internal-yahoo-no-work-from-home-memo-which-extends-beyond-remote-workers/. For the Cali Ressler and Jody Thompson quote, see Elizabeth Weise and Jon Swartz, "As Yahoo Ends Telecommuting, Others Say It Has Benefits," *USA Today*, February 26, 2013, available at www

.usatoday.com/story/money/business/2013/02/25/working-at-home-popular/1946575/. For Mayer's own take on her reasoning, see Christopher Tkaczyk, "Marissa Mayer Breaks Her Silence on Yahoo's Telecommuting Policy," *Fortune*, April 19, 2013, available at http://fortune.com/2013/04/19/marissa-mayer-breaks-her-silence-on-yahoos-telecommuting-policy/.

71 **One IBM/BYU study found that people able to work from home on occasion, and set their own hours:** "Telecommuters with Flextime Stay Balanced up to 19 Hours Longer," Brigham Young University press release, June 1, 2010, available at http://news.byu.edu/archive10-jun-telecommuting.aspx.

79 **Vynamic, a Philadelphia-based health care consulting company with a corporate policy—now called zzzMail:** Laura Vanderkam, "Should Your Company Use 'Zmail'? The Case for Inbox Curfews," *Fast Company*, October 9, 2013, available at www.fastcompany.com/3019655/how-to-be-a-success-at-everything/should-your-company-practice-zmail-the-case-for-inbox-curf.

93 **I think of someone like former Home Depot CEO Bob Nardelli:** Ylan Q. Mui, "Seeing Red over a Golden Parachute," *Washington Post*, January 4, 2007, available at www.washingtonpost.com/wp-dyn/content/article/2007/01/03/AR2007010300553.html.

Chapter 4: Make Success Possible

99 **According to a 2013 survey by Accountemps, Tuesday is the most productive day of the week:** "Workplace Productivity Peaks on Tuesday," Accountemps news release, December 16, 2013, available at http://accountemps.rhi.mediaroom.com/2013-12-16-Workplace-Productivity-Peaks-On-Tuesday.

113 **When I interviewed her for a *Fast Company* post, she told me that she considered mentoring "my most important job":** Laura Vanderkam, "Yes, You Do Have Time to Mentor—Here's How to Make the Most of It," FastCompany.com, March 12, 2014, available at www.fastcompany.com/3027490/leadership-now/yes-you-do-have-time-to-mentor-heres-6-reasons-why-you-should.

113 **In *Lean In*, Sheryl Sandberg notes that smart mentors "select protégés based on performance and potential":** Sheryl Sandberg, *Lean In: Women, Work, and the Will to Lead* (New York: Knopf, 2013), 68.

114 **One Leadership IQ poll of thirty-two thousand people found that employees are most engaged and motivated:** "Are You Spending Enough Time with Your Boss . . . or Too Much?" Leadership IQ news release, June 18, 2014, available at www.leadershipiq.com/are-you-spending-enough-time-with-your-boss-or-too-much/.

114 **(a suggestion from time management expert Laura Stack) wearing a funny hat:** Laura Vanderkam, "4 Strategies to Make Your Office a Place Where People Can Focus," Fast Company.com, March 25, 2014, available at www.fastcompany.com/3028041/work-smart/4-strategies-to-make-your-office-a-place-where-people-can-focus.

117 **Amanda Steinberg, founder of DailyWorth, a financial Web site for women:** Laura Vanderkam, "How to Crush Your Next Conference, from Those Who've Crushed

Them Before," FastCompany.com, June 6, 2013, available at www.fastcompany.com/3012424/dialed/how-to-crush-your-next-conference-from-those-whove-crushed-them-before.

117 **In their 2013 book, *Scarcity*, Sendhil Mullainathan and Eldar Shafir use the term "slack" to describe this unclaimed space:** Sendhil Mullainathan and Eldar Shafir, *Scarcity: Why Having Too Little Means So Much* (New York: Times Books, 2013).

118 **When Crystal Paine started the Web site Money Saving Mom several years ago during the economic crisis, it took off fast:** Laura Vanderkam, "How to Combat a Ridiculous Work Schedule and Stop Feeling So Overwhelmed," FastCompany.com, January 23, 2014, available at www.fastcompany.com/3025206/work-smart/how-to-combat-a-ridiculous-work-schedule-and-stop-feeling-so-overwhelmed.

120 **It was Doug Lemov's *Teach Like a Champion*, and it looked at how the most effective teachers keep students engaged:** Doug Lemov, *Teach Like a Champion: 49 Techniques That Put Students on the Path to College* (San Francisco: Jossey-Bass, 2010).

Chapter 5: Be There

125 **As essayist Caitlin Flanagan, author of *To Hell with All That*:** Caitlin Flanagan, "How Serfdom Saved the Women's Movement," *The Atlantic*, March 1, 2004, available at http://www.theatlantic.com/magazine/archive/2004/03/how-serfdom-saved-the-womens-movement/302892/.

126 **When I was conducting time makeovers for a previous book, a homeschooling mom of young children:** Laura Vanderkam, *What the Most Successful People Do Before Breakfast: And Two Other Short Guides to Achieving More at Work and at Home* (New York: Portfolio, 2013), 158–59.

135 **One of my favorite observations in Tina Fey's *Bossypants* is how she experiences genuine bonding time with her daughter:** Tina Fey, *Bossypants* (Boston: Reagan Arthur Books/Little, Brown, 2011), 260.

136 **To be sure, some research has found that children who eat dinner with their families frequently do engage in fewer risky behaviors:** "The Importance of Family Dinners VIII," National Center on Addiction and Substance Abuse at Columbia University, September 2012, available at www.casacolumbia.org/addiction-research/reports/importance-of-family-dinners-2012.

143 **One attempt to find a causal relationship looked at what happened when families changed the frequency with which they ate dinner together from year to year:** Kelly Musick and Ann Meier, "Assessing Causality and Persistence in Associations Between Family Dinners and Adolescent Well-Being," *Journal of Marriage and Family* 74, no. 3 (2012): 476–93. For an overview of their research, see Ann Meier and Kelly Musick, "Is the Family Dinner Overrated?" *New York Times*, June 29, 2012, available at www.nytimes.com/2012/07/01/opinion/sunday/is-the-family-dinner-overrated.html?_r=0.

143 **One survey found that more than 50 percent of U.S. families claimed to almost always have dinner together:** "Most U.S. Families Still Routinely Dine Together at Home," Gallup news release, December 26, 2013, available at www.gallup.com/poll/166628/

families-routinely-dine-together-home.aspx (53 percent claimed it was six to seven nights per week).

143 **But an anthropological study of dual-income Los Angeles families, done by a team from UCLA:** Jeanne E. Arnold, et al., *Life at Home in the Twenty-first Century: 32 Families Open Their Doors* (Los Angeles: Cotsen Institute of Archaeology Press, 2012), 60–61.

157 **According to the American Time Use Survey, the average mother of kids under age six spends a mere thirty-six minutes per day playing with them:** American Time Use Survey, "Table 9. Time spent caring for household children under 18 by sex of adult (1) and age of youngest child by day of week, average for the combined years 2009–13," available at www.bls.gov/news.release/atus.t09.htm.

Chapter 6: Make Life Easier

167 **I recall a feature in *Real Simple* a few years ago in which writer Stephanie Booth:** Stephanie Booth, "How I Transformed My Mornings," *Real Simple*, available at www.realsimple.com/work-life/life-strategies/time-management/efficient-morning-routines.

169 **one Nielsen survey found that households earning more than $100,000 a year made up a higher proportion of coupon "enthusiasts":** "The Coupon Comeback," Nielsen news release, April 13, 2010, available at www.nielsen.com/us/en/insights/news/2010/the-coupon-comeback.html.

172 **I weighed the options too, even writing an article on school lunch fare for *City Journal* that included visiting cafeterias:** Laura Vanderkam, "If You Serve It, Will They Eat It?" *City Journal*, Summer 2014, available at www.city-journal.org/2014/24_3_snd-childhood-obesity.html.

172 **While program quality does vary, these days most school cafeterias have to meet strict nutritional standards:** "Nutrition Standards in the National School Lunch and School Breakfast Programs," *Federal Register* 77/17 (January 26, 2012), available at www.gpo.gov/fdsys/pkg/FR-2012-01-26/pdf/2012-1010.pdf.

172 **Fun fact: when the new nutritional standards went into effect, the average number of daily paid lunches dropped precipitously:** "National School Lunch Program: Participation and Lunches Served," Food and Nutrition Services, USDA, as of October 3, 2014, available at www.fns.usda.gov/sites/default/files/pd/slsummar.pdf.

173 **One recent Harris poll found that 79 percent of Americans claim to at least enjoy cooking, including 30 percent who love it:** "Three in Ten Americans Love to Cook, While One in Five Do Not Enjoy It or Don't Cook," Harris news release, July 27, 2010, available at www.harrisinteractive.com/NewsRoom/HarrisPolls/tabid/447/mid/1508/articleId/444/ctl/ReadCustom%20Default/Default.aspx.

176 **The Pew Research Center published data in 2013 finding that in families with bread-winning fathers and stay-at-home moms:** "Modern Parenthood: Roles of Moms and Dads Converge as They Balance Work and Family," Pew Research Center, March 14, 2013, 45, chart on "Work and Leisure for Dual-Income and Single-Income Couples," available at www.pewsocialtrends.org/files/2013/03/FINAL_modern_parenthood_03-2013.pdf.

179 **women who take three or more years out of the workforce lose 37 percent of their earn-ing power:** Sylvia Ann Hewlett, *Off-Ramps and On-Ramps: Keeping Talented Women on the Road to Success* (Cambridge, MA: Harvard Business Review Press, 2007), 45–47.

181 **International child care placement programs restrict work to forty-five hours per week, and no more than ten hours per day:** "Au Pair Program," information on the J-1 Visa Visitor Exchange Program, U.S. Department of State, available at http://j1visa .state.gov/programs/au-pair.

Chapter 7: Nurture Yourself

199 **Twenty-five years ago, sociologist Arlie Hochschild studied employed women with families:** Arlie Hochschild, *The Second Shift* (New York: Viking Penguin, 1989), 262.

199 **most notably the National Sleep Foundation's annual "Sleep in America" poll, which, in 2007, focused primarily on women:** "Stressed-Out American Women Have No Time for Sleep," National Sleep Foundation news release, March 6, 2007, available at http://sleepfoundation.org/sites/default/files/Poll%20Release%20-%20FINAL.pdf.

200 **Media magnate Arianna Huffington has taken on yet another career, as a "sleep evangelist":** According to her Twitter profile, as of October 2014: https://twitter.com/ariannahuff.

200 **the seven to nine hours per day public health groups have traditionally recommended for adults:** This is a shifting target as new research comes out. For one list of age-adjusted guidelines, see www.webmd.com/sleep-disorders/guide/sleep-requirements.

205 **According to the American Time Use Survey's 2014 report on its 2013 data, the average American sleeps 8.74 hours per day:** American Time Use Survey, "Table 2. Time spent in primary activities and percent of the civilian population engaging in each activity, averages per day on weekdays and weekends, 2013 annual averages," available at www.bls.gov/news.release/atus.t02.htm.

210 **Some large-scale sleep studies have suggested that getting closer to seven hours of sleep per day:** For a roundup of new research, see Sumathi Reddy, "Why Seven Hours of Sleep Might Be Better Than Eight," *Wall Street Journal*, July 21, 2014, available at http://online.wsj.com/articles/sleep-experts-close-in-on-the-optimal-nights-sleep-1405 984970.

219 **Only one in five adults meets the CDC's guidelines for adequate aerobic and strength-building exercise:** CDC news release, May 2, 2013, available at www.cdc.gov/media/releases/2013/p0502-physical-activity.html.

219 **Averaged over the entire American population, people watch almost as much tele-vision as they work:** American Time Use Survey, "Table 1. Time spent in primary activities and percent of the civilian population engaging in each activity, averages per day by sex, 2013 annual averages"; TV is 2.77 hours/day, work is 3.14 hours (plus work-related activities, it totals 3.46 hours), available at www.bls.gov/news.release/atus .t01.htm.

219 **I'd presumed that people with jobs, and people with children, would be less inclined to volunteer:** "Volunteering in the United States 2013," Bureau of Labor Statistics,

February 25, 2014. The volunteering rate for people with children under age eighteen was 32.9 percent, versus 22.7 percent for those without children. The volunteering rate for employed people was 27.7 percent, versus 24.1 percent for unemployed people and 21.9 percent for those who aren't in the labor force. Available at www.bls.gov/news.release/volun.nr0.htm.

219 **which is more than the 2.5 hours a week many public health experts tell us we should get:** "How Much Physical Activity Do Adults Need?" Centers for Disease Control and Prevention, available at www.cdc.gov/physicalactivity/everyone/guidelines/adults.html.

229 **The average American watches ten hours of TV in about three days:** American Time Use Survey, "Table 1. Time spent in primary activities and percent of the civilian population engaging in each activity, averages per day by sex, 2013 annual averages"; the average American in 2013 watched 2.77 hours per day as a primary activity. Among people who watched TV on their diary day, the average was 3.49 hours. Available at www.bls.gov/news.release/atus.t01.htm.

Chapter 8: Savor Space

231 **free time must come only in bits of "time confetti":** *Washington Post* reporter Brigid Schulte, *Overwhelmed: Work, Love, and Play When No One Has the Time* (New York: Sarah Crichton Books/Farrar, Straus and Giroux, 2014), 28 (among other mentions).

231 **Dr. Phil had the sociology professor on his show to defend this statistic to viewers:** "Are Moms Really That Busy?" *Dr. Phil*, episode 1432, March 30, 2010, preview at www.drphil.com/shows/show/1432.

238 **according to the American Time Use Survey, employed mothers with kids under age six watch 11 hours per week of TV as a primary activity, and those with kids ages six to seventeen watch 13 hours:** American Time Use Survey, "Table 8. Time spent in primary activities for the civilian population 18 years and over by employment status, presence and age of youngest household child, and sex, 2013 annual averages," available at www.bls.gov/news.release/atus.t08.htm.

238 **An ATUS project that looked at married mothers who worked full-time found that they watched 9.7 to 10.6 hours of TV per week:** American Time Use Survey, "Table 1. Time spent in primary activities and the percent of married mothers and fathers who did the activities on an average day by employment status and age of youngest own household child, average for the combined years 2003–06," available at www.bls.gov/news.release/atus2.t01.htm.

238 **Scales of human enjoyment place it somewhere in the middle:** For one scale, see Robinson and Godbey, *Time for Life*, Appendix O, 340.

238 **Reading scores better than TV on scales of human enjoyment too:** Ibid.

239 **only 21.3 percent of married, stay-at-home moms with kids under age six read to or with their children on their diary day:** See ATUS reference, above.

241 **Some 27.7 million copies of *The Hunger Games* books sold in 2012:** Diane Roback, "Facts & Figures 2012: Hunger Games Still Rules in Children's," *Publisher's Weekly*, March 17,

2013, available at www.publishersweekly.com/pw/by-topic/childrens/childrens-industry-news/article/56411-hunger-games-still-rules-in-children-s-facts-figures-2012.html.

243 **Anne Bogel, the blogger known online as Modern Mrs. Darcy, devours books at the rate of twelve per month:** Laura Vanderkam, "How Busy People Make Time to Read—and You Can Too," FastCompany.com, February 27, 2014, available at www.fast company.com/3026923/how-busy-people-make-time-to-read-and-you-can-too.

244 **In Sheryl Sandberg's *Lean In*, she recounts an observation from Larry Kanarek:** Sandberg, *Lean In*, 126.

245 **As Nickelodeon says of this programming, "Since being a mom is a 24/7/365 job":** NickMom, "What Is NickMom?" available at www.nickmom.com/what-is-nickmom/.

251 **When I interviewed Peter Shallard, a business psychology expert who works with entrepreneurs:** Laura Vanderkam, "How to Stop Obsessing About Work When You're Not There," FastCompany.com, June 12, 2014, available at www.fastcompany.com/3031757/work-smart/how-to-stop-obsessing-about-work-when-youre-not-there.

Chapter 9: Master the Tiles

254 **Take this quote from an early 2015 article in the *Financial Times*:** Emma da Vita, "Are You as Busy as You Think? Keep a Time Diary to Find Out," *Financial Times*, January 11, 2015, available at http://www.ft.com/intl/cms/s/0/1eef15ea-958f-11e4-a390-00144feabdc0 .html#axzz3Oc19Kc00.

255 **When I interviewed Mark Langley, president and CEO of the Project Management Institute:** Laura Vanderkam, "How to Manufacture More Time in Your Day," Fast-Company.com, February 25, 2014, available at www.fastcompany.com/3026804/work-smart/how-to-manufacture-more-time-in-your-day.

257 **scales of human happiness have put the morning commute at the absolute bottom of the list, with the evening commute not far behind:** Daniel Kahneman and Alan B. Krueger, "Developments in the Measurement of Subjective Well-Being," *Journal of Economic Perspectives* 20, no. 1 (Winter 2006): 3–24, available at www.princeton .edu/~kahneman/docs/Publications/Development_DK_ABK_2006.pdf.

257 **The National Safety Council estimated that in 2012, 26 percent of motor vehicle crashes involved cell phone use or texting:** "Annual Estimate of Cell Phone Crashes 2012," The National Safety Council, available at www.nsc.org/safety_road/Distracted_ Driving/Documents/Attributable%20Risk%20Summary%202012%20Estimate.pdf.

257 **people who think they're good at multitasking generally turn out to be worse at it than those who acknowledge their limits:** David Sanbonmatsu, et al., "Who Multi-Tasks and Why? Multi-Tasking Ability, Perceived Multi-Tasking Ability, Impulsivity and Sensation Seeking," *PLOS One*, January 23, 2013, available at www.plosone.org/article/ info%3Adoi%2F10.1371%2Fjournal.pone.0054402;jsessionid=1C499237E56E-5530B7AB8E8046DA1D46.

259 **A woman once described her long California commute to me in way that made it seem like a visual adventure:** Laura Vanderkam, "Six Ways to Survive a Hellishly Long

Commute," Fortune.com, February 25, 2013, available at http://fortune.com/2013/02/25/6-ways-to-survive-a-hellishly-long-commute/.

261 **A few studies have found that doodling actually helps you pay attention:** For a summary of several pieces of research, see Sue Shellanbarger, "The Power of the Doodle: Improve Your Memory and Focus," *Wall Street Journal*, July 29, 2014, available at http://online.wsj.com/articles/the-power-of-the-doodle-improve-your-focus-and-memory-1406675744.

267 **Here are better ways to use bits of time to bring joy into your life:** For an earlier version of this list, see Laura Vanderkam, "17 Productive Ways to Spend 5 Minutes Instead of Checking Email (Again)," FastCompany.com, November 19, 2013, available at www.fastcompany.com/3021821/work-smart/17-productive-ways-to-spend-5-minutes-instead-of-checking-your-email-again.

Index

Don't miss these other great time management books by
LAURA VANDERKAM...

"*Within a few pages, Laura Vanderkam's book convinced me I had time to read it. Then it convinced me I had time to reread* War and Peace. In *the original Russian. Thank you, Laura, for freeing up my schedule.*"

—Martha Beck, author of Finding Your Own North Star

"*A satisfying reminder of the role of willpower, its influence over daily priorities, and how it can be tweaked to optimize the morning hours, while your mind is still fresh.*"

—Examiner.com

Available wherever books are sold.
Visit lauravanderkam.com.